New Bern
HISTORY 101

The Essential Facts for the Native,
Newcomer or Visitor to the
Colonial Capital of North Carolina

EDWARD BARNES ELLIS, JR

McBryde Publishing
NEW BERN, NORTH CAROLINA USA

New Bern History 101

© 2009 Edward Barnes Ellis, Jr.

Published by McBryde Publishing, Inc.
New Bern, North Carolina

Set in Bookman Old Style
Printed in the United States

ISBN: 978-0-9758700-9-9

Book and Cover Design: Bill Benners

Author's Cover Portrait: Veronica Ellis
Cover Postcard Images: Courtesy of Willard E. Jones Collection

On front cover: Official Coat-of-arms, New Bern, N.C. (adopted 1891)
On back cover: Official Coat-of-arms, Bern, Switzerland (circa 1224)

First Edition
November, 2009

In Memory of
Miss Gertrude Sprague Carraway

Acknowledgements

REGARDING THE BOOK AT HAND, the author's first deep appreciation and thanks is to the invaluable Kellenberger Room of the New Bern-Craven County Public Library. Special thanks are also in order for the New Bern Historical Society, Tryon Palace Historic Sites & Gardens and the New Bern Firemen's Museum. The Southern Historical Collection at UNC-Chapel, the North Carolina Division of Archives and History in Raleigh and the Joyner Library at East Carolina University have been priceless resources as well.

The individuals below have been kind, supportive contributors to this project and friends to its author. Without their assistance, this work would have been impossible.

Thank you, one and all.

Victor T. Jones, Jr.
John B. Green III
Kay Williams
Dean Knight
Mark Mangum
Bill Hand
Dr. Pete Rowlett
Dr. John Butts
Barbara Anderson
Emily J. Dill
Charles Adams
Simon Ellis
André & Michelle Gower
Shannon LuQuire
Sabrina Bengel
Shannon Richards
Bill Benners
Skip Crayton
The late Natalie Sugg

And the world's best first reader, my wife, Veronica.

Finally, please give support to your local historic society and historical preservation group. There is no doubt that your great-grandchildren will thank you for it.

Also by the author

In This Small Place:
Amazing Tales of the First 300 Years of Havelock
and Craven County, North Carolina

Contents

On the Matter of Spelling

THE READER will find Bern—the one in Switzerland—spelled several ways in this book because, apparently, no one knows how to spell it. It had been Bern and Berne and Bärn and several other variations. The preferred modern name seems to be Bern, but it is quite easy to find Berne and references to olden times bring other choices.

The same problem exists for New Bern itself. In doing historical research, whether in indices or on the Internet, it is necessary to check New Bern, New Berne, Newberne, Newbern, and, as Victor T. Jones, Jr., the Kellenberger Room department head at the New Bern-Craven County Public Library, has pointed out to the author, also all of the above with a "u" in the last syllable. We understand that in the late 1800s, a loud and vigorous debate broke out over the proper spelling of the name of the city. Back then, the City of New Bern, the U.S. Department of Interior, N.C. General Assembly and others were at odds over the matter. The legislature won, but some folks may not be satisfied to this day.

We ask the reader's indulgence and forgiveness as we have often arbitrarily switched back and forth herein among these options with neither warning nor embarrassment.

The matter of DeGraffenried, De Graffenried, de Graffenried, even De Graafenriedt, and then von Graffrenried, Von Graffenried and v. Graffenried is just as thorny and problematic. The styling depends on which language is being translated into what. All the choices have been used by impressive writers with solid credentials. Although the "von Graffenried" model seems to be currently most in vogue, one prominent local historian solved the problem by simply calling the town founder—Graffenried. And is his first name Christophe, Christoph or Christopher?

Due to habits established since childhood, the author has chosen to stick with Christopher DeGraffenried with full and complete acknowledgement that opinions vary.

The writing of history has never met with much encouragement in North Carolina. Our first historian [John Lawson] is said to have been burned alive. Should another, in this day and generation, adopt historical work as the sole means of gaining a livelihood, he might meet death in a no less miserable manner—by starvation. But, notwithstanding these trivial obstacles, the work goes forward.

—Marshall DeLancey Haywood
The North Carolina Booklet
1907

es·sen·tial [*uh*-**sen**-sh*uh*l]

adjective
1. Constituting or being part of the essence of something; inherent.
2. Basic or indispensable; necessary: as essential ingredients.
noun.
1. Something fundamental.
2. Something necessary or indispensable.

New Bern
HISTORY 101

The Essential Facts for the Native,
Newcomer or Visitor to the
Colonial Capital of North Carolina

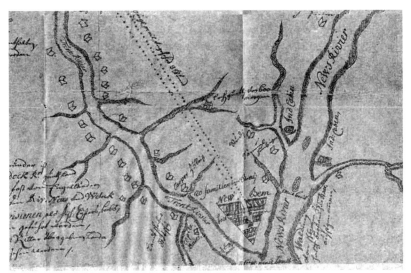

Detail of original map of New Bern colony
University of North Carolina at Chapel Hill

1

A New Bern Tale

INSIDE my childish little head full of porridge, it went something like this: In the beginning—I mean, way back—God took six days to create both the Heavens and the Earth, the stars, the planets, oceans, gazelles, et cetera. Then, on the first Sunday, he rested. The next day, Monday, was 1710. Baron DeGraffenried landed on the Neuse River shore, planted a flag and ran off the Indians. All the rest of history, at least all of western civilization, started from there. I knew some Greeks and Romans were running around somewhere, but the New Bern stuff always took top priority.

Today, following a few decades of study and reflection, the New Bern story is substantially clearer. It's the essentials of this story that I wish to put down here and share with interested readers. This is going to be a New Bern story all the way, but to get it moving I have to tell you a little about myself. I hope you, the gentle reader, will indulge me a few moments before I get to all the essential information.

I was born on Broad Street, October 23, 1950. Kafer Memorial Hospital had been opened the year before in a many-columned mansion a mere baseball-throw from the Hancock Street railroad tracks. My father was a Goldsboro native who volunteered for military service as soon as possible after the Japanese bombed Pearl Harbor on December 7, 1941 and was shipped by the military the entire seventy-some miles to distant and exotic Cherry Point where a short time later he met and, a few years later, married my mother whose family lived at Green Springs on the Neuse River just across the wooden bridge from downtown New Bern. Despite the fact that the happy couple occupied a spacious forty-foot-long trailer in a top-of-the-line mobile home park in Havelock, my Navy hospital corpsman father apparently was not so confident about the medical care available to pregnant ladies at the nearby Cherry Point dispensary. When my mom went into labor, he drove her to New Bern to have their baby.

A boy.

Seven pounds, eleven ounces.

My baby book says the nurses called me "Bright Eyes." Maybe it was an Indian name.

I don't know.

JUST SHY OF TEN YEARS LATER—in the summer of 1960—I stood in front of the same hospital during New Bern's magnificent 250th Anniversary Parade where I jumped from the curb to shake hands with then-Governor Luther Hartwell Hodges, the father of Research Triangle Park. My dad was so excited that he had his finger over the lens of his new state-of-the-art eight-millimeter Bell and Howell movie camera. As a result, there is no visible record of me reaching into the great man's chauffeur-driven convertible, but I have the whole scene in my head—these fifty years later—as clearly as if I were viewing it on the big screen.

The day was bright and sunny. Colorful parade floats glimmered, marching bands high-stepped, drummed and oom-pah-pahed, and thousands of local folks lined the street—smiling and waving—in celebration of the Colonial Capital's birthday. I was wearing my Temple Baptist church-league baseball team uniform as we had a game that afternoon at the Fort Totten field. I considered myself in those days to be the second-greatest second baseman in the world, just behind my hero, Bobby Richardson of the New York Yankees. I doubt my coaches, Chuck Faulkenberry and Robbie Robinson, shared this view of my fielding skills, but I couldn't think of a better outfit in which to greet the governor. My brief contact with the tall, thin, gray-haired leader of the state was the highlight of the day. I had never been more proud.

But the whole New Bern 250th commemoration was a highlight for me. The entire bunting-adorned city went a little wacky for history in 1960. In addition to the atmosphere of joyous celebration and the parade, there were speeches, a play, boat races, dinners and special publications.

My dad moved us to New Bern shortly after I was born and my earliest memories are of our home on Henderson Avenue in Trent Park and my *Leave It to Beaver* meets *Happy Days* existence there. For those of you too young to understand what I just said—Google it. On those un-air-conditioned Friday nights, I could hear the deep-throated cheers through my bedroom window screen when the New Bern High School Bears scored a touchdown.

I mowed grass most of the summer of 1960 and saved my meager allowance to afford two tickets to Kermit Hunter's play about New Bern's founding, *The Third Frontier*. I knew Hunter was famous and had written *Horn in the West* and other major productions. I figured it was a big deal that New Bern had gotten this Lord of Literature to grace its celebration with a work of stage art. I took my girlfriend, Lynn, who lived on the next corner from my Trent Park home, to a matinee performance at New Bern High School. I guess it was my first date. We walked the two blocks to the high school, sat in the balcony and watched the performers strut and fret their hour upon the stage. Hunter's production was elaborate. Except for the colorful costumes, that it went on a long time and that I couldn't follow what was going on, I remember nothing about his play of the beginnings of New Bern. I am sure his characters included Baron DeGraffenried, John Lawson and some Indians. I already knew about them. But, what the heck, I was with Lynn. And we were part of history.

The *Sun-Journal* was full of New Bern's 250th Anniversary. History and lots of it. There were stories and photos and artwork and special sections. Even at nine-point-seven-five years old, I was already in love with newspapers and I ate up every word. A handful of weeks short of my tenth birthday, I was, at this tender age, deep in my heart, already something else: a historian.

MY EDUCATION BEGAN in a one-room, one-teacher first grade class at First Presbyterian Church, about one block from where I was born. My teacher, Mrs. Marguerite Armstrong, specialized in children who were a little too young for the public schools. I missed the age cut-off by eight days. My cousin, Craig Forrest, was one of my classmates. He was about six weeks younger than me. Craig and I were among maybe twenty other kids whose parents felt they were ready for school even if the school board didn't.

Mrs. Armstrong was a wonderful woman; kind, gentle and a great teacher. She taught us to write our letters and to read from the Dick and Jane books. Each day we would write a page of *Our Daily News* with our oversized pencils. I remember how much I loved to make that big first O. *Our Daily News* included such memorable lines as "Today it was rainy" and one or two more facts about our activities. Mrs. Armstrong taught us science with cocoons in Mason jars so we could watch butterflies being born. She taught us arithmetic standing at her giant chalkboard where we added one plus one. It was at the chalkboard where she figured out, and explained to us, whether we were right- or left-handed.

And she taught us history.

Old and gray-haired—like I am now—Mrs. Armstrong walked her little charges across the church yard to the corner of Middle and New Street one day and pointed out the fact that a Presbyterian Church, a Methodist Church, a Catholic Church, a Jewish Synagogue, a Christian Science Church and a United States Courthouse were all sharing the same intersection. Freedom and toleration being taught to six year olds.

I suspect it was from Mrs. Armstrong that I first heard the date 1710. She, and a series of New Bern public elementary school teachers after her, told us over and over again—year in and year out—what a special place New Bern was.

We were taught New Bern history in every grade. We were taken to the town library at the Stanly House which, in those days before it was moved to George Street, was across the road from First Presbyterian. There the magnificent, charming and genteel Elinor Hawkins read us stories and sometimes told us more tales of old New Bern.

From these teachers we learned about the wonderfully named Baron Christopher DeGraffenried—Hollywood could not create a better name—and the wonderfully named Richard Dobbs Spaight and his shoot out—how cool was that!—with John Stanly, son of the wonderfully named John Wright Stanly, and had the date 1710 etched into our collective consciousness.

We learned about Fred the Fire Horse.

We learned about the Great Fire of New Bern

We learned about the Battle of New Bern.

We learned about the Indians.

We learned about Blackbeard.

We were shown the home off East Front Street called Blackbeard's House even though it had been built long after the piratical rascal was dead. We discussed the rumors that Governor Tryon had traded with the pirates, even that there had been a tunnel under Tryon Palace to the river where the governor would consort with the sea-going, black-flag-flying, skull and crossbones loving bandits, all of which later proved to be false.

One year, we kept little journals in which we drew all the famous houses and historic buildings of New Bern. Our notebooks were crammed with drawing and names and dates of Christ Church, First Baptist, First Presbyterian, the Attmore-Oliver House, the Queen Anne Hotel, Gull Harbor and many more. We made field trips to the old homes and the historic sites, gloried in the Firemen's Museum and, best of all, journeyed to the not-so-historic Maola Milk plant where the highlight of the adventure was choosing any ice cream we wanted from the frosty merchandise case.

In those happy summer days, I left home in early morning and rode my heavy solid steel Huffy bicycle, helmetless, all over New Bern. As kids, we had no contact with our parents until dusk unless hunger drove us home for a peanut butter and jelly sandwich. Those PB&Js were washed down with a glass of cream-laden one hundred percent whole milk delivered to our homes before sunrise by the neighborhood milkman.

We chased ice cream trucks. We played, against our mothers' strictest orders, on a huge sawdust mountain in the deep woods where the Hampton Inn is today. In summer, we traversed the steaming desert sand path off Country Club Road to swim at Jaycee Park in the cool wine-dark waters of the Trent River. For pennies, we rolled newspapers at the *Sun Journal* printing plant on Craven Street. We made more money by collecting discarded soft drink bottles and cashing them in at local markets for two cents each and, thereby, subsisted on nickel hot dogs, six-cent Cokes and ten-cent hamburgers.

So, as I completed the sixth grade at Trent Park Elementary School, all was right with my world and I was secure in my paradise called New Bern.

Then—without warning—when I was eleven, my father announced he was tired of the drive to work at Cherry Point. We were moving to Havelock.

He might as well have moved me to the moon.

Now this is not to disparage the city which would become my new home. It is simply to point out that no two North Carolina communities are more dissimilar than New Bern and Havelock.

New Bern was a colonial town.

Havelock was a boom town.

New Bern is filled with stately homes and brick buildings constructed over centuries.

Modern Havelock was built out of anything at hand over a few short years in the 1940s—and because housing could not be built quickly enough for the influx after the establishment of the Cherry Point Marine Corps Air Station—it became the home of one of, maybe, the world's largest collection of trailer parks.

The two cities don't look anything alike. Old New Bern was built for walking with a compact downtown suitable for horses, buggies and pedestrians. New Havelock was built for cars and thus is spread along a five-mile-long corridor of strip centers.

Many New Bern families go back to colonial times.

Havelock is an international crossroads inhabited by sailors and Marines and civilian workers from every state. It is home to an active Buddhist church and has representatives of every ethnic group listed in the U.S. Census except Eskimos. And some Inuit may show up any day now.

New Bern is feverishly historical, but in Havelock the byword was this: *Nothing was here before the base was built.*

This was repeated so often, even in print, that it became common wisdom.

I came to Havelock with great trepidation. But I brought with me my finely honed New Bern elementary school historical training. Even at eleven, I found it hard to believe *nothing* had happened here before 1942—that Havelock was some vast, weird historical void. So I began my search.

In those days, there was a single paragraph of history in the Havelock phone directory. In addition to boldly stating that there had been little to nothing in Havelock before the coming of the Marine Corps, it claimed the place was named for a British general, Sir Henry Havelock, the hero of the Battle of Lucknow in Indian circa 1857. And that was all.

One day I asked my mom to drop me off at the tiny little Havelock Library which shared the space in its squat, square concrete block building with two other government agencies. I sauntered up to the lone librarian like the history whiz I thought I was and asked for everything she had on Sir Henry Havelock. She paused briefly to consider my solicitation and then allowed that there was nothing. Nothing, I tell you. Not a book, pamphlet, brochure or article on the city's namesake.

Because I was so competent at my craft—and because my mom wasn't due to pick me up for another half hour and otherwise I would have nothing to do for thirty minutes—I selected the "H" volume of the Encyclopedia Britannica in which I found a succinct entry on *Havelock, Henry*. To my amazement the article stated that Henry Havelock, British general and war hero, had been born in England in 1795 and died in India in 1857. He had never been to the United States. This great mystery of how a city in North America could be named for a person who had never set foot upon its soil was the single and essential inspiration for a lifetime of historical research.

From tiny acorns...and so forth.

My passion has driven me to endless reading, travel, visitations to libraries and archives across the country, letter writing, research, conversations and interviews with elders and classically trained historians, all of whom have given generously of their time. I have stated elsewhere that I am simply a curious amateur, but I believe that I am a dedicated one. And my dedication has been rewarded by countless hours of entertainment, discovery and fascination.

What I discovered is that the Havelock district does have

an amazing story. It was settled just after 1700, was attacked by Indians and invaded by northern federals. In fact, eastern Craven County has as much history as any place in America and more than most.

For my endeavor, I have been named the Official Historian of the City of Havelock, a rare post, seldom duplicated in any city in the state. I tell people I was named the city historian because of what I do, not the other way around. But I will tell you this plainly. It is impossible to research any community in Craven County without repeatedly and continually being confronted, impacted and amazed by the prominence of New Bern. New Bern is a historical sun, shining so brightly that it blots out the historical stars sharing its sky. New Bern was one of the great cities of colonial America. Its sons and daughters were eminent among the founders of the nation and its story is the essential story of this country and its making.

Others may be more qualified to tell the tales I am about to undertake. But I have chosen to do so because a simple telling of history is for me the best and, hopefully, the most accessible for the interested reader. We will focus on the highlights, high points and hot spots in the story of a community with plenty of all three. In doing so, we will ask and attempt to answer essential questions; share the essential stories; and meet the essential people who make this place unique.

The book is titled *New Bern History 101* because it is intended to be an introductory course of sorts. Those wishing to work on an "advanced degree" can do no better than to accept the challenge of Alan Watson's mammoth achievement, A *History of New Bern and Craven County*. I make no pretense to such skill. My modest wish is to interest and entertain my friends, relatives, neighbors, students and curious lovers of the past with some of the fundamental information about this distinctive and fascinating City of the Two Rivers.

To have witnessed the 250th Anniversary of the founding of New Bern and to have survived to see the 300th is an honor, a privilege and a great blessing. The book you are holding in your hand is a tangible acknowledgement of my joy in having experienced both and having been born in this rich, beautiful and interesting place.

My fervent hope is that when the reader concludes the

final page, he or she will have a fuller understanding of what a remarkable place New Bern truly is, and a deeper appreciation of the many events that have transpired here.

With the introduction out of the way, we are ready to commence.

So here we go.

To begin our quest we must tackle one of the most pressing questions and one of the greatest mysteries in all of New Bern history.

Why do all the bears have their tongues sticking out?

A bear at New Bern City Hall
Photo by Bill Benners

2

Tongue of the Bear

ACCORDING to singer-songwriter Eddy Arnold, American frontiersman Davy Crockett was born on a mountaintop in Tennessee and "kilt him a bar when he was only three." The cleverness of the lyric is based upon the legend that young Davy carved the misspelled boast into a tree after killing his first bear. Well, we cannot excuse the word "kilt" unless Davy was putting a Highlanders' skirt on his furry victim. But the kid may have gotten the "bar" part correct...if he was speaking German.

For bar, or more correctly, bär means "bear" in German.

In 1191, another adventurer, Duke Berchtold V, also kilt a bär, this one on the River Aare in mountainous western Switzerland. The legend claims that the duke—a German nobleman of the Zähringen family—promised to name a new military post for the first animal killed in the hunt. He named the spot "Bären" in honor of his trophy. Today, Bären is a city of 130,000 residents, more than eight hundred years old, and the capital of the country. We know it as Berne, Switzerland, the namesake of this fair city.

The problem, albeit a small one, is that, contrary to popular belief, Bern or Berne or Bären—no matter how you spell it—does not mean "bear."

Bären is the German *plural* form of the word bär. The Duke, it appears, decided to honor all the shaggy-coated honey-lovers everywhere by naming the place "bears."

That's right. Bern means bears.

According to *Muirhead's Switzerland*, published in 1923, "Whatever be the real connection of the words 'bear' and 'Berne,' the figure of the bear occurs in the oldest city seal (1224), and living bears have been kept in Berne at the town's expense since 1513." A study of the matter confirms that the dates and claims about the Berne bears are all over the place. The source above says 1513. Another declares the bear have been there since 1480. Yet another declares that the fierce and victorious Bernese army returned from a 1533 conquest with a living bear as its trophy. This bear, the story says, was placed in the defensive moat circling the city and more bears were added from time-to-time, we suppose, as both a novelty and a disincentive to any enemy's consideration of attempting to breach the city walls. Yet another record, this one left by a writer named Valerius Anshelm, says all this occurred twenty years earlier.

By 1764, "as many as a dozen bears" lived in an eleven-and-a-half-foot-deep "Bärengraben" or bear pit to the amazement of all who beheld them. In 1884, early travel writer Robert Allbut—apparently no bear lover—advised in *The Tourist's Handbook to Switzerland*, "The Bear's Den, near the Nydeck Bridge, is at the east end of Berne. Here are kept some specimens of bears at the public expense, according to ancient usage; and very unwieldy and uncouth specimens they are." The record number appears to have been twenty-four bears kept together in 1913. Regardless of the starting date, suffice it to say that for centuries live bears have been displayed in a series of Berne bear pits which have been the city's number one tourist attraction.

Excepting, of course, when Napoleon Bonaparte swiped

the Berne bears! But that's another story and we'll get back to it in a minute.

To say the image of the bear plays a large role in the city's history is like saying a hurricane is windy. Just like in New Bern, bears are everywhere in Berne. Bears are the city's mascots. The big black bear is the centerpiece of the flag of the City of Berne and the coat-of-arms of the Canton [like a state] of Berne. Bears, in much the same pose as on the flag, have appeared on local coins for at least three hundred years, are embossed on manhole covers and grace fountain statuary, including one fountain where the bear is clad in armor. Street vendors and tourist shops sell all manner of representations of the animals. Bear images decorate city buildings and, as one would imagine, bear statutes abound.

Writing for the *New York Times* in August, 1917, journalist Charles H. Grasty declared of Berne: "This is the city of the bear. Bruin is everywhere—on monuments and 'gateposts,' the coats-of-arms and trademarks, and most of all, in the bear den maintained from time immemorial by the municipality of Berne." Grasty liked the bears and described them thus: "Really there is something kind in Bruin's face as he opens his mouth in what might pass for a smile, taking short breaths, with his red tongue hanging over his lower lip." Having painted this benign portrait, he counters with a horrifying "historically accurate" tale recited to him by a lady of Berne after he "paid a visit to the bear's den."

As she related the story: "On a night many years ago," two British diplomats stopped by the bear's den around midnight after an evening that included dinner and strong drink. "Much under the influence of wine" and being "in a sporty mood, vaulted over the iron rail at the top and then back several times." We know where this is going, right? Sure enough, our daredevil trips on the cane he is carrying and falls twenty feet to the bottom of the bear pit. Good fortune is on his side in two ways, however. The inebriate is uninjured in the fall...and the pit is empty. All the bears are snoring soundly in their sleeping cellar. Neither of the men "was much alarmed," but the fallen man had become instantly sober. He warned his companion to be quiet while he found a way to climb to safety. The problem was that the pit had been carefully designed to keep anything, man or beast, from escaping. After spending considerable time trying to solve the problem, the man at the top—still quite intoxicated and excited—departed to find a rope or ladder. What he returned with instead was a small group of agitated men who discussed a solution to no avail. They decided then to try again for help.

"It was now one o'clock," the woman continued, "and the bears were apparently still asleep. The (men) were gone a long time, knocking on doors and searching fruitlessly. The leader was now in a panic and his own mental paralysis seemed to spread to all who met him. He finally returned, bringing with him a crowd of helpless people, including a policeman. In spite of the warnings from the Englishman, the crowd made a great noise which waked up the bears, and they began to appear in the pit from their sleeping quarters."

The bears slowly circled and surrounded the Englishman. They seemed curious though "without evil designs." They gathered. They sniffed with wet noses. They yawned. But the yahoos at the top kept on yelling, shouting suggestions and cursing the bears. By 3:00 a.m. the bears are appearing more restless and aggressive. Still the crowd had no solution. At long last, a couple of donated coats were torn into strips, a make-shift rope was fabricated and finally the man began to be pulled to safety.

Halfway up the wall, the "rope" parted and the man fell back into the bear pit, raising more gasps and moans and shouts from the ever-growing mob.

All the commotion put the big bears in an ugly mood. They began approaching the Englishman more closely, smelling him longer and even forcefully pawing him. The crowd urged the policeman to shoot the bears, but he refused to do so saying the bears would not attack the fallen man. While this discussion was taking place, another rope was being more carefully prepared by a few level-headed members of the crowd. Again the rope was lowered. Again the man began to be pulled up.

The storyteller concludes the sad, final act: "When his feet were dangling a few inches from the bottom, one of the bears staggered up to him and struck him with his paw in the small of the back. The rope parted and he fell, his spine crushed by the bear's blow. The bears fell upon him and literally devoured the dead body. And then the policeman shot the bear that struck the deadly blow!"

This ferocious tale should bring us, finally, to the matter of the bear's tongue...except we have yet to deal with that bear thief, Napoleon.

Napoleon Bonaparte, as you may remember from history class, was always conquering this and conquering that. One of the places he conquered and occupied was Berne, Switzerland which he took in 1798. Knowing a crowd-pleaser when he saw one, the diminutive general "bear-napped" the Berne beasts and shipped them home to Paris. There they stayed for more than a dozen years, much to the consternation of the Swiss locals. Even though Napoleon had laid waste to Berne and forever diminished its political power, the people had a singular focus. In the negotiated settlement, after years of French occupation, remarkably the people of Berne made the bears a major priority. According to one source, the bear heist was resolved in the following manner: "When peace came, the Bernese clamored loud to have their bears returned and the treaty so provided. These bears of the Berne bear pit are a royal family and can trace their ancestry for centuries."

For all their emotional attachment to the bear, the furry Bernese mascots have received some remarkably questionable and patently unsentimental treatment through the centuries. It's been a rather one-sided deal which the bears have suffered more than enjoyed. In 1891, for example, the city fathers ate one of the bears. For an official feast marking the city's seven hundredth anniversary, one of the "mascots" was slaughtered to provide bear meat for the main course. At one time plentiful and the dominant predator in Switzerland since the last Ice Age, bears were hunted to extinction over a century ago. In the middle of the 1800s, bears were killed in a yearly ritual hunt so the people could enjoy the delicacy of eating bear paws. In 1914, at least eight of them were killed and stuffed to make an arrangement in display "like a carousel of bears" for the city's Zytglogge clock. There are now no indigenous bears in the country. All of the recent Berne bear pit specimens are non-native imports. One of the culture's oldest totemistic and religious symbols, Swiss bears have been long worshiped, but long abused as well. Ironically, the now-extinct bear is still considered the region's king of beasts. Loved to death, maybe.

Taking all this into account, we return to our main question: Why do all the emblematic bears of both Berne, Switzerland and New Bern, North Carolina have their tongues sticking out?

In one word: Ferocity. The Swiss bear, though, is by far the more ferocious. The New Bern bear has been significantly tamed, toned down and maybe even neutered.

Note: See both cities' coats-of-arms on this book's covers.

.

A close look at the Swiss version of the flag or coat-of-arms shows a red field with a diagonal yellow band, colors of the old Holy Roman Empire battle flag. Charging upwards toward the left is a large male black bear. The blazon, or official description for the Berne bear logo, specifies that the long, undulating tongue, out-stretched claws and—how shall we say this?—prominent distinguishing male member are all bright red. Blood red, in fact. The maleness of the Bernese bear is codified in local law. The red panels are said to represent the blood of those who died in battle.

Aroused with claws out, mouth open and tongue outstretched, the symbolic Berne bear strikes an aggressive, threatening, challenging posture, as if about to attack. Its protruding crimson tongue signified defiance, refusal, ferocity, strength; a willingness to bite and claw and drink blood; an entire demeanor intended to frighten away enemies.

The "I'm rough and I'm tough and I don't take no stuff" image perfectly exemplifies the war-like qualities of the Swiss people. Swiss troops were famous for inspiring terror in their opponents. No Swiss force of the period was ever known to have broken in battle or retreated, preferring instead to fight to the last man. The Swiss army *was* ferocious. They gave no quarter, no sympathy, to their enemies. They took no prisoners. Even though it was the custom of the time to spare prisoners who could pay a ransom, the Swiss slaughtered all enemies without mercy. They were ruthless. One source put it this way: "They violated terms of surrender given to garrisons and pillaged towns that had capitulated—not a small part of the fear they inspired sprang from this bloody reputation."

The fierceness of the Swiss army of the Middle Ages had two distinct benefits. The first is that they became the guards of choice for nobility across Europe. At various times for hundreds of years, the Swiss Guards—the name given to Swiss soldiers who served as bodyguards—were employed as household security and mercenary field forces by the royalty of France, Spain and Naples. The French court used Swiss Guards for three hundred and fifty years. These employers realized it was much better to have the Swiss on their payroll than to risk having them as adversaries.

The characteristic ruthlessness of the Swiss military extended to a decidedly commercial attitude about both protective services and combat. The saying was "No money, No Swiss." If they didn't get paid they marched away regardless of the consequences for their hapless employers.

The Roman Catholic Pope himself saw fit to assemble a force of one hundred and fifty Swiss Guards in 1506 to protect Vatican City. The Papal Swiss Guard maintains the role of protectors of the Pope and the Vatican to this day.

The second benefit of the no-holds-barred reputation of the Swiss is that all of their neighbors, from the late Middle Ages up to and including the Nazis in World War II, took a "Don't mess with us and we won't mess with you" attitude.

Thus, the famous Swiss neutrality.

The bear, then, is a perfect emblem for the fierce war-like tribe that is the Swiss. Even the Vikings berserkers considered the bear the fiercest of all beasts. And the bear representing the Swiss City of Berne, the very symbol of the city itself, would indeed have to be the fiercest of its species. With mouth agape, sharp teeth bared, claws ready to lacerate, and a wild, protruding tongue, the lean and hungry Berne boar bear threatens all manner of mayhem if challenged. The warrior bear motif serves as a warning for all to see that the people of the community are strong, vigilant and not to be trifled with.

While Berne's flag has been flying for more than six centuries, a version of the Bernese bear, along with its armorial colors and graphic designs, was adopted by the New Bern city council shortly after a small local delegation helped celebrate our Swiss sister city's seven hundredth birthday in 1891. Here in New Bern, though, the bear has been toned down significantly. For one thing, its red, rigid, rather lewd, maleness has been done away with altogether. The claws have been manicured, drawn in and are no longer the color of blood. Even the shape of the New Bern version is a little plumper and more teddy bear-like, clearly *Ursus americanus*. What remains is the long, odd, undulating tongue made more curious by the lack of the other fearsome parts. It is little wonder that people might question why the New Bern bears stick out their tongues.

Even if the New Bern bear is significantly less war-like than its Swiss cousin, it still has a great deal of utility here in this eastern North Carolina community which sometimes refers to itself as Bear Town. Just like in Berne, bears are everywhere. Our bears stick out of the sides of City Hall, ride around on all the police cars, and even play football on Friday nights. In fact, those Friday night New Bern High School Bears are state football champions at this writing. Here, businesses and flags and banners and half the organizations in town proudly display our more user-friendly bear. Any child touring around town can spot dozens of bear statues and hundred of representations of the familiar yellow, red and black coat-of-arms. With the celebration of the three hundredth anniversary of the founding of the city, the bear has become even more ubiquitous, though some of the new bears are keeping their mouths shut.

Some people don't like that lapping tongue at all. During the late 1950s, someone ripped the bright red metal tongue out of the mouth of the life-size walking concrete bear statue then at the former New Bern High School. "Old Bruno" was built by the city's public works department under the direction of Cedric M. Boyd. A long-time city department head, Boyd stood a bear-like six feet, six inches himself. He is said to have outlined the statue on a piece of plywood and helped all the way through to completion of the realistic seven hundred pound creation. Bruno was built to adorn New Bern's official entry in Morehead City's one hundredth anniversary parade August 7, 1957. The cement over wire mesh bear graced a fifty-plus-foot float accompanied by three or four local beauty queens and won two prizes in the parade competition. After the parade, the board of aldermen voted to give the statue to New Bern High. Made the mascot and displayed at the front entrance of the campus which is today Grover C. Fields Middle School, someone soon attacked and excised the bear's thick crimson metal tongue. Today, Boyd's Old Bruno is on the patio at the new high school where it was moved in 1991. A close inspection still reveals the remnants of the metal tongue now painted black like the rest of the beast.

Regardless of the ancient vandalism, most people love the New Bern bears, tongue and all. Some of the city bears are so honored, they have been officially named.

Two of the more unique bears seem to be piercing the wall of New Bern City Hall. They are black, of course, and have two front legs in walking motion, bulging eyes, bright white teeth and a classic long, red, curling tongue. The city hall building is at the corner of Pollock Street and Craven Street and used to be the United States Post Office. When the city fathers moved their operation from the old City Hall—which had been further down Craven Street toward the Trent River—to the old post office building in 1936, the two bears came with them. The one facing Pollock Street is King William II. That one is named for renowned business magnate and politician William Blades. The Craven Street bear is Crown Prince Albert, named for a former mayor and alderman, Albert Bangert.

Another similar bear is escaping the wall of the old fire department building on Broad Street. Named for William Ellis, a former mayor, alderman and fireman, that bruin owns the moniker King William I.

All three politicians and their namesake bears date from the early 1900s. The bears are appropriately painted, made of copper and cost less than a hundred dollars each when they were delivered in 1914.

Just when you think we must have exhausted all possibility regarding the tongue of the bear, we are confronted with a wild coincidence; a true curiosity of history. For as you will discover, both Berne and New Bern are literally...well, wait and see.

The reason Duke Berchtold selected Berne as the site for his military post in the twelfth century is because it lies on a tight peninsula created by a sharp oxbow loop of the Aare River. The site is described in history books as "a *tongue of land* surrounded on three sides by the river." For eight hundred years, this tongue-shaped peninsula has been the home of the City of the Bears. Berne *is* the Bear's Tongue; literally the tongue of the bear.

In 1905, the historian Emma H. Powell wrote an early, illustrated history of the City of New Bern. In telling the story of Baron DeGraffenried and John Lawson's settlement in North Carolina, she wrote: "They landed in Virginia, and traveled by land to Col. Pollock's, in Albemarle on the Chowan, thence to Bath, and thence to the Neuse, where Lawson located them on his own lands on the Trent and sold them *a tongue of land* between the Neuse and Trent Rivers, called Chattawka, where afterwards they founded the small city of New Bern." She continues by saying, "De Graffenried afterwards bought this *tongue of land* from the Indian King Taylor." Not once, but twice, Mrs. Powell describes New Bern, a place named for the bears, as a tongue of land. New Bern, too, *is* the tongue of the bear.

Amazing! You can't make this stuff up.

Here's a final tongue theory, as good as any we guess, to explain the symbolism of the bear's colorful oral protrusion. We are all familiar with the little marks—the little dashes—drawn around cartoon characters or illustrations of automobiles, for example, to indicate they are moving fast. Suppose, in the same manner, the tongue of the bear represents the sound a bear would make; a big, forceful noise projecting from the mouth. Couldn't it be the artist's representation of the growl?

Well, sure it could. And certainly it is. Our bears are growling. So the next time you see one of the long-tongued New Bern bruins rolling its red tongue too far out into space, listen carefully. You just might hear the roar.

The trial of Lawson and DeGraffenried by the Tuscarora Indians
Burgerbibliothek Bern, Bern, Switzerland

3

What in the World is a Palatine?

ONE OF THE MOST ANNOYING sentences in history appears in every account of New Bern's founding. Some version of it is repeated in books, guides, brochures, articles and all over the Internet.

This is the offending sentence:

New Bern, North Carolina, at the confluence of two large rivers, was settled in 1710 by Swiss and Palatines under the leadership of Baron Christopher DeGraffenried.

They say it over and over and over again like everyone knows from birth what the heck a Palatine is!

We don't know.

And no one ever explains it!

We know what Japanese are. Or Hindus. Or Martians for that matter. But what in the world is a Palatine? How come no one ever tells us? Is it a secret, for crying out loud!?

Well, now we're going to learn once and for all what these pesky Palatines are and a few other things to boot. Because understanding the Palatines, it turns out, will lead to an understanding of what motivated first hundreds, then thousands, then hundreds of thousands and finally millions of people to risk their lives by embarking on leaky, crowded wooden sailing vessels to cross the Atlantic Ocean—the ocean!—and voyage into the absolute unknown wilderness of America.

Why would they have done it?

Crossing the ocean in those cramped, vermin-ridden boats in the 1700s was far more dangerous than blasting off in the Space Shuttle. The survival rate was low. Many times, half the travelers died in misery and wretchedness before they even reached shore. Another half of those wouldn't make it through the first winter. Many of the vessels never made it at all. Instead, they foundered and sank into the watery abyss taking all their passengers with them. Those happy ships arriving at some primitive harbor—after nauseous months at sea—disembarked their lucky survivors into the savage boondocks of an untamed, largely uncharted jungle of briars, swamps and hungry insects where they were welcomed by disease, starvation, wild beasts and wilder Indians.

Why did they do it?

These masses of people were not looking for fun. It was not to satisfy their sense of adventure. Few of them expected to get rich. No, they risked their very precious lives, and those of their loved ones, because they were driven to it. Nearly all of these pilgrims, immigrants and pioneers faced this unimaginable danger because they had to escape something worse than the high probability of death inherent in the voyage to the New World. They had to go because, for many of them, Europe had become something like Hell.

So it was for the Palatines who—listen closely—turn out to be people of one small region of Germany along the Rhine River. Starved, threatened, cast out, war-weary and persecuted, the Palatines were one of the many primarily lower caste European groups willing to die just for the chance to escape crushing oppression and political madness in hopes of finding the faintest glimmer of a promise of freedom across the sea. Many did not know where they were going. They did not know what to expect. Perhaps some had no expectation at all. What they all shared was a deep yearning to flee cities and nations—an entire continent, in fact—that no longer offered a decent existence.

Of the six hundred and fifty poor Palatines who set out for what would become New Bern, more than three hundred died on the way. Many of the others arrived sick and bereft of supplies; so much so that they were forced to barter their clothes and possessions just to have something to eat.

But who did they barter with?

Here's a news flash: There were people here. And lots of them. That's right. Established white settlers were already on the Neuse and the Trent when Baron Christopher Emanuel DeGraffenried and Surveyor-General John Lawson and their horde of Swiss and Germans arrived. Settlement of the Neuse River region had begun twenty years before.

But we are getting ahead of ourselves. Let's regroup for a minute and retrace the steps of the settlers from Germany and Switzerland, through England to Virginia and then to the tongue of land that would become their home.

THE PROBLEMS FOR THE PALATINES began with the death of a genetic oddball. Charles II, King of Spain, sprang from a line of European monarchs so inbred that people who fully understood his lineage would never repeat another rude joke about Arkansas or West Virginia. His father married his own niece. Therefore, Charles's mother was his cousin. And the Empress of Spain was both his aunt and his grandmother.

From early childhood, Charles II manifested physical, mental and emotional problems of the first magnitude. He couldn't chew. His tongue was so large he could hardly speak. He drooled a lot. He walked for the first time at age eight. He never went to school. But when his father, King Philip IV died, Charles inherited the Spanish throne. He was four years old. He assumed full power upon the death of his mother-cousin at age fifteen. The reign was not impressive.

At the time of his ascension to the throne, he ruled over a world-wide empire. His holdings embraced—take a deep breath—all of Spain; most of Italy with Naples and Sicily; the "Low Countries," a wide area of northern Europe encompassing slices of the modern Netherlands and Belgium; a hunk of France; and a share of the Old German Empire including the Palatinate of the Rhine River Valley, the ancestral home of the Palatines of our story; plus Spain's overseas territories in North America, Central America—like, all of Mexico—and South America. Oh, yeah. Did we mention the Philippines?

Despite two marriages, upon his death at age thirty-eight, Charles II left no heir. Among all his other troubles, he was apparently impotent.

Inbreeding among European royalty had been intentionally instituted to keep valuable properties, power and titles within the family. By the late 1600s, nearly all of the rulers of all of the nations and principalities of Europe were genetically related. And, as the old Southern joke goes, the branches of some of their family trees did not fork— literally. For many generations, the primary marriages between and among European monarchs had been cousins to first cousins and uncles to nieces. This led, after a while, to some rather weird characters, many stillbirths, illness and insanity.

Charles II of Spain was disfigured. His portraits show a quite strange-looking individual. His great-great-great grandmother was called Joanna the Mad. His nickname was "Charles the Hexed," as many believed only sorcery could have been responsible for his bizarre condition and traits. American historians Will and Ariel Durant said he was "short, lame, epileptic, senile, and completely bald before thirty-five; he was always on the verge of death, but repeatedly baffled Christendom by continuing to live."

But no one lives forever. When the Hexed One died with no heir in 1700, a giant family squabble broke out among the chromosomally-challenged European monarchs over the matter of who would succeed him. The aptly-named War of Spanish Succession would rage for fourteen years and four hundred thousand people would die. In southwest Germany, the Palatines were caught at Ground Zero.

Though Louis XIV of France is often blamed as the instigator who tried to increase his own power, the list of his kinfolk who also claimed the crown of Spain included Duke Philip of Anjou, Archduke Charles of Austria, Joseph Ferdinand of Bavaria and Leopold I of the Holy Roman Empire. They were all related. Several of them were first cousins.

They all had armies.

And time on their hands.

Combatants in the war were Austria, Prussia, Great Britain, France, the Dutch Republic, the Duchy of Savoy, the Kingdom of Portugal, Spain, the Electorate of Bavaria and Hungary. Battles would be fought all over Europe, Canada, the British colonies of America, Mexico and several countries and colonies of South America. It was fought on land and on the high seas. There is no argument; it was a world war.

In this type of war, of course, it isn't the royal cousins who die. It is the common soldiers, some aristocratic officers and innocent men, women and children. The Rhineland of the Palatines was fought over continually. The countryside was invaded. Crops could not be planted. Business could not be conducted. Cities, towns and villages were attacked, seized and burned. Famine and widespread devastation ensued.

At the same time, some long-term Catholic enemies of the Protestant Palatines—many of them French—thought the war made a convenient moment to settle old scores and a systematic genocide began in some areas. What had long been intolerance, hatred and oppression became arson, confiscation, torture and murder.

So they fled.

Groups of these Protestant refugees became so common in European cities, and so squalid was their condition, that they soon acquired the sobriquet "the Poor Palatines." Between May and November 1709, as many as thirteen thousand people—most of whom were from the Rhine Valley of southwest Germany just across the border from Switzerland—fled first to Rotterdam and then to London. British Queen Anne and many of the leaders of London were at first kind to the Poor Palatines, many of whom squatted along the banks of the Thames River. They were viewed sympathetically as victims of religious tyranny. Such a large group, however, soon became a burden to all who were willing to help and a great debate emerged within the country about immigration in general and the Palatines in particular. While other immigrant groups had quietly integrated into society as skilled laborers and tradesmen, most of the Palatines were simple peasants.

The deliberation and dissension about the Poor Palatines roared from pubs to Parliament. Within the latter institution, word began to spread that the Palatines had been lured to London by promises of free land in America and free passage there as well. The culprits who had created the stampede to England were said to be none other than agents of the Colony of Carolina.

While most of the people who fled to America were forced to do so, there were individuals in the world—as there always were and always shall be—who were adventurers, scientists, buccaneers, prospectors and speculators. Among the characters of this story are English explorer, naturalist and surveyor John Lawson and striving, high-society beneficiaries like Christopher DeGraffenried, a native of Berne, Switzerland. Lawson and DeGraffenried had a loose affiliation and acquaintance with Berne native and soldier-of-fortune Franz Ludwig Michel [sometimes "Anglicized" into Louis Mitchell] and with George Ritter, another Swiss resident who incorporated a speculative stock partnership with several fellow merchants and investors.

Originally there was talk of mining for silver and gold, but the venture soon turned to colonization for which money could be earned by delivering settlers and by sharing in the fruits of their labor. DeGraffenried, "a gentleman of Berne who had met with financial reverses," and Michel, along with the hopeful Ritter, became spirited prime movers—and aforementioned "agents"—in collecting the unwanted poor from the Canton of Berne and the Protestant refugees from the Palatinate of southern Germany.

Michel made the pitch. On August 28, 1709, the Lords Proprietors of Carolina agreed to a deal with the Swiss partners for ten thousand non-specified acres of land in central North Carolina with a twelve-year option on one hundred thousand acres more.

Who were these "Proprietors?"

They were political supporters of the king.

On March 24, 1663, Charles II of England ceded a huge slice of North America to eight men in return for their critical roles in his campaign to regain the throne of England. He granted the eight nobles, called Lords Proprietors or simply the Proprietors, complete and autonomous control of the land known as Carolina—from the Latinized name of his father, Charles I.

Among the eight were men with names and titles still well-known in North Carolina today. Henry Hyde, second Earl of Clarendon, for example, is the namesake of Hyde County and his title, Clarendon, was the name of a main boulevard in New Bern until it was renamed for Martin Luther King on January 21, 2000. George Monck, first Duke of Albemarle, had a North Carolina county, city and sound named for his title, though Albemarle County no longer exists. William, first Earl of Craven, and Sir George Carteret can claim the name of this county and the one next door.

The Proprietors wanted settlers to make their barren land productive and agreed to allow the Swiss to oversee the immigration, provided the Queen would pay passage costs. The men of the Swiss syndicate were known to Queen Anne. In fact, DeGraffenried was one of her favorites. The crown wanted to be rid of at least some of the Palatines and agreed to fund the transportation. DeGraffenried—already deeply in debt—borrowed more money to finance the land purchase. He instantly became a Landgrave of North Carolina, Baron of Bernberg and a Knight of the Purple Ribbon. Lawson, as surveyor-general for the Proprietors, was ordered to lay out the tracts. Ships were arranged to carry the colonists in two groups: six hundred and fifty Palatines to be followed by about one hundred Swiss "paupers and other undesirables."

So far, so good.

When push came to shove, though, the treasury of the crown forwarded only half of what had been promised. The Poor Palatines settlers were supposed to have received supplies for the colony before they left England. Instead, the decision was made by the Lords Proprietors to deliver food, provisions, tools and other supplies upon their arrival in the New World. But the Proprietors did not know with certainty where the colonists were going. Transportation was slow and communication virtually non-existent, so the seeds of disaster were sown before the ships set sail for America.

DeGraffenried leaned heavily upon Lawson who was known to be an expert on the region. Lawson authored an amazing book on its biology, botany, geology, geography and anthropology in 1709. Based on Lawson's advice, DeGraffenried worked industriously, picked hardy and skilled individuals—like house carpenters and masons—for the trip and laid in what supplies he could afford.

John Lawson was a fearless pioneer and explorer. From Charleston, S.C. in late 1700—one day after his Twenty-sixth birthday—he began a little jaunt of five hundred and fifty miles from one Indian village to another across the interior wilderness of both Carolinas where no white man is known to have gone before. "John Lawson, Gentleman," as he styled himself, forded rivers and streams, slogged through swamps, and climbed mountains. By foot and in canoes, he traveled, camping among dangerous beast and voracious insects and sleeping among the "savages." He recorded the entire adventure in a remarkable journal, later published as *A New Voyage to Carolina*, which is fascinating reading to this day.

Teaching Point: Although they have enjoyed better publicity, no one—not Meriwether Lewis, William Clark, Daniel Boone or Davy Crockett—did anything more extraordinary than the explorer John Lawson. A few others had made similar trips before Lawson, but most had taken scores of soldiers armed with blunderbusses, pistols and cutlasses. Lawson took six Englishmen and four Indians through a dangerous unknown land arriving at his final destination with no casualties. On the trip, he gathered a priceless collection of scientific, cultural and geographical information, in the form of carefully-written records, skillfully-accurate drawings and a collection of botanical specimens which set London abuzz for months. To this day the British Museum holds a collection of plant pressings which Lawson prepared and sent back to England.

While DeGraffenried shared the perilous trip on shipboard with the one hundred or so Swiss immigrants, Lawson met the Poor Palatines upon their arrival in North Carolina from England. A common misconception is that DeGraffenried's settlers sailed up the Neuse River in a tall ship and docked at Union Point. In fact, both groups came ashore in Virginia and traveled overland to reach the site that would become New Bern.

When Lawson joined the Palatines to lead them to the Neuse River, he found them in dire straits. Only half had survived the voyage.

Pause a moment and really think about that. You start out with a group of six hundred and fifty people with whom you live at close quarters and see every day. Many are immediate family, relatives and old friends; people from your village. And as you travel you watch three hundred of them wither and die around you. The heartache must have been unbearable.

On top of their other woes, Lawson learned the survivors' ship had been set upon by French pirates shortly before its arrival. Most of the Palatines' already-meager provisions had been stolen. Many of the survivors were sick and weak from the trip. Deaths would continue. Lawson did his best to settle the ill and ill-supplied settlers at and around the tongue of land where the Neuse and Trent rivers join. It was known by the native name Chattawka. Each head of household had been promised two hundred and fifty acres of land and all the supplies needed to make a start on the frontier. Now they found themselves in this "rough wilderness," weak and short of food and tools. They had little or no money.

When DeGraffenried, Michel and the other Swiss arrived in December, 1710, they found "a sad state of things, sickness, want and desperation having reached a climax." The Palatines had been reduced to pawning their clothing and few possessions to nearby white pioneers in exchange for sustenance. Fortunately for the settlers, at least two hundred hardy souls had preceded them into the Neuse-Trent area.

The arrival of DeGraffenried and the healthy, well-supplied Swiss breathed new life into the colony. Spring saw planting with a harvest soon after. The carefully-selected tradesmen and craftsmen were put to work. Soon planks were being cut from native timber for the construction of wood-framed houses. Success might have been within their collective grasp, but trouble was brewing among the Tuscarora Federation—an affiliation of many eastern Carolina tribes—grown weary of the influx of Europeans and intrusion of their way of life.

The first telling event of the on-coming war was the kidnapping of Lawson and DeGraffenried. The pair set off by canoe in the fall of 1711 with two of DeGraffenried's slaves to row them. While exploring the Neuse River some miles north of New Bern, the small group was captured and taken prisoner by a band of Indians who simply walked out into the shallow water and surrounded them.

Forced to the village of Catechna near present-day Grifton, the captives were stripped, bound and interrogated for several days. They were put on trial before a native chief, whose Anglicized name was King Hancock, after which the thirty-six-year-old Lawson was executed.

It was during this time that a savage coordinated attack on settlers in New Bern and the surrounding countryside was launched by the Tuscarora and their allies. They struck white settlements and scattered farms all over coastal Carolina at dawn, September 22, 1711. Hundreds of settlers were slaughtered with unbridled brutality. No one knows how many. Homes were ransacked and burned. Livestock was killed and stolen. Some of the women and children were taken captive.

DeGraffenried said he never learned how Lawson was

killed, but Indian reports later reached another Englishman. He stated that slivers of wood were stuck into the surveyor-general's skin one at a time until his body was covered by the painful wooden projections, like bristles on a hog. Then the slivers were set alight, slowly roasting the great explorer to death.

The execution of Lawson is one of the unexplainable curiosities of history as no one had been more knowledgeable of or sympathetic to the Indians. Before the founding of New Bern, Lawson had lived for three years among the natives on the Trent River with a young Indian servant and a bull-dog. The Indians knew Lawson better than any other white man. He found much to admire among their men and especially their women. He said the European "Daughters of Thunder" could take lesson of passivity and industry from the Native American females. He called the Indians "fine specimens of humanity" and said they were much kinder to the settlers than the settlers were to them. They killed him anyway.

DeGraffenried further states he was set free after making an impassioned speech in which he warned the Indians of his close association with the great and powerful Queen of England who would surely avenge his death. There is another theory: he offered a rich ransom in return for his freedom. His own words tend to support this idea.

DeGraffenried later wrote: "To bring them to a favorable disposition I proposed to make a separate peace with them, promised at the same time each chief of the ten villages a cloth coat, something in addition for my ransom; to the king, two flasks of powder, five hundred bullets, two bottles of rum, a brandy made of sugar."

He said the Indians "wanted that I should send my smaller negro to New Bern, so that everything that I had promised should be brought up to Catechna; but yet not a savage would go with him although I wanted to give him a passport or safe conduct. I told him that none of my people who survived would come back with him, because they were so frightened at the robberies and murders, and my negro could not come alone against the current with a loaded boat."

When DeGraffenried was set free he returned to New Bern and found his colony in ruin. Many were dead and most of the survivors had crossed the Trent River to take refuge in a fortress compound under the protection and leadership of William Brice, namesake of Brice's Creek.

The attacks resulted in a four-year struggle called the Tuscarora War. DeGraffenried would not be around to see much of it. He was bitterly blamed by many colonists for the disaster which had befallen them. They accused him of a failure of leadership. DeGraffenried took umbrage at the settler's carping. His reaction was passionate. He denounced Brice as a usurper and concluded his former colonists were ingrates.

To his credit, even after the accusations and insults, he tried diligently to re-organize the colony. He struggled to acquire supplies, once mounting an ill-starred voyage to Albemarle on which his ship caught fire with the loss of all goods. But, in the end, even his old ally Francis Michel turned against him and he was reduced to hiding from constables carrying arrest warrants for his unpaid debts. It was all too much. No doubt shaken by everything that had transpired, within months—and after less than three years in North Carolina—New Bern's founder permanently abandoned the colony. He returned to his native Switzerland where he remained for the rest of his life.

Like most characters in history, both Lawson and DeGraffenried have had to put up with their shares of criticism. While DeGraffenried is rough on Lawson, other historians have taken well-aimed potshots at DeGraffenried, too.

In his written account of the failed New Bern colony, DeGraffenried saddled Lawson with much of the blame. The baron also blasted Brice, the colonists who sided with him— saying they were wicked and worthless—and Col. Thomas Cary, a political opponent within the larger Carolina colony. But most of his plentiful ire was saved for Lawson.

There is no doubt Lawson was brilliant, dashing and daring, but he has sometimes been characterized by historians as reckless, dishonest, hot-headed, a liar and a cheat. The negative portrayals have been repeated through several hundred years of historical writing. Opinions vary so much that it is interesting to see how Lawson's reputation has run hot and cold through various renditions of his life, and of New Bern's founding.

Most of the criticism can be traced back to DeGraffenried who left the only account of the founding of the colony. In it he had strong words about Lawson. A quick computer search of a portion of DeGraffenried's first-person narrative of his kidnapping and escape from the Indians found not a single positive statement about John Lawson. Instead a long and bitter litany of DeGraffenried's negative comments accumulated.

Lawson "was unpersuasive."

Lawson "got into a quarrel."

Lawson "became rather angry."

He "spoiled everything for us."

"I tried to keep Lawson from disputing..."

"I reproached Lawson."

"I reproached him strongly for his unguardedness."

"I...bitterly upbraided him."

"[H]is lack of foresight was the cause of our ruin."

"Lawson quarreled..."

He "answered with a very disagreeable face."

Lawson "was so impudent..."

"Lawson complaining..."

"Poor Lawson..."

"Unfortunate Lawson..."

These are the comments DeGraffenried made about the man he had known in London where Lawson was well-respected as a representative of the Lords Proprietors. DeGraffenried trusted him enough to follow him halfway around the world. They planned and oversaw sea voyages together. Lawson successfully led some of the colonists across Virginia to the banks of the Neuse River in North Carolina. Lawson taught DeGraffenried about the Indians and served as a sort of ambassador among them. DeGraffenried entrusted Lawson with laying out the streets and lots of New Bern and willingly followed him on an exploration up the Neuse River. But after Lawson's death and the failure of the New Bern colony, DeGraffenried said he lacked foresight, was impudent, quarrelsome, unguarded, angry, and "spoiled everything for us."

Clearly, something had gone terribly wrong between the two. Exactly what may never be known. But, over the years, not everyone has agreed with the censure of the surveyor-general.

"The fact is, De Graffenried, in his account, hurls accusations of cowardice, incapacity and rascality around so general that the truth is hard to get at," commented a scholar writing in 1900 for the Historical Society of Trinity College, now Duke University. "One begins to think that among all this rascality and incompetence, he himself was not untouched, and that this might have something to do with the failure."

Other writers have fired back at DeGraffenried suggesting he was a privileged heir to wealth who led an untidy life. Described by another writer as "handsome and fascinating," DeGraffenried was noted for his ability to charm and was popular both in society and at the royal court. As mentioned, he was a friend and favored associate of Queen Anne. One chronicler, Sheila Turnage in her book *North Carolina*, called him as "a playboy." New Bern history writer Alan Watson, while professionally neutral on both men, said DeGraffenried "lived extravagantly, but made excellent political contacts."

So for DeGraffenried and Lawson—as for many notable figures, ancient and modern—it's not easy being famous.

New Bern historian and author John Green is descended from some of the earliest settlers in the Neuse River basin. He has dedicated a lifetime to the study of all things New Bernian. Green said that DeGraffenried is a hero to many in New Bern and that Lawson's accomplishments were extraordinary.

"He was one of America's greatest explorers and naturalists," Green said of Lawson. "He was certainly the one most sympathetic to the Native Americans. He was the main source on the North Carolina natives because he lived among them and, by the time anyone else wrote about them, they had been wiped out. He was very important in describing them and the early settlers. He was a surveyor—an educated man. He was a respected correspondent with the major naturalists in England. Was he a risk-taker? Was he reckless? Well, he was an explorer. That's what explorers do."

Regardless of modern critiques of men who are now seen only through the telescope of history, both Lawson and DeGraffenried attempted to accomplish something extraordinary. In the process, they each paid a high price for their daring endeavor to create a frontier outpost in the Americas.

Lawson gave his life in the founding of New Bern. DeGraffenried, out of funds, failed to find a new partner and sold his interest in the affair to the wealthy and powerful Thomas Pollock—for whom Pollock Street is named. He returned to the family's Swiss castle just north of Berne. He would inherit the stronghold in 1730 and brood there for the remainder of his days.

For Christopher Emanuel DeGraffenried, the planting of the colony in America was a venture with several objectives. Among them was one of the most common motives in the history of the world. It was intended to undo his personal financial morass as he was "compelled to do something to satisfy his creditors." Ultimately, though, there was no profit.

The cost for the wayward, impoverished European immigrants was that many would die—horribly and soon. The colonists buried at sea or laid to rest by their loved ones beneath Carolina soil were killed by disease, malnutrition and finally, brutal war. There is sad irony in the fact that many of the horrors and torments faced by the Poor Palatines in Europe—the reason for their desperate escape—revisited them and their Swiss neighbors in the New World.

Still, some of these new Americans, shepherded by DeGraffenried and Lawson, did survive the long voyage, the hardships and the carnage. The seeds sown by each of them, with tears and sweat, flesh and bone, continue to yield a rich harvest these three hundred years later.

A wampum belt with figures holding hands in peace
From Great Treaty of Pennsylvania

4

What Happened to the Indians?

> *"I have spoken to many of the Indians about their cruelty, but a sensible king answered me and gave a nice example of a snake. If one leaves it in its coil untouched, quiet, and uninjured, it will do no creature harm; but if one disturbs and wounds it, it will bite and wound."*
>
> —Christopher DeGraffenried

OVER THE PAST FEW DECADES, several extensive archaeological surveys have been conducted at the Cherry Point Marine Corps Air Station. The federal government routinely researches its land for "cultural resources" hot spots. Among the many things the archeologists look for are Native American sites and artifacts.

During the late 1980s, the author asked an archeologist working at the Marine base—about seventeen miles from downtown New Bern—how the professionals selected test sites. He said they used their intuition.

"We look around and think about where a good place to live would be," he said. "A place that might have been sheltered or shaded; near water, but not too close; and with a little elevation for protection from rising water during storms.

It might have some attribute that would make it easy to defend or at least hard to sneak up on. It's sort of like picking a good camping site."

Asked if it was really that simple and straightforward, he added, "After you've been doing this long enough, you just know where to look."

In one study, the archeologists chose, by what this writer suspected involved more education than intuition, seven randomly scattered locations across Cherry Point at which to dig shovel test holes. Cherry Point covers more than eleven thousand acres and the sites were not near one another. They hoped to find something left by Indians at one or two of the sites.

Ready for the pay-off? The archaeologists found Indian material at all seven locations.

Months later, the author was able to look at the printed test data. The scientists had found a single projectile point they called a "lithic biface," but they found many "secondary flakes" or chips left over from making stone tools or arrow points. These were rhyolite and quartz—and quite common.

And pottery sherds. Lots and lots of pottery sherds. In archaeology, a sherd is a fragment of pottery. At one location they found one hundred and fifty pieces. The little ceramic fragments are easy to date. They are classified mainly by the textile imprint patterns applied while the clay was still wet.

Some of the material found at Cherry Point was four hundred years old. One Native American village site had been occupied for at least seven hundred years. But some of it dated to 1,000 B.C. It was three thousand years old.

The writer was amazed. The last set of questions and answers went like this:

"Why did you find so much Indian material?"

"Because Indians were everywhere."

"You mean at Cherry Point?"

"No. They...were...*every*where."

THEY WERE SURE AS HECK everywhere on the morning of September 22, 1711. The warriors of ten tribes swept down upon white villages and scattered farms all over coastal Carolina. Death and savage injury occurred over a wide swath along and between the Neuse, Trent and Pamlico rivers. Histories, written long after the fact, say five hundred Indians attacked and killed one hundred and fifty settlers in the first few hours of a well-planned and coordinated dawn raid. The killing would go on for three days. It was one of the most dreadful massacres of Colonial America.

In the book of Havelock history *In This Small Place*, the writer put it this way: "Had you been in Craven County early that morning you would have been scared. You would have smelled the smoke from burning homes. You would have heard shots fired in anger and possibly screams and shouts. Very probably you would have known some of the victims of the massacre."

The truth is nobody knows how many people were killed or how many Indians were involved. There was no census in 1711. There were no addresses. No cops. No rescue squad. No on-scene reporters. No one knew how many European settlers had migrated down out of Virginia or, by some miracle, made it in boats over treacherous tidal bars barricading the Carolina coastline. There may have been one thousand warriors and five hundred dead settlers. No one knows.

But someone counted eighty dead children.

Someone reported many of the dead women were left kneeling as if in some form of ghoulish prayer while others were pinned to the ground by stakes driven through their bodies. Though it is hateful to repeat, there were awful things done to pregnant women and many, many scalpings. In some of them, the tops of skulls were taken along with the hair. Some settlers died by slow torture.

Surveyor-General of Carolina John Lawson was an eminent naturalist, explorer and author. He was a keen observer of the Indians, living among them for many years. Lawson would be tortured to death just before the dawn raid by the Tuscarora confederation. Ironically, he had written graphically about their methods of torture in his 1709 book *A New Voyage to Carolina*. His words bear consideration.

"They strive to invent the most inhuman butcheries that the devils themselves could invent or hammer out of hell," Lawson wrote. "They esteem death no punishment, but rather an advantage to him that is exported out of this into another world. Therefore they inflict on them torments wherein they prolong life in that miserable state as long as they can, and never miss skulping [scalping] of them, as they call it, which is to cut the skin from the temples, and taking the whole head of hair with it, as if it was nightcap...all which they preserve and carefully keep by them for a trophy of their conquest over their enemies. Others keep their enemies' teeth, which are taken in war, whilst others split the pitch-pine into splinters and stick them into the enemy's body while alive. Thus they light them, which burns like so many torches; and in this manner they make him dance round a great fire, everyone buffeting and deriding him till he expires, when everyone strives to get a bone or some relic of the unfortunate captive."

It was by this final exquisite Indian torture that Lawson is thought to have been exported out of this world.

Back at the massacre that morning, women and children were kidnapped by Indians who crept silently through woods and fields. Cabins and barns were burned. Cows, horses and other livestock were killed, butchered and stolen. Homes were ransacked, property plundered. It was a perfect chaos of screaming, shrieking and horror.

New Bern was particularly hard hit. The small settlement lost between sixty and seventy Swiss and Palatines. DeGraffenried said they were "murdered." The rest had been plundered or burned out. Most of them abandoned the town in favor of the fortified plantation of William Brice on the south side of the Trent River.

But New Bern was only one of the places attacked during the three days of carnage.

New Bern historian Victor T. Jones, Jr. has identified more than eighty-five settlers in the Neuse River basin who pre-date the Swiss and Palatine migration in 1710. In the same year, a group of Welsh Quakers occupied land on the Neuse tributary creeks called Hancock, Slocum and Clubfoot. William Hancock [sometimes spelled Handcock] for whom one of the creeks is named, is also the namesake of a street in modern downtown New Bern. A map exists of a working plantation he owned on his creek in 1707. In the same year, a group of his neighbors were already established on and around what is now Cherry Point:

> Alexander Goodgroom
> Dutton Lane
> Bryant Lee
> Edward Beicheino
> Robert Coleman
> Dennis O'Dyar [also spelled O'Dia]
> Edward Haynes

Amy Thirel [also spelled Thurl]
John Clark
John Slocumb [Handcock's cousin]

Before the Swiss and Poor Palatines arrived, the Trent River was occupied all the way to modern day Pollocksville. There were settlers at what is now Oriental and other parts of Pamlico County. Some of their names are known. Some of them—possibly most of them—never will be.

All of the settler's names above, and the rest on the Jones list, come from colonial government records. It must be remembered that not everyone appeared in those records. But some speculation can be done based upon the known names.

Using typical household multipliers, eighty-five settlers as heads of those households might indicate as many as two hundred and fifty people when wives and children are taken into account. Four per household—not an unreasonable number in colonial times—would put the Neuse-Trent population before DeGraffenried at three hundred and forty people. If we suppose only half the citizens of the time ever appeared in public records, we could double the population to six hundred and eighty. Add to the total the three hundred and fifty Palatines and one hundred Swiss who came with DeGraffenried and it's easy to see there might have been a thousand people or more here in 1711.

However, as we acknowledge, this is just interesting speculation; simply playing with numbers.

However, again, the exercise makes clear one thing the Indians were concerned about. More and more foreigners with different customs, habits, cultures and temperaments were coming day by day, week by week and month by month.

Something had to give.

IT WASN'T JUST THE NUMBERS. It was the attitude.

Lawson said the Indians always fed a traveler while the colonist ignored the needs of the Indians.

"We let them walk by our doors hungry and do not relieve them," wrote Lawson. "We look upon them with disdain and scorn, and think of them as little more than beasts in human form; while with all our religion and education we possess more moral deformities and vices than these people do."

Beyond poor human relations, the colonists seem never to

have considered the idea that Indians had pre-existing property rights. Lords Proprietors's agents simply claimed whatever land they wanted. There were few instances of purchase. Once the land was claimed by the colonists, Indians were no longer allowed to hunt there, and in some cases even near their former land.

The Tuscarora, whose name derives from their words meaning, "hemp gatherers," were a loose affiliation of three main tribes having their own home territories spread across the rivers called Roanoke, Neuse, Taw [Tar] and Pamlico. Indian-fighter Col. John Barnwell said three of their "towns" were on the Pamlico River—the next big river north of and parallel to the Neuse River—but most of their villages were on the Neuse and its many tributaries. Their southern boundary for hunting, fishing and planting may have spread all the way to the Cape Fear River, many miles to the south of New Bern. In 1708, Lawson reported the Tuscarora had fifteen villages and about twelve hundred men of "warrior" age. Barnwell would put the number at fourteen hundred in 1712.

These Indians grew corn, hunted deer and other game, fished the rivers and streams and smoked tobacco. They lived in round-top lodges covered in bark. They made and traded goods including skins, bowls and utensils with tribes as far away as New England. Small groups of the native Carolina people made annual or semi-annual treks to visit the "Five Nations" to the north. They traveled in small groups because a large one might be mistaken for a war party. With the coming of the settlers, the Tuscarora took on the lucrative rum trade, selling the strong spirits to western North Carolina tribes in units measured by the mouthful.

The Tuscarora were also associated with other tribes nearby, some of which spoke different languages. One such tribe was the Neusiok from which the river Neuse draws its name. These were the Indians up and down both sides of the river. Their villages were in modern-day New Bern, Cherry Point, Havelock, Bridgeton and Pamlico County. The Neusiok beat a well-worn path through the forest which ran from the Neuse to the Newport River near what is now Morehead City. From there, primarily in summer, they would fish while visiting and trading with the Core Sound Indians, their "cousins." The twenty-one-mile-long Neusiok Trail is preserved today within the Croatan National Forest.

A list of some nearby "tributary tribes" affiliated with the

Tuscarora would include Neusiok, Coree, Pamlico, Matamuskeet, Bear River and Machapungo.

Lawson considered the Indians to be gentle, generous, smart and hard-working. But, like the snake described by DeGraffenried, they would "bite" if injured.

The colonist are said to have treated the Indians rudely and to have taken land for granted. The nearly-naked, bare-chested Indian women were an almost-irresistible temptation for some of the male colonists. The Indians complained of abuse.

The final straw seems to have been the colonists' enslavement of Indians. Descendants of the Tuscarora now living in New York and Canada maintain to this day that slavery was the major grievance. The practice was common enough that several northern colonies passed legislation in the early 1700s forbidding the further importation of Indian slaves from Carolina. Old Massachusetts newspaper ads offering Carolina Indians for sale have been preserved. Col. Christopher Gale, an associate of both Lawson and DeGraffenried who had visited them at New Bern, wrote after Lawson's death, of thirty-nine Indian women and children being "sent off as slaves."

There is no evidence DeGraffenried, Lawson or any members of the New Bern colony were involved in the practice, though DeGraffenried later claimed his rival Brice was a slaver.

Surprisingly, records indicate a significant amount of patience on the part of the Indians. They even went to court to seek protection from the onerous practices of some of the colonists. Since 1690, courts in eastern North Carolina had been hearing disputes brought by Indians. In 1695, the General Court ordered "the Indians have the liberty to hunt on all waste-land that is not taken up and liberty to pass through lands that are sealed in their going to and from said waste-land, they behaving themselves civilly and doing no injury."

Here is something truly extraordinary.

Shortly before what would become known as the Tuscarora War, the Indian tribes, finding no help in North Carolina, made a formal appeal to the governor of Pennsylvania. Sent via the Susquehanna tribe in 1710, Indian ambassadors including some of the Tuscarora met with two representatives of the governor in an elaborate ceremony. At the meeting, the Indians delivered eight requests. Accompanying each was a beautiful belt of wampum.

Wampum are traditional, sacred shell beads of the eastern Woodland tribes. When we think of them at all, wampum is thought to be money. For the Indians, the value of the belts—some of which were six feet long—was the memories they represented. Each belt made from hundreds of hand-carved whelk shell beads was attached to fringed, hand-woven cloth. The unique patterns and designs of these works of art were created to symbolize marriage, engagement, condolence or some other form of honor. They were also used in treaty ceremonies.

Delivery of the wampum belts to the Pennsylvanians was intended to demonstrate the sincerity of the Indian's appeals and provide tangible evidence of them.

The assembled chiefs asked for friendship; the right to gather water and wood; an end to slavery; the right to hunt; lasting peace; safety in the forest; relief from the fear they had felt for the past few years and the cessation of murder. The Indians said they had come to fear every mouse rustling leaves and they wanted peace. They also asked for help in communicating with the other colonists. Ultimately, they said, they might wish to re-locate to lands in Pennsylvania.

The Pennsylvanians listened carefully to the Indians, but in the end, the native ambassadors were told they should petition the Carolina government about their grievances. As to their request for a future pow-wow, the governor said they needed a statement of "good conduct" from the white Carolina leaders.

But in early 1711, the Carolina government was at war with itself. The peace-loving Quakers led by Thomas Cary—who had been deposed as Carolina governor—were having a shooting war with the Church of England's gubernatorial claimant, Edward Hyde. Cannons and marines were involved in this religious contest with political overtones known to history as Cary's Rebellion.

BUT THE INDIANS were divided as well. The leader of the attack force in late 1711 was the Tuscarora chief, King Hancock of Catechna. Another equally powerful Tuscarora chief, King Tom Blount, refused to engage in the battle against the whites. Whatever their infractions, Blount was enjoying a lucrative fur trade with the colony. But Hancock's forces, along with Neusiok, Coree and others, were more than enough to create mayhem with their September massacre.

With the Carolina government in turmoil, the surviving white settlers appealed to South Carolina and Virginia for help. While Virginia Governor Alexander Spotswood dilly-dallied, South Carolina sent a rescue force headed by Col. John Barnwell. Barnwell would turn out to be both a blessing and a curse.

The original irony is that of Barnwell's five hundred troops, all but thirty-three were Indians. They were members of eighteen different tribes including Yamassee, Essaw and "Flathead" Catawbas—all ancient enemies of the Tuscarora. During his foray into North Carolina, Barnwell would violate both colonial legislation—with unauthorized treaties—and every imaginable law of humanity in his bloody crusade against the Indians.

He and his forces marched across the countryside killing at will, breaking truces, scalping, selling more Indians as slaves and, if DeGraffenried is to be believed, at least once engaging in cannibalism.

At Fort Nahunta [Narhantes] near present-day Goldsboro on January 30, 1712, Barnwell was infuriated by the losses his force incurred. His combatants succeeded in forcing the surrender of Nahunta, the largest and strongest Tuscarora fort, but suffered seventy-three casualties in the process. Thirteen of his men were killed and sixty were wounded. More than half of his dead were from his small number of white militia. He turned his mostly Indian force loose on the captured Tuscarora "putting all the men to the sword" and allowing his men to plunder and take prisoners. Fifty-two Tuscarora men and ten women were slaughtered while thirty were taken prisoner and later sent to Charleston, S.C. to be sold as slaves.

DeGraffenried, who was not present, later claimed Barnwell's forces "in order to stimulate themselves still more, they cooked the flesh of an Indian—in good condition—and ate it."

Barnwell, and his apparently well-fed troops, arrived in New Bern, March 8, 1712, and stayed till the end of the month before moving up the Neuse River and building a fort at a town which bears Barnwell's name to this day. Fort Barnwell was triangular, built between two cliffs and protected by a one hundred and eighty foot-long-wall. Cabins and huts were built inside. This would be his base of operations for the remainder of his stay.

Northern colonists took note of the clash in Carolina. There were rumblings that the Five Nations might move to support the Tuscarora. Had they done so, the Carolina colony might have been wiped from the face of the earth. One governor wrote that, before it was done, the fight between the Carolinians and the natives "would embroil us all."

On April 7, Barnwell moved against Catechna, where John Lawson had been tortured to death. DeGraffenried had seen white prisoners there after the attack on New Bern. Barnwell, during his visit in New Bern, had determined that as many as thirty white women and children might be held there. Indian tradition holds that Barnwell expected "great honor and gifts from North Carolina" if he rescued them. But after two vigorous assaults on the palisaded town, his men failed to take the place. Barnwell decided on another tack. He offered a truce and invited the Indians to a neutral location for a ceremonial exchange of gifts. When the Indian delegation came to meet Barnwell they were disarmed and carried away to be sold into slavery.

The two results of this skullduggery were that the Indians would never settle for another truce and the North Carolina legislature took umbrage at Barnwell making illegal and unauthorized treaties. By the end of 1712, Barnwell had left the state with the colonies still under fire.

During and after Barnwell's campaign in the Tuscarora War, smaller raids continued across the colony. White settlers sent out patrols. William Brice put forces together and carried out his own raids. In one instance, Brice and the settlers attacked some warriors and burned their chief to death. The Indians continued killing as well.

On the Neuse River at the site of what is now the Cherry Point Officers Club, two brothers, Evan and Roger Jones, were attacked and chased through the woods near their home. The young men were the sons of Welsh Quaker pilgrims who had settled near Slocum Creek in 1710. They were working at the family's turpentine distillery one morning in 1712 when the Neusiok raiding party appeared. Evan managed to make his escape into the woods, but Roger was caught and killed by the band of marauders.

AS A SIDE NOTE to the story, no reference is known to this writer of the fate of the white prisoners at Catechna.

And while we are pausing for a side note, let two things be added. The reader should know that a look at four different histories of the Tuscarora War will yield four different chronologies of events with varying details of those events. The most popular histories differ from one another and from the official state version which differs from the modern Native American versions. Part of the problem lies with spellings of sites. For example, Torhuntas, Nahunta and Narhantes are used interchangeably as alternate spellings of one place *and* the location of two different places. We do the best we can to keep things straight.

A NORTH CAROLINA Highway Historical Marker designates the site of the climax of the Tuscarora War. Located on Highway 58 in Greene County, northwest of Craven, State Marker F-37 reads:

NOOHEROOKA
Tuscarora stronghold
Site of decisive battle
of the Tuscarora War
March 20-23, 1713 when
950 Indians were killed
or captured. Site 1 mi. N

Following Barnwell's untimely withdrawal, North Carolina once again called upon South Carolina for help. It came this time in the form of Col. James Moore and another mixed force made up mostly of Indians. Moore learned the Tuscaroras built a massive wooden fort on a branch of Contentnea Creek. The fort called Nooherooka—also spelled Neoheroka—covered nearly two acres with bunkers and tunnels and was well-supplied with food and weapons. Its high-walled "palisade" enclosure was made from tree trunks standing vertical with one end buried deep in the soil.

In March, 1713, the South Carolina force surrounded the fort and began a siege campaign to destroy it. Moore's men tunneled beneath one wall and set fire to the fort. Hundreds of their enemy would be burned alive. Even with this success, it still took three more days to achieve victory. As the marker recalls, nearly a thousand of the Tuscaroras best fighting men were killed or captured. Moore's Indians claimed one hundred and ninety-two scalps.

The capture of Nooherooka broke the spirit of the native Indians. Though skirmishes would continue for years, the Tuscarora War effectively ended with the colonial victory. Many Tuscaroras began streaming out of the region, migrating north toward Pennsylvania and New York to settle among the Five Nations. They were admitted to the alliance as the "sixth nation" in 1722. To this day there is a Tuscarora Creek near the center of Pennsylvania. It is a tributary of the Susquehanna River.

Some went farther, settling in Ontario, Canada.

But contrary to popular belief, all of the Indians did not leave after the war. Many stayed here.

King Tom Blount's tribe did not fight and may have actually helped the settlers. For its loyalty, the tribe was granted a tract of reservation land in 1717 called Indian Woods. Over the next century, most of Tom Blount's people gradually migrated to New York. The State of North Carolina sold the Indian Woods land to farmers in 1828, but the location is still called Indian Woods today. The site is in Bertie County off Highway 17 near Windsor.

Court records also testify that Indians were still here. Thomas Pollock was governor from 1712-1714 and took possession of DeGraffenried's New Bern holdings when the baron went back to Europe. In 1722, Pollock signed an order to call a special court for the trial of John Cope, "A Christian Indian man," of King Blount's Town "for felonious breaking into the lodging rooms" of Pollock's "mansion house." Indians would slowly stream out of the state for the next 90 years. The last ruling Tuscarora chief in North Carolina is known to have died in 1802.

Itinerant missionaries reported Indians living all over the coastal plain well into the 1800s. Many attended services, became Christians and were reported to be living peaceably among their white neighbors. One group of Neuse River Indians is said to have settled in the Harlowe area of eastern Craven County which was a haven for freed blacks and escaped slaves from early colonial days. Some are known to have intermarried with blacks and whites. In the early 1900s, a few people were still living in thatch and bark houses there.

Hostilities did not completely cease with the end of the

war. Coree renegades were known to be living in the Neuse River forests after the treaty was signed in 1715. The Governor's Council learned in September of the same year that the "Core Indians" had "made a Revolt" and wounded a British officer. Troops were ordered to commence the "Entire Destruction of ye Said nation of Indians as if there had never been a peace made with them." There is nothing in the historical record about the Coree after that.

An official garrison of "rangers" would roam local backwoods looking for unruly Indians until 1718.

With the threat from the Indians removed, settlers poured into Carolina in unprecedented numbers. Soon New Bern began to flourish and quickly blossomed into colonial North Carolina's largest and most prosperous city, and became its capital.

In 1800, expatriate Tuscarora representatives came back to North Carolina to ask the legislature for compensation for land they had lost. The legislature established a "lease fund" for the Indians which raised about fourteen thousand dollars. The United States Congress authorized use of the money for the purchase of more than four thousand acres of New York land northeast of Niagara Falls as a permanent home for the tribe. Upon the establishment of the reservation, many of the remaining Tuscarora migrated north to join the Six Nations. Tuscarora descendants live there to this day.

The Canadian Tuscarora gained their land—the Grand River Reservation in Ontario—for their loyalty to England in fighting against the colonists during the American Revolution.

We have said before that history is filled with many inexplicable curiosities. Well, today the Tuscarora Indians have a website. It's www.Tuscaroras.com.

Privateer fighting for a prize off Cape Lookout, circa 1780
Edward Ellis Collection

5

A Revolutionary Tale

*"The country is in a glorious situation for cutting
one another's throats."*
—*Major James Craig, British officer
Wilmington, N.C., 1781*

THE MURDER OF Patriot leader Alexander Gaston was the culminating act of terror visited upon New Bern by British troops, August 19, 1781. The dreadful scene played out in public and in broad daylight on the river's edge near Union Point. His wife and two small children were a few feet away when the unarmed doctor was ruthlessly gunned down by a Tory officer.

The British raid followed six years of struggle that began with the "shot heard 'round the world" at Concord, Massachusetts, April 19, 1775, when colonists first met the king's troops in battle.

It's arguable that North Carolina has not received its due in accounts of the American Revolution. The struggle for independence from Great Britain raged along the Atlantic seaboard from 1775-1783 and resulted in the creation of the United States of America. Representatives of the embryonic state of North Carolina were the first of the thirteen colonies to call for independence. Many historians agree that North Carolinians were early leaders in the rebellion, and that the 1771 Battle of Alamance—where Provincial Governor William Tryon defeated disgruntled citizens called "regulators"—was one of the earliest precursors of the American Revolution.

New Bern had been the seat of North Carolina resistance all along. Those who sought independence were called "patriots" and Dr. Alexander Gaston was among the most prominent of their leaders.

And the most prominent of targets.

The raid on New Bern lasted two days. Contemporary accounts paint it as two days of terror. Led by a British regular, Major James Craig, the city was pillaged and ransacked on a sweep from his base in Wilmington through coastal North Carolina Patriot strongholds. The Craig raid was a savage and wide-spread killing spree by Redcoats and the Tories, the "loyalist" supporters of the British monarchy.

One survivor said "wolves and panthers...were lambs compared to the more savage & wilder beasts of England, and the prowling bloodstained Tories." Another writer said, "Horror and indignation pervaded the land at the murderous deed, and the [Patriots]...cried aloud for vengeance and revenge on their merciless enemies."

Just three months later, the British commanding general, Lord Charles Cornwallis, would surrender the Cape Fear region and Craig would leave for other adventures. Within two years, the King of England would forever cede control of the thirteen contentious colonies. But before leaving, the king's men and Tory sympathizers cut a gore-soaked path of destruction across eastern counties and assassinated a beloved local hero in downtown New Bern.

SOON AFTER Colonial Governor William Tryon moved into the "palace" he built for himself on the banks of the Trent River in New Bern, he was awarded the governorship of New York. His successor, Josiah Martin, arrived at Tryon's Palace in late 1771. He would not remain there long. Nationally and in the Province of North Carolina, colonial-crown relationships were skidding off a cliff. They would soon hit the rocky bottom, catch fire and explode into the American Revolution.

Grievances about the lack of a standard currency, the closure of courts, denial of rights and British outrages against other colonies piled upon the three most troubling issues of the day: Taxation, taxation and taxation. Soon mass meetings, anti-imperial assemblies, rebellious committees and extra-legal congresses were at work from New England to Georgia.

A little affair known as the First Provincial Congress convened in New Bern in late summer 1774. Technically illegal and absolutely extraordinary, it was the first such congress held in America. Nearly every city and county in the colony of North Carolina was represented. The assembly wasted no time in roundly condemning "illegal and oppressive" taxation. It elected its own representatives to attend a Continental Congress and—as we should all know from social studies—those are the folks who would eventually bring us the ever-popular Declaration of Independence.

Governor Martin took note of the maverick congress held under his nose and was sorely offended by it. He would eventually dissolve the provincial congress altogether, but it was too late. The former colonists didn't need him or the king anymore. Rumors soon circulated that Martin was stockpiling weapons and conspiring to foment a slave revolt. After residing at the New Bern palace and in the North Carolina capital for four years, the last colonial governor was forced to flee for his life—disguised and in the dead of night.

And when the grounds of the Tryon Palace were searched by Patriot citizens, they found cannon, guns, ammunitions and explosives—an arsenal, in fact—hidden everywhere from the cellar to a garden. A barrel filled with about three bushels of gunpowder was secreted under a bed of cabbage. The colonial militia would soon make fine use of the munitions bonanza.

In the meantime, there were many more meetings, soul searching and pamphleteering. Pamphlets were to the 1700s what the Internet is today. Printing was big business. And one of the biggest and most vocal printers of them all was in downtown New Bern.

James Davis had worked closely with Governor Tryon. Tryon latched onto Davis early to print the colonial assembly minutes, legal codes, decrees and such. What money there was had been printed by Davis under gubernatorial sanction. The printer founded the *North Carolina Gazette*, the first newspaper in North Carolina. He printed the first book and the first pamphlet in the colony as well—and many more after that. But when Davis turned on the crown, he went full out and never looked back. He was boisterous and bombastic in his printed rhetoric. Davis was wealthy and owned land all over the county. Though nothing was ever proven, more than one person has pointed out that the occupation of printing money might have both special benefits and temptations.

And he had two convicted counterfeiters on his payroll! ...but now we've gone to gossiping. Sorry.

Be that as it may, Davis—though maybe the most vocal— was not alone in his opposition to king and parliament. Two citizens often cited as the most prominent of the Patriot leaders were Richard Codgell and Isaac Edwards. Others in opposition to the crown included Abner Nash, Jacob Blount, Lemuel Joseph Leech, William Bryan, James Ellis, Richard Ellis, John Green, David Barrow, James Coor, John Wright Stanly and William Tisdale. And those were just the ones who got their names in the news.

These men, and many more like them across the thirteen colonies, were known by several names: Patriots Americans, Whigs, Revolutionaries, Congress-Men or Rebels.

And don't think it was just the men. As proof, the women of Edenton, a couple of counties north of New Bern, really aggravated the British in America and England by holding a "tea party" of their very own. Shortly after the faux-Indians attacked the tea ship with little hatchets in Boston Harbor, sympathetic women in Edenton met on Oct 25, 1774 and drafted a resolution. It read:

"The Provincial Deputies of North Carolina, having resolved not to drink any more tea, nor wear any more British cloth, many ladies of this province have

determined to give memorable proof of their patriotism, and have accordingly entered into the following honourable and spirited association. I send it to you to shew your fair countrywomen, how zealously and faithfully, American ladies follow the laudable example of their husbands, and what opposition your matchless Ministers may expect to receive from a people thus firmly united against them."

Penelope Barker, wife of a provincial official, organized it. More than fifty women signed it. And the Edenton Tea Party set all of London a-howl.

These were dangerous times with much at stake. The Patriot colonists were thumbing their collective noses at the most powerful nation on earth, England. And the most powerful man on earth, King George III. All of these people—these American rebels—were putting their lives at risk.

Which brings us to Alexander Gaston.

ငာ ငာ ငာ

ALEXANDER GASTON was of French ancestry, but born in Ireland in 1727. A physician by occupation, he received his training at the University of Edinburgh in Scotland and his experience in medicine as a surgeon in the British Royal Navy. During service with the fleet fighting at Havana, Cuba, Gaston contracted dysentery, a painful, often fatal, inflammation of the bowels. He left service and sailed to the American colonies to recover. After settling in New Bern, he met and married a twenty-year-old England-born beauty named Margaret Sharp.

The Gastons lost their first child in infancy, but in 1778 they welcomed a son, William Joseph, and in 1780, a daughter, Jane. The family owned a town home at Craven and Pollock streets in downtown New Bern, but Gaston also had a plantation of several hundred acres down the Trent River from New Bern on land that is present-day Taberna. Part of the land was purchased from an heir of William Brice, and an adjoining section was purchased at a sheriff's sale.

Gaston practiced medicine in New Bern and also acted as an apothecary, as evidenced by an advertisement he placed in the *North Carolina Gazette* on May 22, 1778:

I have just opened a large assortment of fresh imported medicines, among which there is a greater quantity of almost all the following articles, than I could consume in my own practice in many years, therefore would be glad to supply others, at the lowest terms with what ever they may want, of Peruvian bark, camphire, sweet mercury, opium, rheubarb, jallap, Ipecacuanha, aloes, myrrh, gummastick, magnesia, Spanish flies, Venice treacle, borax, saltpetre, volatile salt of hartshorn, do. of salamoniac, camomile flower, brimstone, and flowers of sulphur, &c &c.

ALEX. GASTON.

Gaston was affable, well-known around town as a gentleman and serious about his politics. Despite having been an officer in the British Navy, he soon became disenchanted with both the crown's attitude toward its colonists, and with the colonial administration's conduct as well.

In 1775, Gaston was a key member of what was termed a district safety committee. Though its function was illegal in the eyes of the crown, the safety committee was charged with organization of militia forces for the conflict they all knew was coming. The militia troops were called Minutemen because they would have to come in a hurry when called. In New Bern, Gaston served with Richard Cogdell, James Ellis, William Tisdale and others. Gaston and company selected Richard Caswell as the local field officer for the recruitment of two fifty-man companies and made him a colonel. Some sources indicate that Gaston was personally involved in the search for and recovery of the Martin arsenal hidden at Tryon Palace.

On February 10, 1776, the New Bern district safety committee played a pivotal role in one of the most critical events of the American Revolution. Word reached the committee that a small army of Scots Loyalists were marching—from the region of modern-day Fayetteville—to the Cape Fear region where they were to join forces with Tories and regulars in Wilmington. That meant trouble. Cogdell called Gaston, Tisdale and Ellis together and the four Patriots agreed on what to do. Caswell and all of his Minutemen were ordered to intercept the Loyalist before they could reach their destination. The New Bern committee sent artillery—some of it from you-know-where—to aid Caswell. They issued orders to surounding counties to send men on the double.

When on February 27, the sixteen hundred Scotsmen and other Loyalists reached the narrow, wooden Moore's Creek Bridge at a swamp about twenty miles northwest of Wilmington, they were surprised by about one thousand Patriots under the command of Col. Caswell and Col. Alexander Lillington. The wily Patriots had dug themselves in, placed cannons at point-blank range, removed boards from the bridge and greased what was left to make the footing slippery. The Scots Highlanders charged anyway across the narrow gap yelling "King George and Broadswords!"

The Patriot cannons and muskets ended the entire affair in five minutes. The Battle of Moore's Creek was over and the repercussions were marvelous for the Americans. Seventy of the king's men lay dead or wounded including their commander and many officers. More than eight hundred were captured. The Patriots secured the rough equivalent of a million dollars in modern-day British pounds sterling, another arsenal of weapons, wagons and supplies.

Only one Patriot soldier died and one was wounded.

Like the local team on a winning streak, the Patriot's popularity soared. Not only did they win this first major victory, but sentiment for independence was bolstered across the state. It was cheered, toasted and bragged about across the colonies as well. For the first time, many citizens believed that the impossible might just be possible.

The spoils of victory were:
> British rule ended forever in North Carolina.
> Recruitment in the militia went up.
> The Loyalists in Wilmington evacuated.
> The state was in the hands of the Patriots.
> South Carolina and Georgia were secured.
> Col. Caswell, now a hero, would be named governor.
> A North Carolina county would later bear his name.
> A city would be named for col. Lillington.
> And Moore's Creek is today a national battlefield park.

Another direct result of the victory was that the North Carolina Provincial Congress—on April 12, 1776, three months prior to the signing of the Declaration of Independence on July 4—issued the Halifax Resolves, the first demand in the American colonies for a full and complete separation from England and its king.

The congress had twice met in New Bern and had then begun to assemble in other places to the satisfaction of the more-rural residents. In Halifax, a committee of delegates, including Abner Nash of New Bern, drafted a list of grievances and demands that was unanimously adopted by the eighty-three delegates in attendance. It read in part:

"Resolved that the delegates for this Colony in the Continental Congress be impowered to concur with the delegates of the other Colonies in declaring Independency, and forming foreign Alliances, reserving to this Colony the Sole, and Exclusive right of forming a Constitution and Laws for this Colony..."

The complete Halifax Resolves appears in the Addenda of this book.

All of it was the result of success in a critical, single battle of the American Revolution.

Teaching point: The unhesitating, forceful execution of responsibility by the four-man safety committee in New Bern has been acknowledge repeatedly by historians as a key to the victory at Moore's Creek Bridge—and all that flowed forth from it.

But there was an unanticipated consequence of the victory. The four members of the New Bern district safety committee, including Alex Gaston, had become marked men.

ଔ   ଔ   ଔ

JOHN WRIGHT STANLY had the heart of a pirate.

The list of vessels his New Bern-based fleet seized in a few years following the Moore's Creek Bridge victory is enough to make Blackbeard blush. But Stanly was a legal pirate. With the Continental Congress short of naval vessels, certain individuals were sanctioned as "privateers" and allowed to prey upon enemy vessels, both military and merchant. Stanly was a young and skillful businessman, knowledgeable in shipping. He married the supreme New Bern Patriot leader Richard Cogdell's daughter, Ann.

So Stanly and his fleet were hunters after lucrative prey. His hunting grounds were off Cape Lookout and Ocracoke

Island, the choke point all vessels had to cross on every Atlantic seaboard shipping route.

On September 26, 1777, Stanly's privateer, *Nancy*, commanded by a captain named Palmer, captured a British merchant vessel off Cape Lookout. The sailing ship was brought to New Bern and its rich cargo of ivory, one hundred slaves from Guinea and other valuable cargo was sold at auction. The vessel itself was either sold or put into the Stanly fleet. The crew, per standard procedure, was given safe passage on another vessel to an agreed upon destination.

The same month, the *Bellona* under Capt. Henson and the *Chatham* under Capt. Pendleton, took the schooner *Actason*, the brig *Elizabeth*—loaded with indigo and lumber—and another vessel of unknown name. They even captured another privateer, the British ship *Harlecan*.

Not wanting to miss out on the action, Patriot leader Richard Ellis and several other New Bern merchants partnered with Stanly to further outfit the *Bellona* from its existing twelve cannons by adding sixteen more guns. Thus armed, the ship would be a match for any British naval vessel it might encounter. And any merchant ship seeing all those barrels was guaranteed to roll over and play dead.

Many New Bern residents were ready to go a-pirating. Part of the motivation was harassment of the enemy, but there was money to be made as well. One local dinner was interrupted by word of British prize. A group of young men, including future governor Richard Dobbs Spaight, jumped from the table to give chase. Alas, that one got away.

But, dozens of ships and their rich cargoes were seized over time and the wharfs near New Bern's Union Point bustled with valuable prizes for sale. Buyers came from all over the eastern seaboard and lodged in New Bern waiting for a chance to bid on the confiscated goods. Within a short time, John Wright Stanly would occupy the largest mansion in town—not counting Tryon Palace, of course.

His banner year was 1780.

Stanly's privateer *General Nash*, a massive twenty-gun monster, took the two most staggering prizes imaginable. In September, off Ocracoke, Captain Deshon seized a big merchant vessel from Scotland piled to the gunnels with valuable goods, and another from the West Indies loaded with rum and sugar. The cargoes of the two vessels, sold at the

New Bern waterfront for 50,800 pounds sterling, well into the millions today.

In the next two months, *General Nash* took three brigantines-rigged vessels off Ocracoke: the *Aggie*, the *Prince of Wales* and the *Kattie*.

John Wright Stanly, who had once been in jail for debt, became New Bern's wealthiest citizen. New Bernians loved the action. The waterfront was bustling. The town was well supplied with all possible commodities. There was plenty of rum. Money was flowing and times were good.

In London, however, the British Admiralty was not the least bit amused by the success of American pirates.

CR   CR   CR

IT WAS CALLED a punishment raid.

The "sixteen Rebels in a house" bayoneted to death on April 12 would surely have agreed with that. To the farmers who had large herds of cattle stolen, it certainly felt like punishment. To those murdered, those whose homes, barns and plantation houses were burned, to the more than fifty women who were abused, and to citizens whose property was "indiscriminately looted," Craig's raid and killing spree had all the earmarks of punishment all right.

James Henry Craig was thirty-three. The career military officer would one day be a major general. He would be knighted and known as "Sir James." But in 1781, the British officer carried the rank of major. As a captain in New England at the beginning of the war, he was wounded twice. After a trip home to England carrying official reports of the New York campaign, he returned as a major in 1779. Serving under General Cornwallis, Craig was among those who had managed to re-occupy Wilmington after the hot contest at the Battle of Guilford Courthouse in 1781. With their resident Loyalist cohorts, they were back in control of North Carolina's largest city and its largest port for the next eight months. Craig and his Tory commander, Captain John Gordon of the N.C. Independent Dragoons, had free reign. They made a ruthless pair. A witness at the time called Gordon "that infernal Tory." One report said that Craig "continues his ravages for thirty or forty Miles up the Cape Fear with little or no Opposition."

The country was bitterly divided during the years of

70

Revolution. About one-third of the population was loyal to the crown. About a third were active seekers after independence. The remainder hoped to survive the conflict. Craig and Gordon apparently reveled in the divergence of opinion.

"The country is in a glorious condition for cutting one another's throats," Craig said.

Craig's arrival often forced a citizen to reveal his true allegiance for the first time. When the king's troops arrived in a given area, a Tory—who had previously hidden his loyalty to the crown—might step forward to help. Likewise, a citizen who had quietly favored independence might take a stand against the British raiders. When Craig departed, these newly-discovered sympathies could lead to reprisals by either side. Glorious throat cutting might ensue.

In particular, Craig was intent on capturing and killing prominent Patriot leaders. On one of his forays, Craig caught two big fish: Patriot leader Cornelius Harnett and militia Brigadier General John Ashe. Both were badly treated and imprisoned in a "Bull-Pen" made of rails situated in a hole on the north side of Wilmington's Market Street. Neither would survive imprisonment. Later, a county would be named for Harnett. Ashe contracted a lethal case of smallpox while in captivity. A county would be named for his family.

Seeking a larger canvas on which to paint with his bloody brush, Craig proposed to Cornwallis that he be given twelve hundred men for a sweep through eastern North Carolina rebel strongholds. He was thinking of Kingston—as Kinston was known before the revolution—and New Bern and other places where they knew the names of the thorns in the royal side. He wanted to plunder the towns and destroy things; kill rebels and capture their leaders. Cornwallis gave him eight hundred regulars and Tories and told him to recruit as he went along.

Craig had an object in mind. He intended to round up the Patriot gang causing so much trouble in New Bern. He knew their names: Gaston, Cogdell, Edwards, Leech and others. But there was one in particular he wanted dead. John Wright Stanly.

North Carolina Governor Thomas Burke warned his militia commanders not to risk their troops fighting Craig in a major battle. Instead, forces under Gen. Alexander Lillington sniped and harassed Craig's force, not making direct contact until August 17. Understanding the Redcoats were headed for New

Bern, Lillington tried desperately to stop Craig at Webber's Bridge on the Jones County line between New Bern and Pollocksville. Despite being short of both men and ammunition, the Patriots killed three and wounded five of Craig's men while taking no casualties of their own. But the skirmish was not enough to stop the advance of the larger British force. On its march, Craig's troops continued to be met by token hit-and-run opposition. He considered the tactics unmanly, more suited for savages than for real men. He was angered, but undeterred. Then, outside New Bern on the day of the local raid, a Patriot sniper killed the "infernal Tory" Gordon. When his raiding party—estimated at four hundred men—swept unexpectedly into New Bern on Sunday, August 19, it was on a rampage. The town would be occupied and ransacked for two days.

New Bern leaders had not believed the British enemy would attack the city because Lillington's troops would stop them. The Patriots were wrong. Warned shortly prior to the arrival of the Redcoats, most of the Patriot leaders of New Bern managed to hide or flee the city. Dr. Alexander Gaston was leaving town, too. He took his family—his twenty-six-year-old wife, Margaret; young son, William; and baby, Jane—to the New Bern waterfront where a boat awaited them. Gaston planned to go downriver to the family's plantation house and there ride out the British storm.

He was too late.

ભ   ભ   ભ

ONE OF THE OBJECTIVES for the foray into New Bern was to damage the shipping that had been causing so much havoc off Cape Lookout and to seize supplies. As a force of troopers under command of Capt. John Cox descended on the docks, Gaston was recognized. With his life in danger, Gaston made the agonizing decision to leave his family on the dock. In an instant, he leapt into the open boat and a servant boy frantically began to row.

From the wharf, the British soldiers fired repeatedly on the unarmed Gaston. Margaret pled vigorously for his life. Little Jane was only one year old. She must have been in her mother's arms. Little William was not quite three. The soldiers continued their inaccurate fire as the boat moved farther from the dock forcing the young rower over the side and into the river.

His boat adrift in the Trent River, Gaston was wounded, but still alive when British Capt. John Cox arrived on the Union Point wharf. Cox angrily reprimanded his soldiers for their poor marksmanship and called for his own musket.

"Please spare my husband!" Margaret Gaston pleaded on her knees before the Redcoat officer.

Cox kept his eyes on the unarmed father of the young woman's small son and daughter. Tears were streaming down her face. Looking up at British officer, she begged again, "Oh, spare him."

Cox was unmoved.

Carefully, slowly, he steadied the musket over the crying woman's shoulder. He took his time; settled the sights on the chest of Dr. Alexander Gaston and fired.

The heart of the New Bern Patriot leader was pierced by the bullet. The body toppled backwards, a lifeless form in the bottom of the small boat.

They held the town in terror for two days. British troops burned homes, seized about sixty slaves and stole horses. They left "ruin, ravage & distress" in their wake, according to one witness. The soldiers cut down masts and rigging of vessels in the New Bern harbor, vandalized and destroyed cargo including a valuable three-thousand-barrel salt shipment. They tried to collect lead for the pressing of bullets from the gutters of Tryon Palace. The Patriots had already removed and hidden most of the metal.

But they could not find the privateer Stanly. As luck would have it, John Wright Stanly had accepted an invitation to visit a friend—in Philadelphia. His absence saved his life, but it could not save his ships. During the war, Stanly is known to have lost fourteen vessels. Some of them were burned during the Craig raid at Stanly's private Neuse River wharf.

When they'd had enough of New Bern, the raiders headed for Kingston. Along the way they ransacked and burned several large plantation homes. The owners would get revenge by burning the homes of nearby Loyalists.

Eventually, the raids ended. Within months the British would be gone from Carolina and in two years they would be gone from the country forever. They would never return to New Bern. The war would end. Peace would finally come.

Sir James Henry Craig went on to other battles against the

Dutch in South Africa and the natives in India. He was promoted to major general and then was made governor-general of Canada. He would die in London in 1812.

During and after the American Revolution, some Loyalist left the country. Kingston dropped the "g" from its name, no longer wishing to honor the British monarch. Time passed. Eventually, the wounds of war would heal.

But not all of them.

Margaret Sharp Gaston, the twenty-six-year-old widow of New Bern's Revolutionary War martyr, would wear black every day for the rest of her life. She would never remarry. She raised the children on her own, learned to farm the plantation and prospered.

Margaret had been educated at a Roman Catholic convent in France. She brought her children up in the Catholic faith in a town with no Catholic congregation, priest or church. There would not be one until her son helped found St. Paul's in 1821. Margaret instructed them. Among other things, she taught her children to pray before beginning their school work, asking God to open their minds so they might learn and understand.

She was a strict mother and carefully saw to their education. Of Jane it was said, her mother would never let her sit with her back touching a chair. And, because vanity is sin, she would not allow her daughter to look into a mirror, at least, not when she was around.

With her guidance, young William would grow up to become one of North Carolina's greatest citizens and, possibly, New Bern's best man ever. One writer said, "The education and proper training of her son became the grand object of her existence." The son would become a remarkable jurist, write the state anthem and be universally loved and admired as a great mind and a great gentleman. In giving praise to Gaston's life of achievement, historians almost always point back with praise toward the mother.

In her later years, Margaret kept busy with duties to family, neighbors and her farm. She would care for the ill and indigent, with a special fondness for the old down-on-their-luck sailors that fate frequently dumped off at the port of New Bern. But a family biographer noted she never missed her daily teatime, precisely at 4:00 p.m.

After the war, it was, once more, perfectly acceptable to drink tea.

Richard Dobbs Spaight
N.C. Division of Archives & History

6

The Duel

RICHARD DOBBS SPAIGHT lay bleeding on the ground, his fine clothes stained bright red by the wound in his side. Dueling pistol still in hand, Spaight's long-time antagonist and rival New Bernian, John Stanly, stood some twenty paces away, silent for once. Following months of acrimony and today's extended contest of ritualized gunfire, a marble-sized metal ball from Stanly's weapon had sealed the fate of the three-term governor of North Carolina.

A crowd of witnesses watched in shock and horror.

It was a Sunday.

September 5, 1802.

Spaight's friend and second in the duel, Dr. Edward Pasteur, knelt beside the wounded man, examined him and issued orders to the men who carried him from the field to his nearby town home. Spaight would suffer through the long night and some of the next day, bravely it was said, before passing from this world.

His death would claim a husband and father of three. But Spaight was much more. He was one of the signers of the United States Constitution. He rubbed shoulders and exchanged ideas with men named Washington, Jefferson, Franklin, and Adams. He was a leader of the American Revolution, a veteran of battle and a general. He was New Bern's richest and arguably most prominent citizen, and its largest land and slave holder. He was one of North Carolina's and the nation's most influential politicians. At only forty-four years of age, he had much more to contribute.

Instead, at about 6:00 p.m. on that fateful day, Spaight collapsed upon the dirt behind the St. John's Masonic hall, in what was then the outskirts of town, bleeding from a mortal bullet wound—but dying because of words.

THE AFFAIR, known as the Spaight and Stanly "Paper War," had begun more than a year before. At first, it was a series of tales, gossip and exaggerations carried by friends. Then it became an exchange of hot words, then a torrent of letters, newspaper articles and broadsides. Over the preceding week, the verbal battle reached crescendo and climaxed finally with fire, smoke and hot lead.

Cloaked in choking customs of ancient chivalry and idealized honor, the battle was one of egos, ambition and politics. Stanly was an ardent Federalist in favor of a strong central government. Spaight was an anti-federalist Republican, a believer in state's rights and keeping the central government weak. In today's vernacular, Stanly might be called a liberal in opposition to Spaight's conservative leanings. Spaight had been to the pinnacle of parliamentary success. Young Stanly wanted the summit to himself.

Chided for months by Stanly and exasperated beyond further words, Spaight had issued the "demand for satisfaction" to his twenty-eight-year-old political foe the previous month. Stanly, the heir to a business fortune created by his swash-buckling entrepreneur father John

Wright Stanly, at first demurred after a fashion offering a rambling, somewhat less-than-conciliatory series of explanations for statements attributed to him. For one thing, he had suggested the former governor, an anti-federalist, was a push-over for the opposition Federalist Party saying it controlled his vote. Spaight then implied that Stanly was scum by stating that the younger man was successful only because "froth you know always swims on the surface." There were many other insults and innuendos cast, answered and denied.

The Francis Lister Hawks Papers, microfilmed at the N.C. State Archives, contains no less than eighty pages of the exchanges between and about Stanly and Spaight. The story has been reenacted by Tryon Palace performers. It has been told a thousand times and been written and re-written in thousands upon thousands of words. Nevertheless, no one has summed the matter up more succinctly than the writer of *A Historical Sketch of Newbern*, published in Charles Emerson and Company's New Bern City Directory of 1880-81.

"John Stanly, son of John Wright Stanly, one of the wealthiest and most influential merchants of Newbern at the close of the Revolution, had then just grown to manhood, and was one of the most brilliant intellects ever produced by the South. A federalist by principle and profession, with a quick and inexhaustible genius armed at all points with satire, ridicule and invective, bold even to recklessness in grappling with an adversary...it was inevitable if there was any manhood on the other side, that he would sooner or later come into personal collision with his opponents."

The writer notes that Richard Dobbs Spaight "happened to be the most conspicuous of the Republican leaders, and it fell to his lot to become a victim to the towering ambition and relentless temper of his adversary." As negative a light as the summary shines upon Stanly, the reporter continues by saying "doubtless, both were to blame for the quarrel."

"But it is a sad commentary on the civilization and Christian spirit of the time," the writer concludes, "that two such eminent men as John Stanly and Richard Dobbs Spaight could fight a fatal duel in the very suburbs of

Newbern, in broad daylight of the Holy Sabbath, in the presence of numerous spectators, and yet public sentiment tolerates the crime."

DUELS WITH PISTOLS or swords were commonplace in post-colonial American society, so much so that the conventions of such affairs of honor had been memorialized in a set of rules called the *Code Duello*. No exact record of the events of September 5, 1802 survives. We know that through their seconds—Pasteur for Spaight and Edward Graham for Stanly—the men agreed on the dueling ground and to meet at 5:30 p.m. Based upon the code, Spaight and Stanly, ornamented in sartorial splendor, would have toasted with a glass of wine. They might have shaken hands or bowed to one another. A doctor would have been present to tend to the wounded and to call for an end to the affair when the requirements of honor had been satisfied.

The matching pistols were loaded by the seconds, each for his own man. The typical pistols were fearsome weapons averaging about fifty caliber, a slug more than double the diameter fired today by the military's M-16 rifle. The impact of the ball and the corresponding damage to flesh and bone has been compared to a modern forty-five caliber semi-automatic pistol's hollow-point bullet.

Once the single-shot pistols were loaded, Spaight and Stanly stood back-to-back and, on a count, began to mark off the agreed upon number of paces. At the terminal point, the men turned, took aim and fired at one another. The guns barked. The crowd jumped and smoke filled the air. Miraculously, neither man had been hit.

At this moment, "honor" had been satisfied. In fact, in many of the rituals, the opponents simply fired into the air and retired from the field with the matter concluded. Spaight and Stanly could have done the same, but instead chose another course. They instructed their seconds to reload and the combatants marched off once again toward their fates.

Again the men turned.

Again they aimed.

Once more they fired.

When the smoke cleared after the next set of nerve-jarring pistol blasts, one of the witnesses, Thomas Brown, later to be postmaster of Trenton, noticed Spaight's shot had punched a hole in the collar of John Stanly's coat. Otherwise, the men were unharmed, but Stanly had avoided certain death by no more than two inches.

With no intention of a peaceful resolution, the men moved to have their pistols recharged. But now members of the crowd began to protest, pleading with the men to put an end to the duel. The cries of "Enough!" were met with force from Spaight's man, Dr. Pasteur, who stepped forward and threatened loudly to shoot any man who interfered with the contest. The crowd simmered down.

For a third time, the two duelists counted their paces, turned, took careful aim and blasted away at one another.

Again both missed the mark.

By now, some members of the crowd were frantic. More entreaties were made for a cessation of hostilities. Again, Pasteur blustered and the antagonists ignored the pleas of their friends and neighbors. Once more the hot pistols were reloaded and once more the angry men stepped off their paces.

Three times that day they had fired in anger, yet no blood had been drawn.

The fourth time the guns roar, Stanly's aim is true. Spaight staggered and crumpled to the ground.

THE NEXT PERSON known to have been shot at by John Stanly is New Bern historian and author Bill Hand. Hand's battles with Stanly have been bloodless affairs staged by Tryon Palace for the edification of the local public and tourists. Dressed in period costumes and armed with the appropriate weapons, Hand, playing Richard Dobbs Spaight, has been "killed" by the actor playing Stanly three times.

We asked Hand if his dueling experience and research into New Bern's most notorious affair of honor had given him any insights into what these men were thinking. He said he's almost come to know them personally and contends they are "two very different parties" with two distinct motivations.

"I believe that by the time of the duel, Spaight was just about eaten alive by his anger at being hammered by this young whippersnapper coming after him," Hand said. "He was *steaming*. It was all about honor which was such a huge, huge thing then, and political differences," Hand said. "Stanly was known for a hot temper and a very sarcastic manner. He was also known for his speeches and his highly energetic oratory when he was in the [state] house and in

Congress."

Hand said Spaight "was a little gentler overall, but he could be hot-headed as well when it came to personal attacks. I believe he went into the duel knowing he had a good chance of getting killed. There he was, walking in leaving behind a wife and several children and a whole household but, in that day, honor was such a *huge* thing, you did sacrifice your family for it. I don't think [this matter of honor] is something we can even comprehend today."

"Stanly, by my understanding of his whole life and his whole attitude, was a manipulator," Hand said. "And he was the one calmly and coolly building this thing up. I think it was very pre-meditated on his part. We know that there had to be some extreme hostility from Stanly toward Spaight because Stanly is known to have harangued Richard Dobbs Spaight, Jr. and reminded him over and over how he killed his father. He would continue to mock [the son] for years."

Hand, who shares the name, but is not related to a long-time local family associated with dentistry, hails from Pennsylvania. Asked why he had left his native state, he explained with a single word: "January." Always fascinated with days gone by, the critical mass of New Bern history has created for Hand, if not a full-time occupation, a nearly full-time pre-occupation with the story of the Colonial Capital. Hand pens a regular column for the newspaper, writes books and teaches history at the community college. He has been a "character interpreter" at Tryon Palace, playing Colonial Governor William Tryon and his favorite character, Reverend Drury Lacy, a minister here in the 1800s. He also served as the director of character interpretation for the Palace where he put together the annual Spaight-Stanly duel re-enactment.

Following the duel and death of Spaight, Stanly had to flee the state. Dueling was technically illegal especially when a standing state official was killed. In begging the North Carolina governor's pardon from his safe haven in Virginia, Stanly characterized himself as the injured party claiming to have been forced into his course of action. Hand finds it odd that Stanly was supported in his eventually successful plea for clemency by William Gaston, a brilliant New Bern-born attorney and judge.

"Strangely, one of his best friends was William Gaston who was probably the nicest guy this town ever produced," Hand said. "You wonder what kind of fire and ice relationship they had because they were extremely close. Gaston later saved Stanly's home when it was about to go up for a tax sale after he suffered a stroke. He saved him a couple of times. Years later, Gaston gave a beautiful, eloquent speech at his funeral. They were very, very close. It's curious to think of these personalities and how they mixed."

After gaining his pardon, Stanly's stature actually grew. He was repeatedly elected to state and national office gaining finally the position of Speaker of the North Carolina House of Commons.

Within months of Spaight's death, the North Carolina legislature passed a new and stronger anti-dueling law. It placed sanctions on office holding and income on anyone participating in a duel or aiding the participants of a duel. This made the duelist's second responsible as well, possibly a reflection on the role Pasteur played in the recent tragedy.

Stanly was both unaffected and unrepentant. He would later encourage his brothers, Thomas and Richard, to take part in duels. Thomas killed or was killed—depending on the historical source one consults—in a duel over a piece of cake he "playfully tossed" into a cup during a party splashing liquid on a man's coat. That one was fought in Virginia because of the new laws of North Carolina. Richard Stanly died in a sword duel in the West Indies.

After losing his seat to political opponent William S. Blackledge, John Stanly could not resist sniping and initiated an open verbal brawl in which deadly language was bandied about. Stanly said "however else deficient" Blackledge was, he had the only attribute his party required: "A belief in the infallibility of Mr. [Thomas] Jefferson." Blackledge, of course, did not have the option of the pistol, such gun play having been banned by the new law. Then again, he may have considered the reference to Jefferson a compliment, no matter how back-handed.

Again in 1810, John Stanly was involved in a long and very public war of words with another man calling him a "lyar," scoundrel, coward and hypocrite. This time John Spence West was the victim of a long Stanly essay in the newspaper in which Stanly used some of the identical words Spaight had used against him years before.

Despite the venom, Hand said Stanly flourished politically and in business for the quarter century following his duel.

81

The affair did not appear to affect his law practice in New Bern.

"To a great extent, it's party politics," he said. "The people on his side are not impacted and would privately cheer him for having knocked off a big guy from the other side."

More than two decades after his famous gun fight, Stanly was in the North Carolina House of Commons delivering a speech when he was hit by a massive stroke which ended his political career. He survived eight years, but the illness took him out of public life and left him incapacitated until his death in 1834. He was buried in the Cedar Grove cemetery.

WITH THE TWO-MAN WAR concluded, sympathetic supporters transported the mortally-wounded Spaight to his townhouse. His wife, Mary, and their two sons and a daughter, supported by friends and other family members, cried, worried and passed the long, sad night in whispered conversation.

The big lead ball had cruelly driven cloth, flesh and metal into his body. One source says Dr. Edward Pasteur acted as his surgeon, but nothing is known about his treatment. It has been reported that the still youthful Spaight knew he was going to die, but faced his "dissolution" bravely. Bearing up under the agony of his wound, he confronted his impending death, one witness said, "with all the fortitude imagination can conceive."

Spaight lived to see the daylight dawn on September 6, 1802, but it would be his last.

The tragic outcome shocked and angered many people both in New Bern and across the state. The impact was greater at home. The widow was overcome with grief and depression. The loss of her husband, compounded by all the implications of the entire sordid affair, was more than Mary Leach Spaight could bear. Beyond heartbroken, she was nearly—if not actually—driven mad by the dreadful episode. Formerly a social matron of the town, she withdrew into a black melancholy that left her and her children prisoners at Clermont, their palatial and once-merry plantation home on the Trent River. Friends and neighbors worried that the reclusive Mrs. Spaight would ruin her own health and that of her young family. She refused visitations and kept the children locked behind closed doors. For most of the next eight years, she remained cloistered in her gloom. She died, still in mourning, long before her time.

Upon her death, family friends who had kept constant watch all along, ministered tender care to the Spaight children. All three, Richard Dobbs, Jr., Charles and Margaret, would survive to lead long and productive lives. The sons, in particular, were important contributors to the flourishing community and successful participants in local government. In fact, the eldest son, the one named for his father, would scale the political heights to also become governor of North Carolina—despite being harassed all his life by John Stanly.

THERE ARE no sources regarding the detailed nature of Spaight's wound. What is known from a letter, a newspaper account and other references is that Spaight was shot in the side—which side is unclear—and that he did not immediately succumb to his injury, but lived into the next day. What is also known is that duelists tended to stand sideways to their opponent to present a smaller profile than would normally be the case facing head-on. This typical stance would mean the ball entered Spaight's torso somewhere between his hip and his armpit. Otherwise, the wound would have been said to be in the head, arm, shoulder, hip or leg.

Dr. Pete Rowlett classified being asked to determine a cause of death for a man shot two hundred and seven years ago as his "weird phone call of the day." Nevertheless, the retired New Bern emergency room doctor who served for more than a decade and half as Craven County's medical examiner agreed good-naturedly to give it a go. Presented with all the known facts about Spaight's gunshot wound and subsequent demise, Dr. Rowlett ticked off the possibilities.

Not the heart, he said. If the bullet hit there, or even near there, say clipping the pericardium—the sack around the heart—Spaight would have died quickly, if not instantly.

Not a major vein or artery. He would have bled out in a hurry, probably not making it home.

Not the intestines, as peritonitis, an infection caused by the leakage of fecal matter or stomach contents, would have taken about three days to kill the victim.

Ditto for a general infection. Spaight didn't live long enough for infection to have been the cause of death.

Rowlett considered the lung a possibility. "You can breathe with one lung," he said. But then again, the chest could fill with air, a condition called pneumothorax. Or with it might fill with blood, known as hemothorax. Either would leave no room for the lungs to expand and put deadly pressure on the heart.

After regarding major possibilities, Dr. Rowlett came down to the liver.

"It's most likely that he died from a soft organ injury," he said. "That would have caused him to bleed out slowly. The liver would be slow and would keep him bleeding all night."

Dr. John D. Butts is the state's chief medical examiner. From his Raleigh office, Dr. Butts agreed with the weird phone call theory. He said he receives must of his weird calls on Friday, but even though this call was a Monday, he agreed to play along.

"You've got a lot of flexibility there," he said, beginning to focus on the slim number of facts, thinking out loud that "he could have been wounded anywhere." But then Dr. Butts began the same thought process as Dr. Rowlett—not the head, not the heart, not a major vessel, not the intestines—and came to a similar conclusion.

"It's possible it was the lung, but that's unlikely," he said. "I just looked at a fellow today who had been stabbed in the chest. They tend to pretty rapidly exsanguinate and die in a relatively short period of time."

After considering the suspected caliber of the bullet and the muzzle velocity of black powder guns, Dr. Butts had one alternative theory: "Maybe the bullet didn't penetrate deeply enough to kill him right away, but did some soft tissue and organ damage by shattering a rib and sending bone fragments into various places."

Then Dr. Butts asked a new question, one raised earlier by Dr. Rowlett: Was the governor right-handed or left-handed?

On that matter the historical record is mute, but we do have excellent samples of Spaight's penmanship many of which are his "paper war" letters to and about Stanly.

Professional handwriting analyist Barbara Anderson of Las Vegas is a forensic document examiner. She is nationally-known and has served as a consultant to *Fox News* and *The History Channel,* and testified as an expert witness in scores of legal cases. Though numerous samples of the deceased governor's handwriting are available, Anderson told the author that his dominant handedness "cannot be determined with any degree of certainty." She said "there are too many variable" and although many lefties slant their letter backwards, many don't, and many righties slant backwards, too.

"There are actually two ways to write left-handed," she said. "Some people hold the pen the same way right-handers do. Then there are people who write over the top of their letters." Other forensic handwriting experts agreed. One raised other issues. In colonial times, many people were forced to be right-handed and most were taught to write in a very precise manner, almost a type of calligraphy which masked their "handedness." Governor Spaight's handwriting was quite precise and uniform.

Emily J. Dill of Raleigh, a top expert in the same field, agreed, saying "There is no actual way to tell. There may be some indicators, but it's certainly not something you could testify to in court."

The issue of right or left-handed was raised by both doctors for the same reason. If Governor Spaight was hit in the right side, his wound might have been liver-related, Dr. Rowlett said, "but if left-handed, the spleen would have done the same thing."

Chief Medical Examiner Butts went with the laws of probability. He noted that since about ninety-three percent of people are right-handed "you can hardly go wrong going with the right side."

Both agreed it is doubtful Spaight's wound would be fatal today. "It may well be true that he would have lived," Rowlett said. "It seems like he had plenty of time, but with medical care in that age, there is no telling what kind of treatment he may have received. For all we know, they may have bled him."

Dr. Butts said a modern emergency room should have been able to save Spaight's life. "You would have hoped with that much time someone could have been able to do something for the man," he said.

Regardless of the cause of death, the duel robbed New Bern and North Carolina of one of its most vital, brilliant and successful citizens. There is no telling what Spaight might have accomplished had he lived a full life. While Stanly continued to live in his own unique way, in the end, his health soured and he was left a damaged man. Today he is most remembered for having killed Richard Dobbs Spaight.

POSTSCRIPT

HERE IS YET ANOTHER of those wild historical curiosities—this one involving the Spaight and Stanly duel.

Battling furiously in World War II, the United States undertook a massive shipbuilding campaign from 1941-1945. At shipyards around the country, in addition to manufacturing heavily-armed warships, the nation embarked on the titanic task of creating the world's largest fleet of cargo carriers. Called *Liberty* and *Victory* ships, these huge ocean-going haulers measured one-third longer than a football field and were required to supply the critical needs of U.S. combat forces around the world.

An old military maxim says, the amateur studies tactics while the professional studies logistics. Logistics, of course, is the art of getting things like food, clothing, weapons, ammunition and medical supplies where they are needed when they are needed. Without these tools with which to fight, a battle is lost before it even begins.

By war's end, 2,751 Liberty ships and five hundred and thirty-four Victory ships were built in eighteen yards around the country. One of the shipbuilding operations was in North Carolina at the Port of Wilmington where nearly two hundred and fifty of the vessels would be christened. The first Liberty ship built at Wilmington took nine months to complete, but the workers quickly streamlined the manufacturing process. The tenth ship took less than four months. By the nineteenth such ship, there was only two and a half months from keel-laying to launch in the Cape Fear River. Joining the fleet September 23, 1942, was one named the *USS Richard Dobbs Spaight*.

By the fifty-ninth Liberty ship, the North Carolina Shipbuilding Company workers had enhanced efficiency to the point where the entire process from raw steel to four hundred and forty-one-foot-long transport required just thirty-nine days and—you guess it—the *USS John W. Stanly* hit the seas.

The Liberty ships went into service around the world hauling vital freight to U.S. fighting men. Many of the vessels and their crewmen made it through the war. Others were not so fortunate. On March 10, 1943, with less than six months in service, a German submarine operating in the Indian

Ocean put a torpedo into the side of the *Richard Dobbs Spaight*. U-182, commanded by Captain Nicolai Clausen, made the attack in the Mozambique Channel off Durban in southern Africa. The blast folded iron and steel deep into the bowels of the ship. All but one crew member were able to abandon the burning freighter which was then finished off by gunfire from the enemy sub. The Germans questioned and rendered aid to the *USS Spaight* crew before continuing its patrol. The two boatloads of survivors—forty-two of forty-three merchant sailors and the entire armed guard of twenty-four—endured a three-day passage of the open sea to a South African port.

The crew of U-182 did not fare as well. Two months later, depth charges from the destroyer *USS MacKenzie* sent the Nazi sub to the bottom of the Atlantic Ocean off the coast of Portugal. Captain Clausen and his five dozen officers and crewmen lost their lives.

The *USS Stanly*, however, survived the war. It initially ran Atlantic routes between U.S., African and British ports. By war's end it had been around the world and seen service in the Leyte Gulf, at Guadalcanal and Manila. In 1947, the ship was sold to the Norwegian government and renamed. It was renamed again when it was sold to Italy in 1954.

In the end, the *USS Spaight*, pierced in the side, was lost at an early age in 1943. The former *USS Stanly*, disowned after long service, ended on an Italian scrap heap in 1969.

For more biographical information on Richard Dobbs Spaight, John Stanly, John Wright Stanly and William Gaston, see Chapter 16, Essential People of New Bern.

Aftermath of Great Fire of New Bern, 1922
New Bern Firemen's Museum

7

Fred and Other Burning Issues

WIDE-EYED, the child stared into the squat glass case. A single questioned pinged around inside his head.

"If they loved him so much, how could they cut his head off?"

Simultaneously attracted and repelled by the sight, the youngster continued to gape at the exhibit. As semi-grisly as the whole idea of decapitation was in the immature mind, slowly a softening began. Some slight easing of the initial sentiment was set in motion by consideration of the big brown eyes. The—what was it?—sweetness there? And the impressive nose. And the strong, broad forehead worthy of a Roman noble.

Before long, a grudging admiration was emerging for the

determination to preserve the story of the fire horse—the selfless sacrifice of a hero named Fred—who had given his life answering a fire alarm. And through the years, the careful work of the taxidermist lo those many years ago became a physical manifestation to this author of the ardent genius of a community to save and savor and safeguard the most intimate details, the precious artifacts, the sacred memories, the strong, sad and bittersweet emotions—all the facets of the legacy, the heritage, yes, the *history* of a single eastern North Carolina town at the nexus of twin rivers.

Fred answered alarms for seventeen years until the day in 1925 when his big heart gave out as he rushed to answer yet another call for help. The men of the Atlantic Fire Company, no doubt heartbroken by the loss of their long-time companion, decided that stuffing the head of the faithful old fire horse would be a fitting tribute. And so today, more than eight decades later, Fred—his coarse brown hair and dark mane offset by a finely-worked bridle—is the most noted feature of the New Bern Firemen's Museum.

So it is that the author himself has, over many years, introduced his own mystified children, and those of others, to the unique token of respect for Fred the Fire Horse at the Hancock Street museum. And now he has lived long enough to begin again with grandchildren passing along the intriguing story of a time when volunteer fire company's water-pumping machines were pulled by these magnificent animals upon dirt streets to bring relief to those in peril and to battle the city's long-time, merciless rival—fire.

THE WOODLANDS around New Bern are filled with a variety of towering pine trees. Some of the more familiar ones are Long Leaf, Short Leaf and Loblolly. The lesser-known Pond Pine is a curious, dwarf, stunted tree found skirting the edges of nearby wetlands and in abundance in the deep recesses of the 156,000-acre Croatan National Forest's pocosin swamps. One of the smallest varieties of pine, *Pinus serotina* opens its cone and releases its seeds after it has been burned over by a forest fire. So natural are wild blazes in the ecology of the local woodlands, the Pond Pine has evolved its survival technique by waiting for the flames. The tree has been shaped by fire.

In the off-chance the bear is ever retired, the Pond Pine might be a fitting emblem for the city because fire has played a lead role in shaping New Bern as well. There's the matter of one in 1922 called "The Great Fire." There are the many historic structures like Tryon Palace, Clermont Plantation, Christ Church and, in more recent times, the Governor Tryon Hotel that have been consumed. There are the fire companies, Button and Atlantic; a story unto themselves. And there's Fred, as we have mentioned, a hero to generations of New Bern school children.

Although hundreds of fires have immolated property and life here during colonial times, the Civil War and into the modern era, all pale in magnitude to the inferno that swept through New Bern on Friday, December 1, 1922.

In a paragraph above, we paid a sincere tribute to the genius of a few professional but mostly amateur historians who have preserved New Bern's history. No finer example of that effort can be pointed to than the one led by people like Mary Barden who recorded the details of the 1922 fire which destroyed so much of the city and changed its face forever. Not only were survivors sought out and interviewed, not only were those interviews tape-recorded, but they were painstakingly and meticulously transcribed. Even lectures about the fire have been recorded and then type-written, double-spaced. All of this material is today filed, indexed and protected within the innermost confines of the main New Bern library. More recently, an African-American history tour has risen from those long-ago ashes with its own research and perspective on the participation and loss of so many in the early twentieth-century black neighborhoods. Many facts and details of New Bern's Great Fire of 1922 shared herein have been preserved by these laudable efforts.

CR CR CR

IT WAS WASHDAY.

In the poorer, predominantly black section north of Queen Street, Friday was the day the little campfires were built. Normally tended with care, the fires heated water in big iron wash pots where clothes were boiled and stirred with sticks or hand-hewn paddles. One of the washday fires burning that overcast, cold and blustery first of December was behind an unpainted wood-frame home on a crowded, narrow lane called Kilmarnock Street.

Like so much else in history, accounts and memories vary.

But in a reliable version, the folks doing the washing were drawn away from their fire that fateful day by something big, something amazing. The Roper Mill was burning down.

New Bern was and had always been a big lumber town. Along the Neuse River at the northern head of Craven Street, immense wharves, saw mills and warehouses had been used by a series of lumber companies for longer than anyone could remember. In 1922 the plant—New Bern's largest industry— was actually operated by the Rowland Lumber Company, but in the past it had long been owned by Roper Lumber and many people, as people will do, still called it the Roper Mill.

The first sign of trouble was when an alarm sounded just after 8:30 a.m. Fires at lumber mills were not uncommon considering all the combustible material. There was sawdust, trim waste, finished boards of all types and sizes, some dried, some full of sap. Here, at North Carolina's largest sawmill, there was a jumble of wooden buildings; everything from plank sheds to timber shelters to a wood-frame metal-roof structure big enough to host a football game. Fires, when they happened, were usually handled by the plant's three hundred workers, sometimes with the help of the nearby volunteers.

Today, however, there was an unexpected wild card.

The wind was blowing a gale out of the south. What might have been a small, manageable blaze was fanned by a stiff breeze which built to forty-five knots. Before the long, long day was over, people who were there swear the gusts hit seventy.

Small at first, the fire was fed by the high wind. Soon it was big enough that every available fireman and every piece of the city's firefighting equipment was fully engaged. The smoke was heavy. Flames crackled fifty feet in the air contrasting with the steel gray sky. And the blaze roared loudly as it quickly spread. If the lumber company was lost, Fire Chief James K. Bryan thought, it would surely be one of the biggest fires the city had ever seen.

At that moment Bryan could not imagine, nor would he have believed, that this would be the smallest of the day's three fires.

Word of the spectacular sawmill inferno spread like fire itself through the neighborhoods and across town. Soon citizens were coming from all directions. A couple of them were people from Kilmarnock Street who left their washing to hurry up Queen Street and see what all the hubbub was about.

There was a second wild card that day.

A sizable contingent of sports fans had left town for the championship football game in Raleigh. New Bern versus Sanford. It was the big game; a really big deal for New Bern. A whole trainload had gone to cheer for the team. Some say it was 300 people. Records indicate it was nearly 400. Whatever the number, the game resulted in the absence of many of the city's able-bodied men. Many of them were young. And some of them were firemen. Most all of them would have come running on winged feet to help fight a fire like the one huffing and puffing at the lumber mill. But they did not come. They could not come. They were gone.

At 10:45 a.m., another alarm sounded.

Was that possible?

Hearing the klaxon, Chief Bryan made the decision to disengage a hose truck from the hellacious beast on Craven Street. He was not going to send a valuable pumper until he knew for sure what was going on. He had already sent a crew to answer one false alarm that morning. He wasn't going to do it again. He needed all his equipment where it was at the moment.

Arriving at Kilmarnock Street, the hose truck driver, A.L. Deal, discovered another alarm was, indeed, all too possible. Coals blown from an untended wash pot fire had ignited dried groundcover setting an old wooden fence ablaze. The dry fence boards were going up like kindling, snapping and popping under the strong encouragement of the wind. Sparks were flying and the roof of the nearest house was already beginning to smoke.

The men went quickly to work and just as quickly discovered they had left the Rowland blaze without a hose nozzle. Expelling some blue words almost as hot as the flames, they hurried back up the long street for the proper gear.

Another version of the story says the Kilmarnock blaze was begun by embers coaxed up and out of a chimney by the high winds. No matter if it was the wash pot, a chimney fire or both, sparks soon landed on the wooden shingles of the home of Henry and Hester Bryan near Five Points on land where Craven Terrace would later be built. Almost all the houses for many blocks around had wooden shingles. The shingles, it turned out, were just a little more fire resistant than tissue paper.

Neighbors fought the Bryan's fire in vain by handing buckets of water to a man on the roof. A witness said "a gale was blowing and the blaze started racing across the roof's wooden shingles with lightning rapidity. The man on the roof scrambled down—just in time."

When the firemen returned some minutes later, they were properly armed and ready for battle. But it was too late. Three homes were fully involved. Fanned by gusts which could nearly blow a man off his feet, the fire assumed a life of its own. It swirled skyward, a scorching tornado sucking up oxygen and spitting out hot embers. Driven backwards by searing heat, the bewildered men witnessed the flames— coaxed to demonic fury by the wind—bounding from house to house.

Soon, startled people were running through the streets, some clutching small children. Others tried desperately to drag their precious possessions outside. The street began to fill with furniture, trunks, clothing and even pianos, much of it destined to burn in place. Men were shouting and women were crying as the conflagration hurdled over homes. The volunteers gave it all they had, but it would have been easier to stop the tides. Soon the crackling nightmare was jumping across streets and eventually street-to-street in a tremendous firestorm like none of them had ever seen.

"Flaming shingles, careening on the breast of the gale, flew through the air for blocks and set widely scattered conflagrations," wrote Raleigh *News & Observer* reporter Joe Gaskill McDaniel. "It was an awesome sight—completely unbelievable. Pitiful humans screamed everywhere like trapped animals fleeing from a flaming forest."

More fire alarms whistled distress. Church bells began to ring out alarms of their own.

All over town panic prevailed. With flaring shingles and glowing embers raining down far and wide many feared all of downtown would be lost. Others could see the tsunami of combustion headed their way and grabbed whatever they could carry.

"It's right funny the things we saved," Eleanor Jones Carr would later recall. She was a child at the time of the great fire. Her father was out of town. "So my Uncle Jimmy opened a locked drawer and got a pint of whiskey and took a pistol," she said. "I took my bicycle and my doll, and mother took silver, and that's all we took." With fire only minutes away, they still carefully locked the front door.

Confused people of all ages were running through the streets barely staying ahead of the flames. Some wept. Some moaned. Most moved with a wide-eyed, quiet intensity. Some barked orders of encouragement to those around them. Moving ahead also was a parade of horse carts, handcarts, Model T Fords and trucks loaded with furnishings and valued belongings.

Malissa Vailes's mother told her and her sister to hurry and get their clothing off the wall and into a metal washtub. Many homes of the era lacked closets and clothes were hung on wall pegs.

"Mr. Ernest Johnson was going through the neighborhood shouting for people to take their belongings...and go to the railroad tracks," Ms. Vailes said. "He had a big horse-drawn wagon and people put their pianos and big, heavy furniture on the wagon and he took them to the railroad tracks and put them on the flatcars. All the people in our area went and got on the flatcars. No roof. Just an open flatcar. The engine then pulled the cars way out at the end of the tracks, out by Oaks Road. It was the day after Thanksgiving and mama said for us to pack all the food we had left...that we would have something to eat."

The young girls and their handicapped mother would spend the cold night upon the car trying to warm themselves with extra clothing. They would not know until the next morning that their home had gone up in smoke shortly after their escape.

Many of the residential areas north of Queen were tightly packed with old run-down houses. More than a few of them dated from the Civil War when freedmen claimed land on the outskirts of town and built rude shelter for themselves and their families. One memoirist called parts of the area "sort of a ghetto." Many of the homes were the property of landlords, black and white. Caleb Bradham, the inventor of Pepsi-Cola, for example, would lose about ten homes in the fire which he rented to black families for a dollar or two a week. Some of the homes, however, were much more substantial and owned by their occupants. Nonetheless, few of them were insured.

The most common roofing material on all the homes was cedar shake shingles, some of which were fifty or more years old. All over the area, burning embers rained down on the aged roofs.

Meanwhile, the sea of flames roared through Tin Cup Alley and Bern Street; devoured everything at Smithtown and the Frog Pond; took out Elm Street, West Street and Cedar Street. One home after another was blasted, blistered and then burst into a fireball. During the height of the fire, standing homes were turned to rubble and ash in as little as fifteen minutes. The hell storm vaulted George Street. It rolled through Cedar Grove Cemetery. The thick stand of lovely cedar trees which gave the cemetery its name cooked off like gasoline. The mid-town forest fire burned wooden crosses, monuments, caskets and mausoleums.

One man would remember heat so intense it warped the nearby railroad tracks. He was sure the whole town would be destroyed.

The fence around Union Station burned. All the Pasteur Street homes in front of the station burned. The train depot itself was saved by heroic efforts of neighbors who ascended to the roof of the two-story structure and beat out fires started by falling debris. Nothing, however, could save the big overall factory, Nassef Manufacturing, across the street from the depot or two nearby brick tobacco warehouses. Telegraph communication was lost when poles toppled and wires melted. The fire took out the Norfolk and Southern railroad's riverside loading docks, but providentially failed to contact the big fuel storage tanks there.

The front doors of the First Missionary Baptist Church were only scorched, but the fire claimed all of Ebenezer Presbyterian, Rue Chapel and sent the flock of conventioneers gathered at St. Peter's AME Zion Church running for their lives. The burning steeple of St. Peter's, the finest black church in town, could be seen for miles.

New Bern blazed for the next thirteen and a half hours. The inferno would devour twenty-five percent of the city.

It might have taken more if it hadn't been for a crucial decision followed by a little luck.

Chief Bryan was out of options. He called for help from every city he could think of and a number rallied to help. The calls from New Bern have been described as frantic and no doubt they were. Kinston sent a truck on the unpaved highway. It took two hours to arrive. It made town at 3:15 p.m. about seven hours after the start of the fire.

Washington, farther away than Kinston, put a fire truck on a flatbed railcar and off-loaded in New Bern just fifty minutes later. The crew of the Coast Guard Cutter *Pamlico* had been helping since the start of the Rowland blaze and would continue to help until the last ember was snuffed. But as one observer noted, no amount of men and no firefighting apparatus from any small town or big city could have halted the firestorm which was hopelessly beyond control and had been from the beginning.

George Bradham rode the train to Raleigh for the championship game. It was during the gridiron contest, he said, when troubling reports began to circulate among the crowd of spectators.

"We received word there was a big, big fire in New Bern and the town was burning down," Bradham remembered years later.

Some had driven the gravel and clay roads to Raleigh. Most of them left for home immediately upon hearing the news. Those on the train couldn't leave until the appointed time, but, for everyone, the trip home was slow and painful. They would not know the city's true fate for hours.

Many years later, Bradham still remembered his first view of the devastation and—most particularly—the heavy smell of smoke and fire.

"It was a very spectacular thing," he said.

The huge Rowland sawmill, where the first fire originated, was destroyed. Records say two million board feet of finished lumber went up in one of the most colossal bonfires ever witnessed. Observer Ray Hathaway said it was "a scene of total confusion."

"I saw the metal roof collapse," he said of the main mill building. "It just buckled in the middle and fell down."

The wind carried dense choking smoke, sparks and burning debris over downtown New Bern and across the river all the way to Bridgeton. Rowland had a second huge lumber saw-yard up Griffin Street—today called North Craven. Flying embers set the northern yard ablaze as a coup de grâce to the day's events. That fire, the third in a few harrowing hours, was spectacular in its own right. It burned a separate multi-block area just up the river from the first Rowland fire.

Chief Bryan had seen enough.

He made a daring decision.

They'd blow up part of the town to save the rest. He called

for dynamite.

The idea was to deny fuel to the wall of flames by creating a fire break. Once made, the decision was quickly executed. Crews began to blow up undamaged houses at Queen Street and Metcalf. Some say nearly one hundred homes would be leveled in all including a half dozen along Queen which were ripped apart by a stout cable attached to a steam locomotive.

People whose homes were not yet threatened by the fire stood in awestruck disbelief as men placed sticks of dynamite beneath them. To all the other unnatural sounds that day was added the concussion of one massive explosion after another.

Coast Guard officer William Montague was carrying a woman from her home when it was dynamited. With the woman in his arms, Montague saw three men placing explosive charges. He shouted to tell them he was in the building. Rushing toward the door, he yelled to no avail for them to wait. The blast blew Montague and the woman through a wall and into the yard. Although the coast guardsman was unconscious for several hours, by some miracle, they both survived with only minor wounds.

Then, with the approach of dusk, the smutty, dirty, exhausted firefighters and the terrified residents of New Bern caught a break. The wind sheared, settled to a breeze and stilled. Though fires would burn through the night creating an eerie glow visible for miles, the fury was brought under control. The full extent of the damage would not be known till morning.

Refugees of the fire passed the night among tombstones in the Cedar Grove and Evergreen cemeteries. Some slept in boxcars, in stores, churches and an empty fertilizer warehouse. Many residents who still had homes opened their doors to comfort neighbors who did not.

In the nine-tenths of a mile between Five Points and Union Station, a thousand buildings were consumed. The flames did not discriminate between homes, warehouses, factories, churches and stores. Neither did they discriminate between black and white, though it was clearly the black folks who bore the overwhelming, heartrending brunt of it.

By morning, a forty-block forest of chimneys north of Queen Street towered over a thick smoldering floor of hot ash.

And thirty-two hundred men, women and children of New

Bern were homeless. Many of them now owned nothing but the cinder-stained clothes upon their backs.

Referring to World War I which had ended just four years before, a nationwide Associated Press dispatch noted, "The war-devastated towns of Belgium and France hardly presented a more pitiable spectacle of complete destruction than that section of New Bern tonight which was swept by fire throughout the entire day."

The smoke and the glow in the sky had been seen by people forty miles distant. The great fire that day after Thanksgiving 1922 was, and remains to the present, the largest fire of its type in North Carolina history.

There was a final blow to the tragedy. With sawmills, stores and businesses gone, fifteen hundred New Bernians had no place to go to work the following Monday.

But there was a miracle buried in all the bad news. Only one person died in the fire. The single fatality was an elderly black lady too feeble to flee her home.

THE MORNING of December 2, 1922 dawned with most of New Bern in a state of shock. But cool heads began to prevail from the start. By 10:00 a.m., Chamber of Commerce director Harry Jacobs had gathered civic and business leaders. A recovery effort was quickly launched.

Help poured in from across the state. Possibly the most immediately significant were the train car loads of shelter material sent by Brigadier General Albert J. Bowley, commander of the Fort Bragg army base at Fayetteville. Bowley sent sixteen men and eight boxcars loaded with tents, bedding and other equipment. The Norfolk Naval Station delivered a shipment of "one thousand cots and blankets and hundreds of sweaters." The North Carolina National Guard began patrols to prevent looting and help local police maintain order.

Bakeries and restaurants went into full-time operation, many giving away their output to the needy. The Swift and Armour meat companies sent ham. A Statesville milling company sent a train car load of flour. In addition to food and medical support, the Red Cross supplied cooking utensils and household goods. Area cities and towns sent clothing literally by the ton and New Bern citizens worked to organize it all.

Even the President of the United States, Warren Harding,

sent his condolences to Mayor Edward Clark.

For a time, New Bern took on the nickname Tent City. Homeless families were housed in a huge campground of canvas, hard-sided military tents. Each had a stove and each family got two tents set up so the doors faced one another. One was used for cooking and washing while the other was for sleeping. Tents were even provided as meeting places for the congregations of burned churches.

There were several notable effects of the fire.

For one, shingle roofs were outlawed.

In the medical arena, a local health department was created to provide typhoid fever shots and Good Shepherd Hospital was built to provide badly-needed medical care for the African-American community.

The city board made the controversial decision to disallow the reconstruction of homes in part of the burned-out area. The armory building on George Street, which now houses the police department, Kafer Park and an expansion of Cedar Grove cemetery, resulted.

Despite the fact that the lumber mill and several other large employers decided to rebuild, many black families who lost their homes and jobs gave up on New Bern. Most are said to have moved up north.

IN THREE HUNDRED YEARS, a lot of fires might be expected. Individual homes and businesses have been razed. An 1866 blaze called "the Great Conflagration" took out a whole block of Pollock Street. In 1965, local firefighters battled a hot one at the gargantuan Governor Tryon Hotel on South Front Street for most of two days. The ancient hotel was a total loss. The site is now occupied by the downtown branch of BB&T. Other fires will come but, as we have learned, nothing has topped the 1922 disaster. Hopefully, nothing ever will.

And now, at the end of our story, we find you *can* teach an old horse new tricks. Believe it or not, closing in on one hundred years after his death, lo and behold, New Bern's venerated Fred the Fire Horse can talk.

The Amazing Fred started life in Gastonia in 1900. In 1908 he was purchased to pull a big four-wheeled fire wagon for New Bern's Atlantic Fire Company. He hauled the wagon for seventeen years, mostly on reins held by John Taylor, a veteran African-American fireman noted for his skill at handling the big steam boiler. It could pump hundreds of gallons a minute. We say he "held the reins" because all who knew the horse swore Fred could locate a fire all by himself. An alarm for Box 28, for example, would be two tones followed by eight tones. The signal meant a specific location in the city and Fred, they say, had the alarms and their locations memorized.

When one sounded he would race through the streets of town, Taylor hanging onto the reins, and people would wave and kids would shout Fred's name. The horse was known and loved by all.

Sometimes life for a fire horse was a little less dramatic. Fire horses did double duty pulling the sanitation trucks. Fred did his share of trash hauling. But then there were other more glorious days, like the parade for the New Bern Bicentennial of 1910, when Fred was washed and brushed and bedecked with big white ribbons to pull a fancy Atlantic fire wagon for all to see. That impressive picture now adorns the glass museum case displaying his mounted head.

One day in 1925, Fred was on duty when an alarm sounded for Fire Box 57. John Taylor was not at the reins that day. The old veteran had died a short time before of a heart attack. Fred was no youngster himself at twenty-five, but he and other firemen began to hurry to the scene of what would turn out to be a false alarm. On the way, the horse's mighty heart finally beat its last. The noble and beloved Fred stumbled and fell dead in the street.

As we have said the horse head was stuffed and beautifully mounted in a case. Even among the antique fire equipment, the great old photographs, Civil War artifacts, and a remarkable collection of memorabilia, the taxidermal tribute is a highlight of the New Bern Firemen's Museum on Hancock Street near Broad.

And what's more, today, old Fred can speak. That's right. A visitor who pushes a small doorbell switch on the front of his case is treated to a first person—or should we say "first steed"—narrative of Fred's life spoken by the wonder horse himself.

The Tryon Palace Restoration
Historic New Bern Guide Book

8

A Palace Resurrected

"Fire! Fire on them or fire on me!"
—*Royal Governor William Tryon*
Battle of Alamance, May, 1771

THANK WILMINGTON for Tryon Palace.

Brand-new North Carolina Royal Governor William Tryon might have left the seat of government exactly where he found it when he was sent from England in 1764 to take charge of the colony—in Wilmington. However, after Tryon was confronted by a big mob angry about taxes, he decided to move the capital to a place where he was wanted.

He was wanted in New Bern.

In fact, the high muckety-mucks of New Bern had been sweet-talking the military officer-turned-politico for some time. Tryon visited New Bern soon after his arrival in the colony. The local folks went all out. They fired nineteen cannons. They threw him a ball. They dined him. They wined him. They offered to give him a "large genteel" house. They showed him the view.

One New Bernian advised the governor of the "Terrible Horribility!" of the high prices of everything in Wilmington. The printer, James Davis, told him in a bold editorial that Wilmington was gloomy and dismal; that it was nothing but hot, parching sand and stagnant water. They said Wilmington was almost South Carolina and he should move the capital to a more central location. They laid it on thick.

But the best players on New Bern's team turned out to be those rowdy Wilmingtonians themselves. After the tax mob made a scene, Tryon packed his wig and moved to New Bern. Well, not quite that fast. First, he had to build an appropriate residence and government house. That took three years: 1767-1770.

But that's how New Bern became the capital. And how it got Tryon's "palace."

Apparently, Tryon had planned to build something grand all along. How do we know this? Well, he brought his own personal architect with him from England. Not everyone does that. John Hawks, thereby, became the first professional architect in America, or so say the textbooks. Tryon "had the idea early on" to build a structure "to serve as a reminder of the force of the crown," said historian Dean Knight. North Carolina-born, Knight carries the unwieldy title of "registrar, archivist and librarian" at Tryon Palace. Formally degreed in history and education, Knight has been a staff member of Tryon Palace Historic Sites & Gardens since 1990.

From his wonderful, high-ceilinged, appropriately stirred-up office in one of the magnificently-restored homes that today make up the palace complex on Pollock Street, Knight shared some of his thoughts about the Tryon legacy.

Tryon's palace "was such a large, imposing structure," Knight said. "Around here at the time, there was virtually nothing but one-story frame houses, or an occasional two-story framed house, but almost no other brick structures. It made a statement that 'Might is right' and 'I am the representative of the King'."

It is not necessary to look far to find Tryon's mansion and government house described as the most beautiful structure in colonial America. Tryon and Hawks created a majestic

English-style country house in a generic Georgian design. The appealing symmetry of Tryon Palace was and is reminiscent of the magnificent homes of the landed gentry—that would be "the rich folks"—around London at the time. But Tryon's goal seems to have been to exceed the grandeur and architecture of anything even in Europe.

The architect advertised for the finest craftsmen in America to build the striking manor house. He traveled to Baltimore and Philadelphia to find talented brick masons and finish carpenters and other tradesmen. No expense was spared. Tryon squeezed every shilling possible out of the colonial assembly, and he and Hawk spent each one.

According to historians Hugh Talmedge Lefler and Albert Ray Newsome, Hawks's plan "included a brick house of two main stories, eighty-seven feet wide and fifty-nine feet deep, with two wings of two low stories each, connected to the main building by semi-circular colonnades."

As both the governor's home and the colony's capitol, it included an assembly hall, council room and public offices. Over the vestibule door, Lefler and Newsome noted a "somewhat ironic inscription." In Latin, it read: "A free and happy people, opposed to cruel tyrants, has given this edifice to virtue. May the house and its inmates, as an example for future ages, here cultivate the arts, order, justice, and the law." So hoped Hawks and Tryon.

The boys had a little female help with the palace. Tryon—after some infamous youthful dalliances—married quite well. Margaret Wake was a wealthy heiress from one of those big houses in England.

Knight said Margaret Wake Tryon was "a very, very strong influence, not just here, but throughout his entire career." Literature has it that she "demonstrated a masculine mind." She read about and wrote a treatise on fortifications, a subject she may have learned about from her father, an influential member of the largest business enterprise in the world—the East India Company. Margaret "had heard the talk of establishing colonies and fortifications all of her life," Knight said. "She grew up in a household with that kind of conversation." She was well-educated and a good musician. She "played and amazed" people with her skills.

"We have accounts of her managing the household," Knight said. One story relates how she flew into a rage because the palace kitchen was not clean and tidy. Lady

Tryon had the servants throw open all the windows and haul everything out into the yard. The kitchen was then thoroughly cleaned and white-washed. "She was not just a lady of retirement who sat idly by. She was involved in the everyday operation of the household also."

LADY MARGARET'S TEMPER was the least of the governor's concerns, however. By 1770, there were already stirrings of what would become the American Revolution. The whole thing boiled down to taxes and government intrusion into people's lives. In all thirteen colonies, citizens were beginning to think about throwing England over the side and the king along with it. Some of those earliest stirrings were right here in North Carolina.

As primitive as eastern North Carolina was at the time, it was a thriving cosmopolis compared to the western part of the state. In the east, occupations included merchants, lawyers, doctors, tradesmen and craftspeople. Out west, they were still living off the land. "Out west" at the time was just on the other side of what is now Raleigh. According to an official state history authored by the well-respected William S. Powell, the people there were backwoods pioneers seriously rankled by unexplained taxes, exorbitant fines, inconsistent fees for recording documents and surveys, a convoluted court system and general corruption among the king's agents. They hated the way they were regulated and formed committees to talk about this inept regulation. Soon, people were calling this crowd "the Regulators."

The absolute last straw for the Regulators was when they heard their governor was building himself a mansion. These disenchanted farmers from the Piedmont were in log huts, and the crown's agents were coming around with out-stretched hand for taxes to build a palace for William Tryon. Enough was enough. Soon, threats began to arrive that the Regulators were coming to burn New Bern to the ground. Some of the Regulators did burn down the home of a prominent Hillsborough judge, ransacked a few more homes of government officials, and beat or harassed others. More moderate members of the Regulators, however, hoped to negotiate with the royal government.

More than anything else, William Tryon was a military man. He called out the local militia, and when it didn't answer he offered to pay a bounty to anyone who showed up.

Soon he was training several units of riflemen from nine counties. He added to that some artillery and a little cavalry, totaling about nine hundred men and one hundred and fifty impressively-dressed officers. Tryon armed his militia with swivel guns, flintlocks and plenty of ammunition.

The colonial troops met the Regulators in May, 1771 near Alamance Creek, south of modern-day Burlington. There were twice as many Regulators as militia, but the two thousand "rebels" had no leader. They had been leaderless from the beginning. That was their greatest weakness. The vague idea among the rudderless Regulators at Alamance was that Gov. Tryon would be intimidated by such a large crowd, get wobbly in the knees, and give in to their demands.

Instead, Tryon told the Regulator horde to "submit to the government and disperse." The Regulators stood their ground. Tryon considered the armed citizens to be in "a state of War and Rebellion." He ordered them again to disperse and go home, or be fired upon by his troops.

"Fire and be damned," they said.

Tryon ordered his militia to fire. Nothing happened. The militia was made up of people just like the Regulators. They were not British troops. They were trained and drilled citizen soldiers, that was true, but most had come along on this adventure from the counties of Craven, Carteret, New Hanover, Beaufort, Onslow, Johnston and Wake strictly for the pay.

Angered, Tryon rose in his saddle and yelled at his soldiers. "Fire! Fire on them or fire on me!"

They fired on the Regulators.

The Battle of Alamance was over in two hours. The Regulators, of course, were no match for Tryon's well-led militia. In the end, they retired from the field. Accounts vary, but about nine were killed on each side with dozens wounded. Tryon took prisoners, executing one on the battlefield and a few others after trial. Many observers, then and later, concluded that Tryon was heavy-handed, but he had his admirers as well. To his credit, he ordered his own surgeons to care for the wounded enemy and soon offered clemency to all who would swear allegiance.

No more Regulators.

The crown was so pleased with Tryon's performance that he was named governor of New York. Within one year of the completion of the New Bern palace, William Tryon packed his wig again and sailed away with Margaret to New York City.

The next palace occupant was Royal Governor Josiah Martin. Martin didn't know it when he reached New Bern in late 1771, but he would be the last royal governor of the Province of North Carolina. Those revolutionary stirrings presaged by the Regulators turned into a full-blown movement. This time, the revolutionaries had leaders. Some of the names you will remember: Washington, Jefferson, Franklin, Adams, and Lafayette.

Martin took his family and fled New Bern in 1775. Trouble was coming. Eastern North Carolina was crawling with militia called Minutemen. They would come at a moments notice. And they were good soldiers.

Many of them had been trained by William Tryon.

FOLLOWING THE AMERICAN REVOLUTION, four governors of the new State of North Carolina—Richard Caswell, Abner Nash, Alexander Martin and Richard Dobbs Spaight—resided at Tryon Palace. The legislature met there a few times. But when the capital was permanently moved to Raleigh in 1794, the building, already in a state of disrepair, was virtually abandoned by the government and fell into infrequent use.

A dance master gave lessons there and it was occasionally used as a community ballroom. The local Masons held meetings and stored records there. After a fire destroyed New Bern Academy, classes were shifted to the palace for a while. It's also been suggested that the main building was used as a boarding house.

Knight thinks it may have been a little less formal.

"We don't know any of this with certainty, but what evidence we have would indicate—to me anyway—that it was not any kind of organized boarding house, but more like a derelict building where you could go and spend the night," he says. In any event, in February, 1798, a cellar fire quickly spread and devastated the main building. Knight thinks the fire that destroyed Tryon Palace in 1798 could have been started accidentally by vagrants or travelers who bedded down in the basement at night. "Legend, that we think may be true, says the reason the palace burned was because of a lamp falling over into hay, probably used as bedding," he said.

The magnificent central structure was consumed by roaring flames and collapsed to a pile of ash and rubble. Only the kitchen and stable wings remained. The "Kitchen Offices" were torn down after the War Between the States. By the early 1900s the stable had been converted into an apartment building.

With no palace to block its route, a main local highway now followed Broad Street to George Street. George Street, which stopped at the old palace's front gate, was extended through the center of the former palace grounds straight to the Trent River, where it joined a new bridge to Havelock and Morehead City. So the site of North Carolina's first capital became part of a busy thoroughfare. Building sites were sold and a new neighborhood grew up on both sides of the new road. Businesses, including several gas stations, opened. Time passed. Years went by, then decades.

And slowly, the awareness of Tryon Palace—the most beautiful public building in America—waned among many citizens.

CR CR CR

BUT NOT EVERYONE FORGOT.

Kay Williams points to three key people from the earliest days of the restoration effort: Minnette Chapman Duffy, Gertrude S. Carraway and Ruth Coltrane Cannon. Williams is the director of Tryon Palace Historic Sites & Gardens. An English major by education and an industrial engineer by training, she now oversees twenty-two acres of vintage and reproduction properties, a large staff of employees and volunteers, exhibits, collections and events. She's been thinking about the palace and its origins full-time since 1983. The New Bern-born director said the trio of Duffy, Carraway and Cannon started planning for the reconstruction of the palace in the 1920s. She said both their vision and their success were "astonishing." We talked about the women.

Minnette Chapman Duffy moved to New Bern from Tennessee as the new bride of New Bern native Dr. Richard Nixon Duffy. Described as well-educated and bright, she took a strong liking to the city and wanted to learn about its history. To stimulate more activity on the subject, she helped found a precursor of the New Bern Historical Society. "I'm sure she felt a man should chair it, so she got Judge Romulus A. Nunn to be the first president," Williams said.

107

Gertrude Carraway was a promoter with a newspaper background who knew how to network and pull people together. She'd become an enthusiastic researcher, speaker and writer on topics related to local heritage. "Her energy was very important," Williams said. "She was more likely to make the bold move, to go out and meet new people," while Mrs. Duffy was more likely "to provide the appropriate underpinning" for an occasion. Miss Carraway said Mrs. Duffy would throw wonderful parties. She lived in a fine home. Miss Carraway would find the key people coming into town that they needed to cultivate, and invite them to one of the parties. That's how they began to expand their circle of influence.

At the same time, Ruth Cannon was important on several levels. The Cannon name was very prestigious. She had a great deal of interest in history and even had her very own restoration. Mrs. Cannon convinced her industrialist husband to buy an abandoned historic home outside of Kannapolis, in rural Cabarrus County. She began its rehabilitation, apparently at great expense. One day, her husband asked her, "For pity's sake, Ruth, how much more are you going to spend on that house?" So, Mrs. Cannon named their country home—and her first historic restoration—"For Pity's Sake." And kept right on spending.

The Tryon Palace director said Mrs. Cannon "represented the other end of the state." That facet of the relationship had great value. "If Gertrude and Minnette Chapman Duffy had never conceived of this being a statewide project, I don't think it would have ever happened," Williams said. "They were great strategists. The Cannons had a mountain home in Blowing Rock and these early planners would retreat there and have long sessions plotting their statewide plans."

And if parties had been the key so far, how about throwing a really big one?

The New Bern Historical Pageant of 1929 was their creation and "everyone who was anybody in North Carolina was at that pageant." There was a huge parade. There were tours of historic homes, and this is thought to have been the first time New Bern homes had been opened to the public. A pageant of history went on all day. The non-stop entertainment included acting, music, dramatic speeches and elaborate costumes. There was a nineteenth-century carriage pulled by horses to convey North Carolina Governor

O. Max Gardner and other dignitaries. President Herbert Hoover had been invited. [He sent his handwritten regrets.] The evening was capped by a well-attended colonial dance held in a tobacco warehouse. It got a lot of people excited about New Bern.

And it actually made money.

Mrs. William Neal Reynolds, wife of the Winston-Salem tobacco manufacturing dynasty's president, loaned money for the pageant to the New Bern group. "Being good, thrifty New Bernians," said Williams, the money was reimbursed from the proceeds of the event. Mrs. Reynolds returned the money and earmarked it for the restoration of Tryon Palace. That was the first donation.

The Tryon Palace team had two huge obstacles looming on the horizon no one could foresee: The Great Depression and World War II. Four months following the pageant, the New York stock market collapsed. The economic depression would last until the beginning of the war in 1941. The country would experience hard time from 1929 until the U.S. victory in 1945.

"They worked on the project for thirty years," Williams said. But it was during this time that Maude Moore Latham joined the effort. Miss Carraway had known the Lathams when they lived in New Bern.

Mrs. Latham grew up in "somewhat modest circumstances." Her marriage to James E. Latham would prove fortuitous. James Latham started as a local cotton broker and became acquainted with the vagaries of the market. A series of investments in cotton futures made him rich enough to start other ventures, like the King Cotton Hotel in Greensboro. He moved into real estate and successfully developed one of Greensboro's early suburbs, Latham Park. To put a fine edge on things, he became one of the early players in the firms that would become Jefferson Standard-Pilot Life Insurance. Gertrude Carraway "brought Mrs. Latham into the mix" and Mrs. Latham would eventually offer a personal financial legacy that drew the interest of the State of North Carolina.

Her gift would be followed later by other generous contributions, long-time cooperation and support from her daughter, May Gordon Latham Kellenberger.

Kay Williams said that the success of Tryon Palace grew out of a revival in historic interest in North Carolina and a new feeling of confidence engendered by surviving both the Depression and World War II.

"Those challenges actually heightened feelings about saving our history,'" she said.

And then she told this story:

"During World War II, a dinner party was held at the governor's mansion in Raleigh. Gertrude was there. A lot of people were there, including Mrs. Latham. During the dinner party, when everyone was around the table, Mrs. Latham told Governor [J. Melville] Broughton that she planned, upon her death, to give money for the restoration of Tryon Palace—if the state would agree to maintain it and operate it. It was her first public statement of intention. The governor was encouraging and everyone was excited. There was political strategy involved. It was probably orchestrated that she would have done it at that dinner.

"That led to a legislative strategy. Senator [D.L] 'Libby' Ward of New Bern—he was another of the New Bern people instrumental in making this happen—had been an advisor and opened doors for Gertrude Carraway. With Ward's help, she was appointed to statewide boards and commissions and made many contacts. Ward got forty-eight of the fifty senators, to not only vote for the bill, but also to sponsor it. So it obviously passed. That legislation created Tryon Palace Historical Sites and Gardens along with the Tryon Palace Commission to administer Mrs. Latham's money. It also obligated the state to acquire the land. I think it was an astonishing achievement that could have only been done at that time with the groundwork laid by those particular people.

"There was a sense coming out of World War II that the country could do anything. There was a wave of patriotism, and at that moment, preserving history *was* patriotic because we had almost lost our culture. The war made our history more precious. Nothing was too big an obstacle for a country that had won World War II. What are removing a bridge and a highway in comparison to what we had accomplished? I think the palace came out of that. It was *the* moment in time it could be done."

Mrs. Latham died before the reconstruction of the Palace began. Her daughter, May Gordon Kellenberger, stepped in to help guide the project. Before construction started, dozens of homes and businesses had to be acquired or moved. Highway

70 was rerouted and its traffic was directed over a new bridge. The original palace foundation was found exactly where expected, dead center under the old highway. Craftspeople from across the country and abroad were brought to the site, but much of the work was done by the skilled hands of local African-Americans.

The newly-restored Tryon Palace opened to the public in April, 1959. Today, nearly one hundred thousand visitors a year come to visit.

POSTSCRIPT

WORKING A FEW SUMMERS at Tryon Palace changed Charles Adams's life.

A greeter and part-time guide from 1961-1963, he met tourists from across America, rubbed shoulders with famous and influential citizens who helped create the palace, and was schooled by the palace's first director, the inimitable Gertrude Carraway.

"Miss Carraway was a regimented type of person and she thought 'idle hands are the devil's playthings'," he said. "She kept everyone busy. Whenever you came into the [John P. Daves] house where she had her office, you could hear her typewriter pounding upstairs."

Adams expressed unabashed awe at Miss Carraway's life, education, and accomplishments in the Daughters of the American Revolution. During her three-year term as president-general of the National Society of the DAR in Washington, D.C., she became familiar with the organization's "house museum." He said the experience added to her expertise in American decorative art. After she returned to New Bern, Mrs. May Gordon Kellenberger asked her to be the palace's first director.

Adams had a personal connection to Tryon Palace. His father, Raymond, owned a Pure Oil gas station located where the huge back lawn is today. The business was closed and bulldozed during the restoration. Raymond Adams opened a new station on Neuse Blvd. One day in the early 1960s, he told his son he needed to get a summer job, but also told Charles he wasn't hiring at the service station. So, the young college student applied at Tryon Palace. With her assistant,

111

Cookie Ipock, in the office, Miss Carraway quickly informed Adams that all the people she had working at the Palace were ladies. Disappointed, he was almost out of the house when he was summoned back by Mrs. Ipock.

"I don't know what she said to Miss Carraway," Adams said, "but they told me to go upstairs to a closet. There was a colonial costume they'd had made for a film or an advertisement or something. Miss Carraway said that if I could fit into the costume I could have a job. That's how frugal she was. They weren't going to buy another costume, but if I could get that one on...well, I was about a hundred and twenty-eight pounds wet at the time, but that costume must have been made for a child."

Adams said he squeezed into the tight knee-length trousers, but the side buttons wouldn't button. Determined to have the job, somehow he fastened the knee pants anyway and covered his discomfort beneath the accompanying wide belt with a big, shiny, square metal buckle, and a tobacco brown vest. The outfit included a v-neck white shirt with full sleeves and wide cuffs which slipped on over the head, and long cotton socks. The colonial look was completed by a dark, tri-cornered hat.

"They stood at the bottom of the stairs as I made my entrance," he said. "I felt like a pogo stick coming down the steps, knowing I was going to pop a button or a seam."

He made it to the bottom without incident.

He was hired and, after his mother, Maebelle, altered the trousers, worked at Tryon Palace each summer while he was in college. Asked what his first job was, he said, laughing, "I was an ornament."

Actually, he stood at the big front gate in his eighteenth century costume, greeted visitors and had his picture taken—a lot. Every Sunday, he'd spend part of the time redirecting people from out of town who were looking for the world-class buffet at the Governor Tryon Hotel. Adams said the Governor Tryon, located at South Front and Middle Street, and the Sanitary Fish Market in Morehead City, were two of the best places to eat on the coast.

"They'd drive down and misread the directional signs that read 'Tryon Palace *Restoration*' thinking it said 'restaurant'."

Adams remembers vividly that Miss Carraway required him—like all the other volunteers—to learn and memorize everything about Tryon Palace.

"We had to memorize thirty-seven rooms, room-by-room, with all of their contents. We had to memorize everything from the history of the palace to the botanical names of the flowers," he said. "Gertrude made my brain like a Rolodex. I had to know everything about the furniture, the silver, the crystal, the styles, the manufacturers, rugs, the woodwork, textiles. Everything. Every detail."

The strict training would pay off later.

With the help of a committee, Miss Carraway created scripts that were repeated by guides for each group visiting the palace. Volunteers and staff were required not only to learn the scripts perfectly, but also had to speak them in a specific amount of time. The Carraway method provided consistent information for all tourists, and kept them moving on a precise schedule.

Adams said that on busy days, he was allowed to take visitors through the third floor and basement, but never through the key first or second floors. Miss Carraway would allow only her most knowledgeable and polished guides to conduct tours through those two floors in the very heart of the palace.

"The famous people I met there were just wonderful," Adams said. Some were world-class collectors of art and antiques. Ima Hogg was one. Miss Hogg (1882-1975) was a member of a wealthy east Texas family involved in oil, agriculture and real estate. The family promoted philanthropic projects, including historic preservation. She was also a collector of the same type of furnishings that the Palace was looking for, so she would come to visit.

Mr. and Mrs. Henry Francis du Pont also spent time at the Palace with some frequency. Henry du Pont (1880-1969), a trained horticulturist, was also an expert in early American furniture and decorative arts. He specialized in Federal furniture. A member of the prominent du Pont family, he was an avid collector of American antiques and later helped Jacqueline Kennedy renovate the White House. His wife, Ruth (1891-1967), was a descendant of palace architect John Hawks.

"That was her connection," Adams said.

He remembered that Mrs. Ruth Cannon of Cannon Mills would come from Kannapolis, N.C. with two limousines, one for her and one for her nurse. Mrs. Cannon (1890-1965) was the wife of Charles A. Cannon, president of Cannon Mills, then the world's largest textile maker. Mrs. Cannon was a history buff and original member of the Tryon Palace Commission. She took a particular interest in the development of the palace gardens.

At the time, the women in charge of the palace were buying furniture, artwork and furnishings all over the world. Adams remembered Virginia Horne, a commission member who lent her advice to acquisitions for the collections.

And, of course, Mrs. Kellenberger was there.

His hard work under the Carraway system paid big returns. "It was actually very good for me personally," he said. "Very definitely."

Adams, the first male ever hired at Tryon Palace, had planned to study architecture. Instead, because of what he was taught by Miss Carraway at Tryon Palace, he switched his college major to interior design. For most of the last four decades, he has been an antique dealer and appraiser. His expertise in the business of old treasures and collectibles includes the areas of fine art, china, crystal, silver, period furniture and nautical artifacts. Today, his shop, Adams on Castle, is part of Wilmington, N.C.'s thriving antique district.

Adams's future took a new direction one day many years ago all because Gertrude Carraway gave him a chance to work at Tryon Palace. And because...he didn't split those knee britches.

Fighting at the Fort Thompson line during the Battle of New Bern
Edward Ellis Collection

9

Civil War: The Flood of Tears

YOU COULD ALWAYS count on John.

The leading men of New Bern were calling for a special train and John D. Whitford was getting one put together for them. It was Sunday and trains didn't run on Sunday. But today—of all days—they needed a train and Whitford was getting it done.

In 1861, New Bern had no telegraph. The closest operator was at Goldsboro, source of the Atlantic & North Carolina Railroad line. The railroad's massive black steam locomotives towed their loads by morning sun from Morehead City to Goldsboro and made the reverse trip promptly at 3:00 p.m. But not on Sundays and the men simply could not wait until

115

tomorrow to hear the news from Charleston.

When the three o'clock train left Goldsboro the day before, Saturday, April 13, 1861, Union troops inside Fort Sumter were still holding out. The opening salvos of artillery had been fired by the freshly-seceded Confederate States of America before dawn on Friday, and the last word to reach New Bern said the cannons in Charleston were pounding the island fort non-stop.

So it was war.

The extra locomotive and passenger coach arranged by Whitford, president of the A&NC, left New Bern loaded with the most prominent men in town. They would have to spend the night in Goldsboro and return the next afternoon, but curiosity and excitement trumped a little inconvenience.

Whitford went with them. He was secessionist all the way. Though the election was yet to come, the men on the train would be instrumental in sending Whitford to the state convention in June which would officially withdraw North Carolina from the Union. But North Carolina was already on the way out and they knew it.

Whitford was a businessman; one of the town's finest. One day he would be mayor. During the war, he would do his duty as an ordinance and transportation officer, and make a name for himself leading raids against Yankee forces around New Bern. He'd be a colonel by the time Dixie had finally given its all. They'd call him Col. Whitford for the rest of his life. But all that was in the future.

Today, North Carolina was still a star in the flag of the United States of America. But those aboard the special train rocking its way toward Goldsboro knew the days were numbered.

With the road only three years old and straight as an arrow, with no other trains on the track that day, with a load of only one passenger car and all the men anxious for news, do you think John Whitford might have told the engineer to let the iron horse run?

When the train pulled into the Goldsboro station belching carbon and steam, the men saw the citizens of the town crowding around in animated conversation. The telegraph office was in the depot and the place looked like market day. The streets were full of country people. Horse buggies and mule carts lined up from here to yonder. It was as if the air was full of sparks; excitement enough for all the senses.

In minutes, Whitford and company knew. The news had come to Goldsboro after sunset the previous evening. Fort Sumter had fallen.

The island fortress in Charleston harbor had been hammered by artillery for thirty-four continuous hours after refusing a polite request for surrender. It looked like no one had been killed except some poor Southern soldier when a cannon exploded during celebratory firing after the fact. But Charleston ladies and gentlemen sat upon porches and balconies of their stately waterfront Battery mansions, watching the fireworks while repeatedly toasting the beginnings of war.

At the depot, the telegraph key was pounding like a jack hammer. That's how news and information moved. And there was plenty of it. One telegram tapped to Goldsboro on Monday morning was from North Carolina Governor John W. Ellis. The governor ordered Capt. M.D. Craton to assemble his company, the Goldsboro Rifles, and go seize the coastal island citadel, Fort Macon. It was much easier said than done. Craton's men were scattered all over hell and gone, some of them many miles out into the boonies. Gubernatorial telegram in hand, Craton grabbed his roster and began gathering his flock. By some miracle, at three sharp when the train left for the coast, the captain had all his one hundred and two green recruits present and accounted for. Their uniforms were not uniform, but they were armed to the teeth thanks to the fifty seven dollars recently appropriated by the Goldsboro city council.

Another telegram got the crowd even more animated. Read out loud from the platform, it announced that Abraham Lincoln, President of the United States, was issuing a call for seventy-five thousand troops meant to crush the Southern rebellion.

Capt. Craton and his Goldsboro Rifles shared the eastbound train Monday afternoon with Whitford and the other leading lights of New Bern. And almost all of Wayne County was on hand to see them off.

What Craton didn't know, and wouldn't until he arrived in Morehead City, was that Fort Macon had already "fallen." Capt. Josiah Pender had jumped the bureaucratic gun so to speak. On his own initiative, he had taken his seventeen-man militia, the Beaufort Harbor Guards, over to the fort on Sunday. The single man there, the caretaker, Union Sgt.

William Alexander, answered their knock at the gate and calmly handed Pender the keys to the place.

In Goldsboro, the locomotive whistle was heard all over town as the big wheels began reluctantly to turn. There was waving, hugging and cheering as the trainload of hometown soldiers headed off to meet destiny. Good-bye. Good luck. Craton, Whitford and the rest returned the vigorous waves of hats and hankies through open windows as the cars jerked and began to grumble down the tracks.

Among the many people in the crowd that unforgettable afternoon was twenty-two-year-old Jim Hollowell. Hollowell was a newspaper reporter who would soon join the Confederate artillery. James M. Hollowell would survive the war by forty seven years and become a trusted Goldsboro businessman and state representative. In 1909, he remembered the day this way.

"Bless you, those were exciting times," he wrote. "The people were stirred as I never saw them before, nor since. That day I saw the first tears of the war, as the wives, parents, sisters, brothers and friends stood at the train to bid the soldier boys goodbye; but alas, the tears that day were but the beginning of the floods of tears that followed in the next four years."

ᘓ   ᘓ   ᘓ

FOR A FEARLESS SOUL standing on South Front Street near the Hancock Street railroad line that afternoon eleven months later, the entire range of human emotion was on vivid display. Tears, elation, agony, caution, terror and resignation were a gaudy exhibit in exquisite disharmony with raging fires and cannonballs fizzing overhead.

People were crying and running. Those who did not believe the Yankees would come were there with those who did not believe the Yankees could win.

The wounded and bleeding hobbled up the tracks trying to reach the getaway train before it chuffed out of town. Two bewildered men struggled to carry a big rag-doll fellow who appeared to have already cast away this world's cares. The newly-issued, newly-defeated Confederates were streaming ahead of the Union forces, the embodiment of disbelief; their startled eyes showing much more white than normal. A heavily-armed steamer coming alongside the wharf ejected men in clean blue uniforms. They gaped warily at the rag-tag randomly-clothed farm boys who, though still armed, conveyed the lowly countenance of the steadfastly surrendered.

Dense anvils of smoke rose above the city. It was rising thick and dark on the other side of the river, too, where the North Carolina forces had recently been rudely introduced to well-drilled Yankees. Something had gone wrong, badly wrong, at the forts over there. Who ever heard so many guns?

The fire close by, just across the tracks, was fueled by cotton and barrels of tar and rosin. It was serious business. Some would claim it was intentionally set by the retreating losers as a last desperate act. But no one knew for sure or would ever know who set the fires. With so many artillery shells flying around who could be sure of anything?

For the next hundred years, they would say the defeated rabble set the railroad bridge ablaze as well, but any damn fool could see that a fire boat aimed at the Yankee fleet had gone askew and careened against the tar-soak pilings.

Cannon shells exploded with ground-quaking concussion. Union gun-boats were firing wildly in the general direction of the fleeing rebels. They were doing more damage to woodlands and nervous systems than anything else.

Despite danger and mayhem, joyous clusters of black people who had been slaves a few hours before savored freedom for the first time, and they liked it. Happy as lovers at jubilee, they were laughing, holding one another and offering praise to the Almighty. Tears wet some of their faces. One man stopped to pick through a trunk of clothing spilled upon the dirt street by fleeing townspeople.

There were bullets flying, tears streaming, bombs detonating, dense smoke rising and dark hands clapping in unbridled joy. Running feet. A horse with no rider. A train whistle. And death. Lord have mercy!

Welcome to New Bern. March 14, 1862.

CR CR CR

LAWRENCE O'BRYAN BRANCH was no general and he knew it. At least not yet. He had attended a military school when he was younger, but that was all academics. He had served an Army stint during the Seminole War fighting renegade Indians in Florida, but being a private soldier in a bush war

119

was quite a different matter than the one at hand. Following the fall of Fort Sumter, though, the embryonic Confederate government reached out for leadership wherever it could be found. Many successful civilians were called to military service. And Branch was nothing if not a success.

By the time of the Battle of New Bern, in which he would be the commander, brand-new Brigadier General L. O'B. Branch had attended the University of North Carolina at Chapel Hill, graduated first in his class at Princeton University, owned and edited a newspaper, practiced law, run a railroad, served in the U.S. House of Representatives and been offered and declined an appointment as Treasury Secretary of the United States. He was barely forty years old.

Youthful and tall, sometimes with a neatly trimmed chin beard, O'Bryan Branch exuded manly good looks, the visage of a natural leader. Intellectually gifted and well-spoken, he was the man any organized assembly would naturally elect to be its leader.

Eighteen days after the Confederate flag rose over the Charleston, S.C. fort, the North Carolina native donned the gray uniform of private. Four months later, he was elected colonel of the 33rd North Carolina Troops. Four months more and he was a general. With stars on his collar for less than sixty days, he witnessed his own personal nightmare unfolding on a flat battleground south of New Bern.

What looked to be the whole Union army descended upon the raw, untried Confederate troops, and even though the Carolinians defended a massive earthwork, they were out-numbered three-to-one. That's what the textbooks at West Point said was needed by an attacking force to have an even chance against well-entrenched defenders. While there was a dearth of West Point training on the gray side of the line, the Union side was awash in the world's most advanced military knowledge. All four of the Union generals at the Battle of New Bern were alumni of the United States Military Academy at West Point. One of the Union commanders would one day be its superintendent. All of the troops under their commands had been drilled and trained in West Point theory.

The bluecoats broke the center of the Confederate line. There were numerous acts of gallantry by the Confederate force defending its home, but the plowboys, deer hunters, merchants and bankers were quickly overwhelmed. Many ran in panic.

Branch had probably seen a few men die in battle. He was certainly seeing plenty more today. For the relatively small forces involved, the casualties were high, at almost eleven hundred. One reliable count put the Union dead at ninety with 384 wounded and one missing. The Confederate death toll was sixty-four, with one hundred and one wounded and four hundred and thirteen either missing or captured.

Following the battle, one Union soldier would call the southerners "imbeciles" for "losing such a fine line of works." But Branch knew that was not the case. His troops were out-numbered, out-gunned and out-trained; like a high school team up against the big leaguers. It had been a mismatch. The meaning of the higher casualty figures for the Union was that the blue generals were willing to put more pressure on the Confederates, to hit them harder than they could stand, until their line collapsed under the strain. Right out of the textbooks.

Branch would *learn* today; gleaning what he could from the whipping. He had the makings of a fine general and was later considered to be a rising star among his peers. He would be denied the chance to prove his potential. He'd be dead in six months; killed instantly by a Federal sniper's bullet at the Battle of Antietam.

ભ ભ ભ

THE PREVIOUS DAY, March 13, 1862, a Union fleet of five dozen vessels disgorged thousands of men at Slocum Creek near Havelock, just below the outer line of Southern defense. After scaring off a small force of cavalry dragoons, the Union army marched up the rail line and old road to New Bern until they met resistance from gray-back pickets.

Though the invasion was a Navy operation, the ground troops were under the command of Ambrose Everett Burnside, a lifer who, after fifteen years in the U.S. Army, had reached the rank of major general. Tall, trim, and balding with a round, pleasant face, General Burnside's most distinguishing feature was a unique hedgerow of muttonchops. Thick as dark steel wool, the beard whizzed down from his temples almost, but not quite to his chin, where it arched suddenly to join at the mustache. "Burn," as the general was called by friends, took a lot of time with his crazy shaving job. Soon, others would emulate his weird beard and create a style called "burnsides." With the English language being the fluid creature it is, the general's invention was eventually twisted into the word "sideburns." Despite the fascination with his facial hair, the general was fully military in bearing, carriage and thinking.

Burnside was more of an administrator than a battlefield warrior. He did not lead from the saddle, but was both fortunate and skilled at selecting excellent sub-commanders. The Indiana native, just thirty-eight at the time, oversaw the battle plan for the New Bern operation, but left the fighting to his three combat-seasoned subordinate brigadier generals: John G. Foster, Jesse L. Reno and John G. Parke. This trio of superb professional soldiers led the troops ashore and marched them in three columns to New Bern.

Burnside set his headquarters in the rear, away from the treeless killing zone the rebels had cleared for several hundred yards in front of their fort. He would survey the operation on horseback occasionally riding up among units under the subordinate commands to give a compliment or some fatherly encouragement. The men loved him. But once the battle commenced, Burnside was a spectator.

Today would be glorious. The second of his three campaign objectives was within his grasp. Roanoke Island was in hand already. New Bern was teetering as he watched. In a few days, he and his staff would execute a plan for the re-taking of the citadel frowning over the ocean port of Beaufort: Fort Macon.

Hopefully, Burnside savored the glorious moments well. While he would survive the war and have a successful career in business and politics—even becoming the first president of the National Rifle Association—his military fortunes were headed for the rocks. Caught up in President Lincoln's search for the perfect commanding general, he would be promoted beyond his level of both comfort and ability. He candidly asserted that he would not do well with greater authority and when it was thrust upon him anyway, at Antietam and Petersburg, he met his own low expectation. After the disaster of Petersburg's Battle of the Crater, they plucked off his wings and set him aside with the assessment that Burnside would have made a great colonel.

The always-smiling, wild-bearded general would die suddenly of a heart attack at age fifty-seven in Rhode Island sixteen years after the Confederate States of America surrendered at Appomattox Court House.

ભ્ર   ભ્ર   ભ્ર

AMONG THE MEN in one Union column—Gen. Parke's—was a young officer named Levi E. Kent. Capt. Kent served with Company F of the 4th Rhode Island Infantry Regiment. Young Kent was homesick. He was ill with a stomach complaint that lingered through much of the campaign. But he could still write. Kent was an avid diarist. He was a good descriptive writer even if spelling had not been his favorite school subject. He kept a journal throughout his entire military service and there was an air of excitement in his entry of March 12, 1862, the day the ships prepared to sail to God-knows-where.

From the steamer *Eastern Queen* anchored in Albemarle Sound, Kent recorded the weather as "splendid." He found all the troops "in good humor." They were several weeks beyond their first battle and the fleet's first victory at Roanoke Island. Since then, they had been going nowhere. Everyone was excited by the activity and signs of preparation on all the ships even if they didn't know where they were going.

The "rumer," Kent noted in his unique spelling, was that either "Newberne & Norfolk" was the next likely target. He also noted sadly that his friend, Capt. Clias A. Tillinghast, had received a letter from his New York home conveying news of a brother's death on some distant battlefield. Within a few days, the Tillinghast family would be sent the news that another son, the young captain himself, had fallen in the fight for New Bern.

"On the night of the 12th we laid at anchor just above Slocoms Creek in the Neuse River," Kent wrote in his journal. "On the morning of the 13th, the force was landed at the mouth of Slocoms Creek by the light draft Steamers & Launches and a march commenced toward Newberne."

The Union armada covered much of the river off what is the present-day Carolina Pines golf course. The fleet has been described as a "motley one." Fourteen large transport ships were accompanied by just about everything the Navy could spare that didn't have a hole in it. There were shallow draft steamers, barges, sailboats, tugs, and ferries. During that day and some of the next, after brief cannon bombardment of the vacant shoreline, the fleet disgorged between eleven thousand and fifteen thousand men, depending on what source is consulted. Either number is huge—amounting to the population of a small town—and more men than Gen. Douglas MacArthur would use for the massive invasion of Inchon during the Korean War of the 1950s.

Small skiffs were used to ferry the men ashore in what amounted to an amphibious assault. After moving as close to the beach as possible, the men jumped into the water and waded ashore. Some landed on sandy beaches; others in a stands of tall, thick marsh grass; others in blue gumbo mud. Once on dry land, a color guard planted Old Glory and unit flags as rallying points for the disembarking troops. Soon the lines were formed for the march toward New Bern.

"Dry land", though, was a matter of opinion. Burnside's soldiers marched in the rain all day. Sometimes it was a regular deluge. The roads were heavy with mud and it was a hard slog especially for the artillery troops who had to find a way to move unwieldy cannons through the mire. It was weary and tiresome work.

Capt. Kent's first halt for rest was near a deserted farm house between the landing site and Croatan. Kent said the farm family had fled. He and his buddy, Lt. Charles Greene, took a look.

"The troops before us had turned everything upside down," he said. "The furniture once nice was a complete wreck. A piano was being pumped to its utmost & was sadly bruised. Some few articles of food were left to which the boys helped themselves & somebody brought Greene & myself some pickles that were good."

During and after the battle, Union forces routinely ransacked homes and looted whatever struck their fancy. Union military governor of North Carolina Edward Stanly condemned his own troops for the ransacking and pillaging of Craven County. Stanly said the blue jackets stole everything that wasn't nailed down, shipping much of it north. He noted entire libraries that were crated up and shipped as well as valuable rugs, artwork and antiques. Even a thoroughbred horse worth a small fortune was smuggled out. Noting that the countryside suffered the most, one soldier wrote his family and told them everything had been picked clean and the county outside of New Bern was "a desert."

The blue wave continued to march through rain and drizzle looking for Confederate resistance. At about four in the afternoon, they reached "quite an extended earthwork of the enemy, which covered the railroad, the county road, and terminated in a formidable earth fort upon the bank of the Neuse."

The first Confederate earthwork was at Croatan and had been deserted shortly before the Union forces arrived. Several earthwork forts lay between Slocum's Creek and New Bern. Union forces noted that no guns were in position except at the river. They were impressed with the earthwork and thought it was unoccupied because it was unfinished.

"Probably in a few days, this extension work would have been in shape to have given us great trouble and held us in check for awhile," Kent said.

In fact, Gen. Branch had ordered all the Confederate forces back to what would be the battle site, the Fort Thompson line. Branch simply did not have enough men to occupy all the fortifications built below New Bern.

After moving through these massive unoccupied earthworks, some of the Union troops rested for about a half hour in a grove of pines. They were tired from tromping through and slipping on mud. More than a few, Kent included, hoped this was their stop for the night. But they were kept moving along the approximate route of today's U.S. 70 toward New Bern. They marched until dark when the blue advance force came upon "the rebel pickets."

At dawn on March 14, the day of the Battle of New Bern, nearly everyone woke up cold and drenched to the bone. It had rained all night. Heavily.

"Lt. Greene and myself 'slept together' between two logs," the captain wrote. "We slept upon my blanket covering us with his. We were completely soaked & the water [rose] to three inches deep where we lay. The camp fires had blazed away all night and many—probably less tired—had sat about them."

Within minutes, the force was on the move. Before long, they were approaching Fort Thompson, the earthworks stronghold where the rebels would make their stand. Kent soon found himself "in front of another line of rebel works in the midst of musketry and cannon." Sharpshooters were sending little deadly gifts their way.

The battle for New Bern had begun.

125

Confederate troops in retreat at the Battle of New Bern
Edward Ellis Collection

10

Civil War: A Blue Wave

"I am not anxious for a repetition of the doings of the 14th but wish it might please God to stop the rebels in their career of madness and return them peaceably to their homes."

— *Capt. Levi E. Kent*
Company F, 4th Rhode Island Infantry

FOR ANYONE with even a shade of wistfulness or nostalgia for the glories of the Civil War, an excellent antidote is consideration of a cannonball's effect on a human body.

Typical battlefield cannons launched an iron ball the diameter of a man's open hand with fingers spread. The size of, but much heavier and more dense than a bowling ball, the projectile could mow a group of living men down just like bowling pins. Instead of simply knocking them over, however, the balls tended to separate heads, arms and legs from bodies, or torsos from the rest. In the choice position of firing down a line of marching men, a dozen could be decapitated at a time. There is nothing wistful or nostalgic about that.

The standard bullet of the day was the Minié ball, or minie ball, a cone-shaped hunk of soft lead about the size of a man's thumb. The minie ball was extremely lethal and inflicted terrible wounds. The huge caliber rounds, when they did not kill outright, splintered bones of arms and legs resulting in a high rate of amputation.

These cruel operations were carried out in the open field with neither anesthesia nor antibiotics by attending surgeons huffing away with bone saws. Sometimes after battles, it was said the bone saws could be heard ringing above all else. A doctor who could remove a limb and sew a flap of skin back over the wound in less than fifteen minutes was considered by the suffering soldier to be a hero. The awful procedure became so common that doctors from the Civil War onward have lived with the nickname "sawbones." The number of these wounds, and the number of amputees afterwards, was unprecedented in the history of warfare.

The battle commenced on the level plain across the Trent River about five miles east of New Bern, which today stretches from Taberna toward Carolina Colours. The day of fighting would claim the lives of one hundred and fifty-four men. It would leave four hundred and eighty-five wounded. Some of the lucky wounded would recover, but many would suffer for life. Some of them would die days or even months later.

For example, the steamer *Eastern Queen* made a run from New Bern back to New York City in May, 1862, about two months following the battle. Aboard were one hundred and four of the most seriously sick and wounded men from New Bern. There were even a few with lingering, unhealed wounds from the early February fight at Roanoke Island. The ship arrived in New York on May 9. William Carrington, a soldier with Company E of the 51st New York Infantry—after surviving his battle wound for weeks and living through an ocean voyage back to his home state—died just as the ship reached the wharf.

CR CR CR

ON THE MORNING of March 14, 1862—the day of the Battle of New Bern—the Confederates were arrayed along a line blocking the advance to New Bern beyond the railroad and all the way to the Neuse River. The Union column, including Capt. Levi Kent's group, first moved from the main road toward the rail line, passing "very near the center of the enemy's line of works."

If anyone understands the earthworks Kent saw that morning in 1862, it's Mark Mangum. Mangum led the preservation effort that created the New Bern Battlefield Park. He's extremely well-versed in the local clash of blue and gray and has a strong affinity for study of the five-year conflict between the North and the South.

Falling in love with the Civil War came naturally to Mangum. The winter camp of Robert E. Lee's army was on the Virginia farm where he grew up. The Mangums owned land at battle-torn Brandy Station near the Rappahannock River. Over a hundred battles were fought within a fifty mile radius of his home. The downtown New Bern businessman, who came to the Colonial Capital as a banker in the 1990s, said a passion for history came naturally in his family. Many relatives fought in the Civil War, all on the side of the South. The family has a deep military legacy and he inherited the gene. He's been a life-long student of the war.

In his top floor office at the Galley Stores and Marina on East Front Street, Mangum said he's not a historian. He calls himself a historic "preservationist" and says he has been a Civil War re-enactor since 1987. Invited to sit on the board of the New Bern Historical Society, he was asked in 1999 to chair a committee to plan the preservation of battlefield remnants near Taberna.

In answer to a question, Mangum explained what the Federal force faced when it came out of the woods early on that rainy day headed toward New Bern from the direction of Havelock. The Confederate line was anchored on the river by Fort Thompson. Fort Thompson was a huge earthwork on the Confederate's far left wing—the Yankee's right side—meant to protect the river channel. It originally had thirteen guns. From Fort Thompson, running toward the west was an earthwork line, a long "ditch" from which the dirt had been piled in front.

Today, part of this original battle line is still intact. The visible divide slices through the county fairground. Mangum said what most people see as just a ditch is actually a century-and-a-half-old remnant of the battle.

Historian and author Richard Sauer described the line this way. "The interior of the line consisted of logs, covered with dirt on the side facing the enemy," he wrote in his book on the Burnside expedition. "The resulting ditch in front of the line was at least six feet wide and six feet deep." Add to that the four-to-five-foot height of the berm and, in places, the Union soldiers might have had an obstacle ten feet tall facing them. This mile-long man-made hill bestowed upon the southerners the distinct advantage as a defensive force firing from behind solid, protective cover.

In 1862, the earthen line was straight as a rifle-shot from the river all the way to the Atlantic & North Carolina Railroad tracks, a distance of one mile, Mangum said. On the opposite east side of the tracks, the right wing of the Confederate line, was a large swamp. Therefore, one end of the battle line was anchored by a fort on the river; the other end bogged down in a nearly impassable swamp. Because the Yankees would not be able to penetrate this natural obstacle, the Confederates knew they could concentrate all their forces along the earthwork line and leave the natural marsh and quagmire barrier undefended.

In front of this fortified line, all the trees had been cleared for a distance of three hundred and fifty yards. The clearing created a long, open field-of-fire which enemy soldiers would have to cross. With no cover, and the North Carolina troops fighting from behind their berm, the Yankees would have quite a challenge. The clear, free-fire zone and lack of cover for the Union gave the southern fighters a significant advantage.

Mangum said battle planners for the southern forces had estimated that forty-six hundred men would be needed to defend the line. About two weeks before the battle, the southerners learned something amazing. The Union troops had taken Roanoke Island by going through, not one, but two "impenetrable" swamps. Based on the intelligence report, the decision was made to pull the eight hundred and fifty-man Twenty-sixth North Carolina—under the command of Zebulon Vance—from the main defensive line. They were tasked with creating a fortification west of the railroad track along Bullen's (or Boleyn's) Creek. Vance was a political commander with no practical military training. However, his sub-commander, Lt. Col. Henry Burgwyn was a Virginia Military Institute-trained soldier with a personal zeal for fortifications. Burgwyn joined the service with the recommendation of one of his professors, Thomas "Stonewall" Jackson. Only nineteen, he would become known to history as the "boy colonel."

Probably under Burgwyn's tutelage, the Twenty-sixth used the natural undulations of the ridge and ravine topography to create a strong defensive line. They, too, cut down all the trees for three hundred yards—nearly a thousand feet—and then, days before the battle, they dammed the creek and flooded the entire area. The result was more than three feet of water around the creek with floating logs and jagged limbs set as obstacles guaranteed to break up the Yankee advance.

"They would have never lost that position," Mangum said. One knowledgeable and high-ranking military officer who visited the site in recent times suggested that nothing could have crossed the Twenty-sixth's defensive line until the most current generation of modern tanks. And it was not crossed on March 14, 1862.

In fact, Mangum believes the Federals knew they couldn't get through—that they had intelligence gleaned by spies to that effect—and the forces directly opposing the Twenty-sixth simply held their position until the anticipated break-through happened at the railroad track.

The railroad was the weak point. Along that formidable line of earthworks, near the Confederate's right wing was a gap created by the railroad tracks and the creek. It was about three hundred yards wide. The gap was necessary. The trains had to run from Morehead to Goldsboro and back. Even so, the southern forces knew the gap was a danger as well. They had planned to plug the hole with artillery, but, by plain bad luck, the cannons did not arrive in time for the battle.

A brick yard was near the gap. Wood's Brickyard was the site of one of many kilns in the area where native clay soils were formed and baked into building material. Wood's covered about an acre not including the many open clay pits that had been dug over many years.

Wood's Brickyard, just east of and beside the vulnerable gap in the Confederate's massive earthen berm, was where the Battle of New Bern would be lost. While the lack of cannons was bad luck, a much more serious failure in planning was in play. Guarding the gap—the weakest point in the line protecting New Bern—was a battalion of local militiamen. Under the command of J.H.B. Clark, the men were virtually untrained; some were poorly armed with personal weapons like shotguns and squirrel rifles. And they had been together as a military unit all of two weeks.

The railroad gap was one problem. The ill-prepared militia was another. And a third problem would plague Gen. Branch that day. Though necessary, the movement of the Twenty-sixth North Carolina created a serious consequence. Branch needed forty-six hundred men to cover one mile of entrenchments. He only had four thousand. Pulling troops out of the line to defend the swamp left him even more badly short-handed. With the Twenty-sixth ordered west of the railroad tracks, Branch's fighters on the line were reduced to about thirty-one hundred riflemen to control an area that required fifty percent more.

A smattering of rifle fire had been going on for some time. A group of Confederate cannoneers were ready to enter the fray. Captain A.A. Latham's men had been watching a concentration of federals moving their way. When the artillery captain judged the time was right, he ordered his guns to open fire. Immediately after Captain Latham's gray-clad gunners began to deliver their solid shot and exploding rounds on Union General Foster's men, matters heated up very quickly.

Here they come!

Under the dark, cloudy sky, a blue wave began to appear before the defenders' eyes. Gunfire and ordnance exploded from all directions. Then, out from the forest like some dream come to life, the Confederates saw at first hundreds and soon thousands of Yankee soldiers approaching quick and double-quick.

The first advantage went to the Carolina forces. Effective artillery volleys sheared sickening gaps in the blue lines. Some blue units were completely halted by bullets and cannonballs. Others rocked and wobbled before regaining enough composure to continue the forward pressure.

With little sleep and after slogging through miles of knee-deep mud, Levi Kent was beyond tired.

"I was so completely exhausted that all my movements were sort of mechanical," the young captain remembered. "I moved more like a machine than a man and I almost feared the machine would break down. But it kept up and held together through it all for which I am thankful."

Bullets whined all around Kent and his brothers-in-arms. They could see dirt flying, smoke rising. When the big shells burst in dirt or trees the men felt the concussion in their guts. Shots rained down around Kent and his men but many passed harmlessly overhead.

෴ ෴ ෴

MARK MANGUM related details of a story about one unfortunate officer of the Twenty-sixth North Carolina.

At about 11:00 a.m., during the thick of the fighting at the Battle of New Bern, a federal sharpshooter was scanning the battlefield through binoculars. From his secure position, his eyes fell upon a cluster of southern officers huddled up for an impromptu conference. One of them appeared to be a colonel. But another one of the rebs, he saw, had a little Confederate flag stuck in the side of his hat. The rifleman picked the man with the rebel flag.

Taking careful aim, the Union marksman put a minie ball into the officer's head.

Maj. Abner B. Carmichael had been with recruits from the western part of the state. He was commanding parts of three companies during the battle. At the moment of his death, Carmicheal's girlfriend, who had traveled with him to New Bern, was waiting in town.

She had given him the little flag...for good luck.

෴ ෴ ෴

MOVING THROUGH some young pines, the Union company around Capt. Kent continued to be fired upon by Confederate marksmen. After assessing their situation, they hurried down a grade to the rail line. With part of his force in light woods and part behind the railroad embankment, Kent's colonel, Isaac Rodman, had completed his orders. Now they waited for further instructions from Gen. John G. Parke, one of Burnside's subordinate commanders. While on hold, Rodman carefully scanned the area around him.

He could see the Confederate flanks being attacked by forces under the other commanders, Gen. John G. Foster and Gen. Jesse Lee Reno. Both Rodman and Kent observed that the forces in the Confederate center were withdrawn to support the two ends of the line under attack. "The enemy had withdrawn everything from his centre," Kent said. "This was our fortune."

Union General Jesse Reno's troops found and exploited the weakness at the gap in the rail line. But they met stiff resistance from four companies of the 33rd North Carolina. These men had been ordered forward to fill the void being created by the wavering militia. Reno led them as they charged and the untried militia broke and began to retreat.

The men of the 33rd met Reno with all they had. Moving to protected positions close to the railroad, they called upon their deep-seated obstinacy to block the federal's forward progress. One end of the 33rd's line was commanded by a Confederate officer, Maj. W. G. Lewis.

Lewis and his men fired a volley directly into Reno's advancing men. They were answered in kind and soldiers fell dead and wounded on both sides of the skirmish line.

"Our loss was greater at that point than any other," a fellow officer would later write of Lewis's efforts. "He had to fight to his front, right, and left, but still maintained his position. No one could have behaved with more coolness, bravery, and determination than he, and he deserves the praise of every true countryman for his action."

They tried with all their might to hold back the blue flood. Several of their officers were killed in a matter of minutes. All along the mile-long line, men were falling by the dozens.

The Union fleet, which had been paralleling the movement of its troops, was firing at a steady pace, blindly at times, over the tree line along the river into coordinates they believed were occupied by the rebels. Some of their shots fell among their own Union troops that morning.

A wild cacophony of death and destruction played itself out for the next three hours as some in New Bern watched in hope and horror from the captain's walks on top of their homes.

At the railroad gap, the defenders held on bravely.

One of General Parke's corps, led by Colonel Rodman, and including Capt. Kent, was preparing to deliver a telling blow.

The collapse of the Confederate center, manned by the most inexperienced troops, is noted in all accounts as the major failure of the defense of New Bern. Kent was there when it occurred and witnessed it with his own eyes.

Kent's group now had nothing directly in front of them. They were under fire, but he indicates the musket fire was ineffective, mostly falling short. "They peppered at us but did not seem to reach us fairly," he said. "What few shots reached us passed well over."

Fierce fighting continued all along the line. Some of it was hand-to-hand. In places, the Union advance was bitterly repulsed. One group of 24th Massachusetts soldiers seized a cannon from Confederate hands, but was driven back over the big earthen berm by a charge of southerners. They left several of their dead behind. In the rain and smoke, men continue to feel the sting of steel and lead, or drop lifeless with no sensation at all.

Without orders to do so, Kent "joined by Capt. Buff...went up to the breastwork and, digging steps with my sword, I mounted it."

Kent "could distinctly see the rebel colors on my right on the hill and the heads of a few men...their colors [the rebel flag] I could distinctly see planted on the very line of works on which I was standing."

Meanwhile, Rodman and several other officers had been conferring and decided to charge their portion of the Confederate earthwork. With the order, the men began to roar and yell or, as Kent said, "and up the hill we went with a tiger and a yah!"

The charge startled the Confederate defenders so badly that they stopped fighting and began a hasty retreat.

"The rebels evidently thought bedlam was not only loose but upon them," Kent said. "They did not stay to receive us but their backs and heels were shown instead as they retreated on a double-double quick, through the woods."

In his journal, Kent proudly underlined the following words: *The Colors of my Company were the first planted upon the rebel works.* The feat was particularly satisfying because among other things, Kent was in charge of the Color Guard, the soldiers who carried, displayed, and protected and, in this case, planted the Stars and Stripes.

The fight was continuing in places. Reno's men were still laboring to dislodge the stubborn opponents across the tracks. After twenty minutes rest, Kent's group was ordered to move and assist Reno. As they charged across the railroad tracks, they came under intense fire and begin to rush from one pit and berm to another, firing as they went. The movement of new forces to the fray caused the rebel resistance to collapse. Though effective, the charge had a steep cost for the Union army with twenty killed and wounded. This is where Kent's friend, Capt. Tillinghast, was fatally shot.

Kent says the 5th Rhode Island Volunteers mounted a charge down the railroad near "a sort of brick yard." They attacked and routed the Confederate riflemen "in their pits that peppered us while we stood on the railroad before the charge." Here another of Kent's friends, Lt. H.R. Reice, was killed.

The appearance of the Stars and Stripe on the New Bern side—clearly the wrong side—of earthwork was visible by North Carolina forces all up and down the line. Some began to retreat in good order. Others simply ran for their lives. Soon Union troops were pouring in by the hundreds.

Among the wounded Union officers, Kent knew, "Capt. Bill Chace has a shot through his cheek and Lieut. Curtis of my company, a wound upon his shoulder."

Watching his men retreat and Yankees occupying his works, General Branch knew the battle was over. He sent couriers scurrying with orders for his officers to cease resistance and save all the men they could.

Kent said the fort was now in Union hands from the railroad to the river. On the other side of the railroad, the fighting continued as the rebels contended "obstinately" against Gen. Reno's forces.

Gen. Parke's troopers, including Kent, began regrouping on the top of the fort's hill-like wall. At that moment, Gen. Burnside himself, having witnessed the successful attack, charged up on a horse. He asked the men if they were the 4th Rhode Island Troops. "Being answered in the affirmative said 'I knew it.' And away he rode to prepare a new job for us," Kent related.

The Battle of New Bern was nearing its end.

"The rebels now put for Newburne," Kent said, "and across the river burning the railroad and highway bridges behind them. On followed our forces, Foster in advance, and the gunboats followed up the river. With our advance we soon had [General Foster's] entire brigade in the city."

Kent reports that "near the City we found several encampments of the rebels just as they had left them in the morning when they moved down the road to give us battle."

In one of these deserted camps, Kent made a temporary home and completed the entry in his journal.

He made a final assessment of the Battle of New Bern that is particularly poignant:

"This is our second engagement [Roanoke Island was the first] and far the most severe. I am not anxious for a repetition of the doings of the 14th but wish it might please God to stop the rebels in their career of madness and return them peaceably to their homes."

ભ ભ ભ

FOR YET ANOTHER of those curious, ironic anecdotes of history, consider how things turned out for Colonel Isaac P. Rodman, leader of the charge that broke the Confederate line.

"Rodman's soldierly movement was the culminating point of the day," a Union officer wrote in one of several reports extolling his action at the Battle New Bern.

Other accounts, while uniform in praise, leave it unclear whether he consulted superior officers before his attack. One said he had permission, "barely." Another indicates he made the decision on the fly.

"The charge of the 4th Rhode Island under the impetus of Rodman was decisive at New Bern, and earned his promotion to brigadier general a month later," one U.S. historian reported. "At the New Bern battle, Rodman offered to assault the center of the enemy line, perceiving an opening where the railroad crossed the Confederate entrenchments. He had barely received permission when he led the 4th Rhode Island on an impetuous charge, breaking the Rebel line and capturing nine pieces of artillery."

The historian of the 9th Corps would later state, "Colonel Rodman, with a fine soldierly instinct, perceived that the enemy's line could be there successfully pierced, and his prompt and daring spirit suggested that, without losing time in waiting for orders, he should take advantage of the opportunity so fortunately offered."

Whether he followed orders or not, Colonel Rodman fought like war was his natural habitat. He leaned into the fury of battle and came out a hero—and brigadier general.

Capt. Levi Kent's immediate superior, Rodman was a paradox in boots. First of all, Isaac P. Rodman almost declined military service. He was a Quaker. Quakers reject war and their pacifism is built upon the bedrock of personal nonviolence. Strongly conflicted, he decided in the end to strap on a sword, load his pistol and fight for the Union.

In doing so, the warrior, credited with leading the bloody charge that broke the back of the Confederate army at New Bern, had something else to think about.

His middle initial stood for "Peace."

ભૂ ભૂ ભૂ

SO WHY did the North Carolina troops lose?

"They were just out-gunned," Mangum said. "You had four thousand troops against eleven thousand troops. The weak point fell. The federals rolled them up with no problem and that was the end of it. They fought very valiantly for many hours and then they had to finally give in and retreat. But, you know, the way things turned out is a mixed blessing because if our troops had hunkered down and the federals had besieged New Bern, we wouldn't have New Bern here today."

A naval cannon-pounding and fires set by friendlies and marauders could have easily taken out all of what are today the irreplaceable historic homes and artifacts of New Bern. But the city was not destroyed. As far as infrastructure goes, the occupation would be benign.

So, Union soldiers made themselves at home in the City of Twin Rivers. Levi Kent was one of them. Kent had made no entry in the journal from March 13-18, 1862. He'd been too busy. During that interim, Burnside's fleet arrived off Slocum Creek, marched to New Bern, won the battle and mopped up afterwards. When he put pen to paper March 18, he was happily ensconced at "Rebel Camp Lee," a former Confederate campground "near Newberne, N.C." Kent said, "Our little Army has again made its mark and routed the rebels from a position they considered secure."

His outfit made itself comfortable in a rebel camp that was all set up and ready for occupancy after the Confederates marched away from it to meet the Union in battle. In camp, the victors found stacks of kindling and firewood, food and cots made up and ready for sleeping. In places, campfires were still warm.

After the battle, victorious Union troops bivouacked all over New Bern and along the banks of the Trent and Neuse

Rivers, including several deserted Confederate camps. Officers, including Burnside, bedded down in the finest homes of the city.

On March 17, Kent went to see New Bern with his fellow officer, Lt. Charley Greene.

"It is a pretty little town and must have been a lovely place in time of peace," Kent said. "Several valuable buildings were destroyed by the rebels as they passed through on their flight."

He reported that in New Bern "one of the enterprising sutlers," the traveling vendor and merchants accompanying the Yankee fleet, opened the Gaston House hotel, renaming it the Union House. The Gaston House was a large three-story brick hotel on South Front Street between Middle and Craven.

"Its bar is well-patronized," he said. "Capt. Belger, whose battery is quartered in the city, invited us to the Union House where we had a good lunch and glass of blackberry wine which we were very thankful for its medicinal qualities."

After visiting "places of importance" in the city, he and Green "went down to the wharf and foraged a boat." They found a couple of the recently-freed slaves to row it down river "to our good old *Eastern Queen.*" At the ship, they enjoyed a bath, had a "change of under clothing," a lunch of hard tack before returning to their camp near New Bern.

"We arrived back at rebel 'Camp Lee' about nine [o'clock] in the evening after a very pleasant day," he said. "We were soon comfortably snoozing in quarters."

The Yankees would snooze comfortably in New Bern, more or less, for the next three years.

ભ   ભ   ભ

THEIR REST would be disturbed from time to time by the likes of Col. John D. Whitford. The reliable railroad man and future mayor would conduct merciless raids on Union forces outside of town during the remainder of the war. He would live to write a rambling history of the city.

Three Union men would be awarded the newly-created Congressional Medal of Honor for their actions on the New Bern battlefield. Private Orlando E. Caruana, a native of Malta, rescued a wounded color sergeant and retrieved the unit's flag, carrying them both across the field under heavy fire from North Carolina troops. Sergeant John D. Terry was from Boston. In the thick of the fight, he lost a leg to cannon fire. With disregard for both the gravity of the wound and his own safety, he continued to command and encourage his troops until carried from the field. James Harry Thompson was born in England and entered military service as a surgeon at New York. Although it was not his duty, the doctor volunteered to scout enemy positions and carry orders "under the hottest fire."

Generals Reno and Branch would be dead soon, transported from this life on other battlefields. After some dramatic combat failures, Gen. Burnside would resign from service to work full-time on a new brass-shelled rifle he invented, the Burnside carbine.

A Confederate snare drum was wrenched from the hands of a drummer boy during the Battle of New Bern. The beautiful infantry drum was decorated with a gold star wrapped by the words "The Old North State." A twenty-three-year-old private from Massachusetts would carry it home as a souvenir of war. L.L. Lamb wrote both his name and his initials on it. In 2006, the Tryon Palace Commission would pay an auction house $28,000 so the kidnapped drum could finally be brought back home.

The commander of the Twenty-sixth North Carolina at New Bern, Col. Zeb Vance would nearly drown the day of the battle when he tried to swim forty-foot-deep Brice's Creek on horseback. But he didn't. Six months later, he'd no longer be with the Twenty-sixth. He'd be the Confederate governor of North Carolina. Following the war, he was elected governor again and lived to be a major political force in the South.

The Twenty-sixth itself was not so lucky. It would go down in history as the unit with the highest battle casualty rate of the war, or maybe any war. At Gettysburg the next summer, more than seven hundred of its eight hundred troops would be killed or wounded. At one company's roll call after the first day of battle, only one man answered. Vance's second at New Bern, Henry King Burgwyn, Jr., now a colonel in command of the Twenty-sixth, would be counted among the dead. His last words were, "The Lord's will be done." He was twenty-one years old.

Captain Levi Kent, the informative diarist of the Battle of New Bern, would survive the war and return to Rhode Island. He would marry, have children and support his family as an insurance adjuster. He'd live to be an old man.

Bombardment of New Bern by Union Fleet, March 14, 1862
Harper's Weekly

11

Why the Yankees Wanted New Bern

NEW BERN GUY goes into the Smithsonian. Have you heard this one? Well, this special Smithsonian exhibit is called "America in Motion." Railroads, transportation, shipping, that sort of thing. He sees—there in the center of the exhibit—four antique prints. Large prints. Huge, Huge. You know, Smithsonian Huge Prints. And these prints are the major ports in the United States in 1860; old style drawings of ships sailing in and ships sailing out. The ports in the Smithsonian prints are the Great Lakes's harbor of Detroit, and the Atlantic Ocean seaports of Boston, New York City, and—ready for this?—New Bern, North Carolina.

That's right. Believe it or not, at the beginning of the War Between the States, New Bern was one of the most important ports in the country.

Everyone in town has seen the big bank murals of the

antebellum Port of New Bern or those old nicely-framed prints with all the sailboats and steamships in the river off Union Point. Those images are not exaggerations. Although the treacherous and deadly sands of the Outer Banks had been a huge handicap in the early days of settlement, by the time of the War Between the States, shippers had figured out how to move a lot of goods through those narrow inlets.

By the early 1860s, New Bern was the second largest town in North Carolina after Wilmington. It was a port town. It was a railroad town. The Atlantic and North Carolina railroad connected New Bern to the vital port of Beaufort in the east, and all the rest of the country to the west.

New Bern shippers had world-wide connections with the flourishing trade to the West Indies and all the major ports of the East Coast. The federals were intent on stopping commerce at every Confederate port and cherry-picked their way around the Atlantic and Gulf coasts. New Bern was high on the list of targets.

It was also the center of all commerce for a ten-county area surrounding it. Most important of all, those ten counties, for which New Bern was the hub, produced four times the raw goods of the Shenandoah Valley. That bears repeating. The famous Shenandoah Valley produced only one-quarter the goods and produce that flowed through New Bern. And the Shenandoah was nicknamed the "Breadbasket of the Confederacy."

Few natives or newcomers understand today what a machine of production the New Bern region was. But people around Abraham Lincoln understood. The Union leadership knew that if they could control New Bern, they could control the region and all of its production. They might not have the goods for themselves. That was true. But they could deny all the meat, vegetables, raw materials and other goods to their enemy—and that was motivation enough.

"Anybody who's been in eastern North Carolina knows that we are farmers," said historic preservationist Mark Mangum, who outlined the theory above. "We're farmers and always have been. Everything from cotton to corn, beans, anything they could use. Hogs, meat. It was enormous. New Bern was a major, major supplier. And that's not to mention pitch and tar products."

"Gathering turpentine," as the industry was called, required the tapping of sap from the native pines trees. The tar, pitch, turpentine, rosin and other products harvested or distilled from the sap produced commodities used in the construction and maintenance of wooden ships. At one time, the naval stores industry was as lucrative as the oil business is today. Some of the "farmers" in the ten-county area, for which New Bern was the outlet, grew nothing but pine trees.

Hundreds of thousands of barrels of these "naval stores" were shipped from New Bern in the years before the war. In a single year more than four million gallons of tar, pitch and turpentine were shipped from Craven County. These products were so ubiquitous that one census reported one-fifth of the men in a section of the county were employed as "coopers." A cooper is a barrel-maker. Such was the volume of naval stores that twenty percent of the labor force was engaged in making the barrels for its shipment. Lumber and finished wood products completed the inventory of raw good supplied by the Port of New Bern.

The writer of one early history noted: "Hundreds of acres are being planted in peas and potatoes, which after harvesting will again be covered with valuable crops of cotton and corn." The writer further noted that "the Neuse and the Trent, the great highways of interior commerce for the city, are being rapidly opened."

The two rivers—these "great highways" of water—carried the goods of a significant slice of eastern North Carolina to New Bern's doorstep. Many cities had a single river bringing in commerce from a single corridor. New Bern had two. These rivers allowed products of all kinds to be barged to New Bern by-passing dirt roads which were impassible at some times of the year.

Compared to other parts of the Atlantic coast, eastern North Carolina was sparsely populated and always had been. It was, however, a highly-productive area of significant prosperity. It was a big slave-holding area, too.

The equation for the federals was easy. It went something this: Here lies a rich area of the South. It is a great contributor to the commercial well-being of the Confederacy. From New Bern, we can control half of the state's waterways. It will put us behind the lines of Gen. Robert E. Lee's rebel forces and open a port where we can come and go as we please. We will have a base of southern operations where we can harass and demoralize the enemy. The region is sparsely populated and therefore will present little resistance. And a percentage approaching half of the population is made up of slaves who will not resist us at all.

And, there was a political reason.

Early in the war, matters were going very badly for the Union. Lincoln needed a victory. And he needed it right away. The odds appeared good that both New Bern and Roanoke Island could put two "plus signs" in the win column for the Yankees. So they sent ol' Sideburns down. With eleven thousand buddies.

In the author's previous book, *In This Small Place*, the relative lack of population in eastern North Carolina—resulting in relatively light resistance—was explained with an imaginary trip back in time.

Imagine you are a shoemaker who wants a new life in America. You have boarded a small, leaky wooden sailing ship in London in, say, 1753 and are about to voyage across the ocean with your precious family and all your worldly goods. Perhaps the captain gives you your choice of sailing to:

1) The Port of Boston, or
2) The Port of Charleston, or
3) "The Graveyard of the Atlantic."

Which would you choose?

Trust me. Number Three was an unpopular selection.

The long, curving coast of North Carolina, the aforementioned "Graveyard," has always had a string of barrier islands broken only by a series of shifting and treacherous inlets. Add to that three sets of shoals running straight out into the sea; Diamond Shoals off Cape Hatteras, Cape Lookout Shoals off Beaufort, and Frying Pan Shoals off Wilmington. In some places, the water may only be six inches deep many miles offshore. They did not call it "Cape Fear" for nothing. Add to that the frequency of hurricanes and the powerful Gulf Stream, a river of warm water in the ocean driving northward with its foggy, stormy weather, and you wind up with more shipwrecks than National Geographic can fit in tiny print on a three-foot map of the North Carolina shoreline. Pirates, like Blackbeard, called it home because few would chase them here. But even Blackbeard lost his flagship near Beaufort. Call it a destination of last resort.

Other modes of transportation, of course, were foot, horse or wagon. If you were coming from the north or south on muddy dirt roads, when you reach North Carolina you must swing *wide to the west to avoid a parallel series of huge rivers with accompanying swampy terrain for miles on each side. Crossing these rivers was difficult, dangerous, and, if you had to hire someone to ferry you across, expensive. The Cape Fear, the Neuse, the Pamlico, and the Albemarle rivers were huge impediments to travel and still are. The State of North Carolina recently spent $100 million for a bridge to cross the Neuse at New Bern. Even today, to cross the river from Havelock to Pamlico County you have to go by state ferry.*

So, few ships sailed here. Most travelers walked west around the rivers. Most settlers simply did not come here at all. President George Washington traversed the region in 1791 and wrote in his diary that in eastern North Carolina he had "passed through the most barren country I have ever beheld." Although it is rapidly changing, to this day eastern North Carolina is among the least densely populated areas from Boston to Key West.

So, the federals outnumbered the local force by three-to-one, as we have previously noted. The Union had a relatively easy time taking New Bern. But the Confederacy never stopped wanting it, and its goods, back in the southern marketplace.

"Throughout the war, there were constant battles and constant efforts [by the South] to take New Bern back," said Mangum. "There were three separate instances when the Confederates tried to take New Bern back and failed."

The last such attempt was in early 1864, when—on direct personal orders from General Robert E. Lee—Confederate officers and men tried to re-capture Union-held New Bern. Fighting ranged up and down the railroad from Newport to New Bern with action at Havelock, Croatan and at other places in Craven County. Thousands of troops were involved.

The following dispatch was sent by Lee to Major General William H.C. Whiting in Wilmington, N.C., January 20, 1864:

> *Head Quarters 20 Jan*
> *Genl.—An attack on Newbern is contemplated by the forces under the command of Gen. [George] Pickett. The time will be between 25th and 30th inst. I request you will give all the assistance in your power, especially by threatening simultaneously with your troops south of the Cape Fear, the enemy's position*

so as to prevent their reinforcing Newbern. Gen Pickett will telegraph you the day, by which you will know what is meant. Commit nothing to the telegraph on the subject. Keep the matter secret.
Very respectfully, your obedient servant,
R.E. Lee, General

Though hard-fought, the attempt failed. Gen. Pickett blamed his subordinate commanders. Historians have blamed Pickett. Apparently, Gen. Lee blamed Pickett also as his command was handed to another general a short time later. The major success of the attack was the burning of a famous federal gunboat, the *Underwriter*. About two dozen former Confederate soldiers who had taken up arms for the Union were captured and executed en masse at Kinston. But a gunboat and some deserters was not what Lee was after. He wanted New Bern back.

"They didn't try this with every other place they lost," Mangum said. "There was good reason for that. New Bern was a very strategic place or they would not have taken it so early in the war. [The battle of] New Bern had much more importance than it has been given credit for. It was not very big and it's not very well written about, but this battle was probably one of the most important strategic battles in the war. Period."

To secure its investment of time and blood in taking New Bern, ten forts were built by the Union to protect the city, including the massive star-fort, Fort Totten, west of downtown. One of General Ambrose E. Burnside's sub-commanders, John G. Foster, took charge of the "Department of North Carolina" after Burnside was sent to the Virginia frontlines. Now a major general, Foster's strength was beefed up to nearly twenty thousand troops. He began a series of raids to sow destruction and create chaos in the greater New Bern commerce area.

John Gray Foster, who oversaw occupied New Bern, was an interesting man. After graduating fourth in his class, he served as a U.S. Army engineer. In one of those curious twists of history, he helped construct Fort Sumter in the harbor of Charleston, S.C. And, on April 13, 1862, when railroad president John Whitford and the other head men of New Bern were wondering what was going on in Charleston, John Foster was *inside* Fort Sumter which was under heavy artillery bombardment by the Confederates. He endured all thirty-four hours of the non-stop barrage. Following the fort's surrender, he was returned to Washington, D.C. and promoted to brigadier general. Ears still ringing, no doubt.

Foster, a New Hampshire native, was born in 1823. He served with distinction in the Mexican war where he fought in a half-dozen battles, was badly wounded and promoted twice for bravery. He later became part of Maj. Gen. Burnside's three-man brain trust at age thirty-eight—with generals Reno and Parke—and exhibited excellent command skills at the battles for Roanoke Island and New Bern.

Over the next few years, Foster's forces prowled constantly hitting places like Tarboro, Goldsboro and nearby Whitehall, Kinston, Gum Swamp, Greenville, Pollocksville, Trenton, Swansboro and Rocky Mount; all places that had done business with and through New Bern before the war. All were agriculture and forest product centers.

Once, at Washington, N.C., Foster was in command of an expedition when Confederate Gen. D.H. Hill surrounded the town and demanded its surrender. Foster is said to have replied, "If you want Washington, come and get it!" Hill withdrew.

Foster didn't try to occupy or control anything other than New Bern, Beaufort and the railroad in between, though. Instead, all over the multi-county no-man's-land east of Goldsboro, the federals cut telegraph wires, burned bridges, tore up railroad track, burned pine forest, killed livestock, destroyed farm goods and knocked down fences.

It was economic warfare, pure and simple.

Foster's regiments attacked Confederates wherever they could find them and were likewise attacked by their opponents. More than anything else, though, the countryside was stripped and denuded by Union troops bent on punishing the "rebels." Farm production was disrupted as much of the population retreated to the relative security of Southern lines. Many former New Bern residents sought refuge in Goldsboro and Wilmington.

And sometimes the Confederates themselves had to live off the locals, too. Addison P. Whitford, who survived the war in Craven County, was quoted in the New Bern Historical Society's *Journal*. Whitford reported that "periodically both Confederates and Yankees came by the plantation."

"They took all the livestock and most of the other food like salt meat and corn," he said. "Once both Yankees and Confederates had been in skirmishes, and they took most of Ma's linens for bandages. We kept our cattle and hogs hidden in pastures in the woods."

One time the family heard the federals coming and shooed a young mule out of the barnyard to prevent the Union troops from stealing him. Whitford reported: "The mule was never captured. One Yankee swore he would get him, but he run himself out without success."

Foster would later assist Gen. William Tecumseh Sherman in his infamous March to the Sea, specifically aiding in the capture of Savannah. After the war, he began the study of underwater explosions and wrote a classic reference on the subject called *Submarine Blasting in Boston Harbor*. The Union general died and was buried in Nashua, N.H. in 1874. He was fifty-one.

Although Foster moved on to other duties during the war, the federals remained in New Bern to the bitter end. Some stayed longer, never returning to their northern homes.

The end of war found the riches of this southern breadbasket all but destroyed. The Confederate dollar was worthless and prices were astronomical. All commodities were in short supply and locals hunted rabbits and deer to have a little meat. Some people went back to tapping the pines trees to raise some ready cash, but the demand for naval stores was on the wane as the world shifted from wooden sailing vessels to metal-hulled steamships. The hateful period after the war, called Reconstruction, was anything but. It would take the South about a hundred years to get over it.

The former Union soldiers who stayed in North Carolina suffered the economic privation and political turmoil along with everyone else. They married, had families and slowly assimilated into the culture. Others spent time at home, but having grown accustomed to the South, later returned to New Bern. And, over time, they kept on coming. In fact, God bless them, more are coming back all the time.

After all these years, the Yankees *still* want New Bern.

Some folks believe New Bern's Cedar Grove Cemetery is haunted.

12

The Baron Sees a Ghost—A True Story

IN THE SOUTHERN VERNACULAR, you could say New Bern is eat up with ghosts. Blackbeard's ex-girlfriend is supposed to be "hanging" around every Halloween. He is said to have used a noose on her pretty neck to keep her quiet about treasure. It's *always* treasure with these pirate guys.

Then there are all the angry Confederate soldiers eternally agitated because their Cedar Grove cemetery graves were robbed last century. That's three hundred ghosts right there. By our count, three whole companies of the transparent rebels prowl nightly seeking revenge.

And don't get us started about Cedar Grove itself when all

of our grandmamas told us not to get dripped on under the Weeping Gate—or we'd be the next ones pushing up dandelions or daisies or whenever it is you push up from down there.

New Bern mansions have chains a-draggin' and a local house of worship has a spectral preacher who has trouble with electricity. They say the reverend keeled over right in the middle of a sermon and has been blowing church fuses ever since.

There have been plenty of opportunities for "ghost production" in New Bern. There's the Indian War which dispatched hundreds of pioneers and Native Americans alike. We have Revolutionary War martyrs. Plenty of ghosts were generated by the Civil War too. Local ghost tour guides say there are thirty-five ghosts from that War of Northern Aggression alone, and that's in addition to the Cedar Grove crowd. Don't forget yellow fever. And then there have been duels, and executions, and bloody murders galore.

It's enough to frighten a shipload of Vikings.

There's a ghost in the balcony of the old Tryon Theater that used to be the Kehoe Theater on Pollock Street now the home of the local drama group. New Bern has ghosts that dance a pretty minuet to eerie music, ghosts inhabiting city buildings—probably addled former taxpayers—and ghosts prowling the streets on nights dark as the inside of a skull. Folks claim to have seen full-grown ghosts, old geezer ghosts and little kid ghosts, one of them named Dorothy. And there seems to be a lot—a lot!—of angry wives. They are the scariest of all.

In fact, there are so many spooky haints out there that Dottie Hollatschek has put a whole book together on them. If *Ghost Stories of New Bern* makes the little hairs wiggle on the back of your neck, don't blame us.

One guy who deserves ghostdom is John Lawson, also known as The Flame. But there are other explorer ghosts like Arthur Barlowe, a lot of phantom sea captains and feisty girl ghosts like Mary Oliver.

There are so many ghouls and poltergeists in New Bern that, as most of you know, you can take a tour to see them up close and personal...or at least hear about them.

Most of these spooky tales are repeated in good humor with the intent to entertain, but there are people here in River City who will swear in hushed voices that there are

149

ghosts and spirits, and even witches working magic—*magic*, they tell you!—of the kinds both black and white.

Some of these goings-on, which you may not know about, were witnessed by New Bern's founder, Baron Christopher DeGraffenried. The baron wrote a lot of stuff and some people believe every word. Others say you could tell the guy was lying 'cause his quill pen was moving. But if there is one thing we believe, it's his story about the Indian ghost told by him as the gospel truth in his book, *Account of the Founding of New Bern.*

The baron says the Indians, too, practiced some form of powerful magic. The Christian colonists were convinced the savages were in league with the devil. And DeGraffenried cited several examples of what they were known to do. Here, he tells three stories; one about a ghost and then some Indian "conjuration." Finally, the baron turns the tables and uses a little "white" magic of his very own.

So turn down the lights and listen up.

THE BARON said it happened at the Indian burial of a deceased widow woman. The woman had been ill and the native "priests," or medicine men, had come to her bark house. She was laid upon a pallet of skins, covered by a patterned blanket. Long gray hair combed smooth. Face old as rocks. The medicine men went through "all sorts of figures and antics." They made "conjurations." They gave the sick woman dollops of foul-looking medicine. None of it seemed to help.

Next they blew into her mouth. They puffed their breath so hard it made "a frightful roaring" noise.

DeGraffenried said he knew from experience that if the old Indian lady had recovered, there would have been "indescribable rejoicing." This was not to be. Instead, the old woman died before his very eyes. Immediately, there commenced, from many voices, "a sad howling, enough to frighten anyone."

Her grave was prepared by the tribe with tender attention to detail. A bark arch was fashioned over it. Her body was carried by the two native holy men. They stood over the grave and lamented while making a "funeral sermon after their fashion," the baron said.

They told of the good deeds and the well-lived life of the departed sister. They comforted her relatives with soft words.

But they did other things DeGraffenried did not understand; all sorts of "strange conjurations."

"In short, there is much action and chattering so that I have seen the priest or conjurer all in a sweat," he said. "But this happens if a good present is expected."

When the ceremony ended, the family bestowed upon the priest "pendants of wampum" made from beads of mussel shells. They were white, purple and yellow. This was the pay for the head medicine man.

The baron took the time from his story to comment that the Indians are ingenious with the use of the colorful hand-carved wampum beads. He said they attach them to clothing, especially deerskin trousers, and make necklaces with them.

"They know how to knit and to weave them so skillfully and ingeniously through one another, with all sorts of figures, that it is to be wondered at," he said.

Then he saw the ghost.

When the ceremony was accomplished and the grave had been closed and carefully covered "something marvelous took place which I myself saw."

"A pretty fire or flame of about two candle-light size went straight up into the air," he said, "as high probably as the longest and tallest tree, traveled again in a straight line over the hut of the deceased and so farther over a great heath [an open field], probably half an hour long until it disappeared in the forest."

DeGraffenried was amazed by what he had seen. But when he expressed his astonishment to the Indians, they laughed at him "as if it was nothing new to them." And no matter how he asked, they would not tell him what it was that he had seen. He continued to ask around and no one would answer him directly. They would only say it was a good sign for the old woman.

The baron considered all the possible explanations. It could not have been an ember blown on the wind or some "sulphurous vapor out of the earth," because it lasted too long. It was "too much for me," he admitted.

Sometime later, the baron was at a meeting with the Carolina colony's governor, Edward Hyde. A council was in session about Indian relations and several chiefs and two dozen other Indians were present. During the deliberations, DeGraffenried's eye kept falling upon an old Indian who had the appearance of a conjurer, shaman, or priest. Something kept drawing him to the old man's face. Skin wrinkled as a Chinese dog. At an opportune moment, he approached the Indian and asked him about the light he had seen at the funeral.

The Indian listened. He then gathered the others. They spoke among themselves and, at last, two of the oldest came to him. They said few would understand what he had seen. But *they* knew. Then the two white-hairs told a story that seemed to him "like a fable."

They whispered that only great men—mostly old experienced chiefs—could see what he had seen. They said the "little fire is the soul of the departed." If the person has led a good life and conducted himself properly, the light goes into a good creature. If not, it turns into a villainous smoke and goes into "an ugly and miserable creature."

The old medicine men told DeGraffenried it is possible to catch the fire. And some have done it. If a good man sees it, they said, and runs quickly and catches "this wonderful thing" he will become "the best conjurer or magician and can do all sorts of wonders." He who does so has the power "to invoke the devil or send him away."

They also told him some things about a small spider and a mouse that he did not understand, but the departing spirit he had seen with his own wondering eyes...he understood that.

HAVING GOTTEN his explanation about the ghost of the deceased woman, DeGraffenried presented another example of "conjuration" among the Indians.

He said a ship captain on the Carolina Sound was transporting a group including several Indians in his small sailing vessel when they were becalmed. The ship came to a stop on the flat, still water. Not a breath of air stirred. It was hot. They baked in the sun. After some time of making no headway at all, one of the Indians "said he could probably procure a good wind, and was willing to do it." The steersman had few provisions aboard. He knew these waters and understood they could be stuck in the sound for quite a while. He badly wanted to get the boat moving again so he "left it to the Indian."

Be careful what you wish for.

In only a short time after the Indian began his chanting and antics, there came such a strong wind that the ship's captain was thrown into a panic. The craft nearly capsized. He had to reef down the sails and it was all he could do to keep the vessel upright, but they were soon moving at great speed. With darkened sky, whistling gusts and monstrous seas, the ship's keel cut deeply through the waves while the steersman wrestled with the helm. Wishing desperately for less wind, he had no choice but to deal with the small hurricane manifested by the native sorcerer.

In no time they were at their destination. The wind slackened and the ship made a safe landing.

"The captain assured me," DeGraffenried said, "that he received such a fright on this account that as long as he lived he would no more use such help."

AND FINALLY, there's the one about the time his neighbor smashed the devil statue. In this one the baron unleashes a little "white" magic of his own.

"At New Bern where I settled and started the little city," he remembered, "I observed another custom among the Indians who lived there before us, which was somewhat nearer Christian worship."

The Indians built something like altars and this particular one he said was "very cleverly and artistically" made out of twigs woven into an arched dome. There was an open space in the middle where an offering could be placed. At the center of "the heathen chapel" were places where they left spirit gifts of wampum and coral beads.

On the eastern side of the chapel hut—the sunrise side—was an impressive carved wooden mask. The face was painted half red and half white. It was on a pole and wore a type of crown. The pole had red and white rings on it. This mask represented "the good divinity."

On the opposite side, toward the west, toward night, was another mask with a gloomy face.

Carved of wood.

High up on a pole.

Painted half red and half black.

You guessed it.

The devil!

And DeGraffenried—world class humorist that he was—could not resist adding "with whom they were better acquainted."

Now the plot thickens.

One of the baron's tenants, a strong man with a humorous, whimsical and somewhat odd personality, was coming home from chopping wood. While walking past the crude Indian chapel, he was riveted by the two carved images. He stared at the faces. First at one. Then at the other. He realized immediately that one represented "the good God" and the other was the image of evil. Then he was struck further when he realized that the savages had painted the devil himself red and black! The beloved red and black! The very colors of his precious hometown of Berne, Switzerland!

Fury seized him.

"He was so embittered at it that he cut the ugly image in two with his ax," the baron said. He smashed it. He bashed it. And he went home and began to tell the tale and brag about his deed saying he had split the devil himself in two with a single blow of his mighty ax.

DeGraffenried, being one of the guys, laughed a little about it as the story was told. Then at the same time, he admitted having a feeling of foreboding.

Maybe he was clairvoyant. For sure enough, faster than you can say *smash a devil,* who should show up but the local Indian king backed up by some headmen and a shaman or two; and the whole gaggle of them mad as, well, the devil. The chief was huffing and puffing. He called the chapel vandalism "a sacrilege and a great affront." He "complained bitterly."

Despite all his foreboding, the baron tried to handle the matter lightly. He told the chief and company that only the devil had been damaged and hurt, not the Good Spirit. No great injury had been done, he argued with a smile.

"I treated it as a joke," he said.

He told the chief that if the good one had been smashed he would have adjudged a serious penalty on the offender, but in any event he would personally see to it that "such vexation should not happen to them anymore."

Arms folded, eyes glaring, the Indian king was not buying what DeGraffenried was trying to sell. He could see the baron was making light of the blasphemy. This only made him angrier. DeGraffenried knew that when these savages were angry, anything could happen. He had seen the results with his own eyes.

Thinking fast, he changed his tone and said the matter made him angry too. Yes, it did. And, by Jupiter, if the good king or his men could point out the culprit who had done the abomination he would have him punished immediately.

This they could not do.

The king settled down a little.

The baron offered him something to drink.

The king said the Indian equivalent of "whatever."

"I gave the king and those with him rum to drink, which was a kind of brandy made of distilled sugar waste," the baron said.

Now, any Alcohol Law Enforcement officer can tell you that rum made from sugar—sugar rum—is corn liquor. Moonshine. White lightning!

"In these parts [sugar rum is] very common and healthful if one drinks it with moderation," the baron explained.

He and the chief and his new pals sat around together and consumed a "moderate" amount of the healthful white beverage.

"I was very friendly with them," he said, "so that they went away from me well-contented and satisfied."

Just like magic.

Crayon portrait of Francisco de Miranda
Bizzell Memorial Library, University of Oklahoma

13

A Venezuelan's Treasure

> *"Miranda was a man of the eighteenth century whose genius lay in raising the consciousness and confidence of his fellow Americans. Although he prided himself on being a soldier, his greatest battles were fought with his pen."*
>
> —*Daniel Florence O'Leary*
> *Aide-de-camp to Simón Bolívar*

ALEXIS DE TOCQUEVILLE wrote the classic *Democracy in America* in the 1830s. The book is fairly well-known to students of history. It's a travelogue as well as social commentary by the young Frenchman who visited the United States to see for himself what had been created by our Founding Fathers.

Less well-known, but no less fascinating, is a similar book, *The New Democracy in America: Travels of Francisco de Miranda in the United States, 1783-84*. It was translated from Spanish to English by the University of Oklahoma Press in 1963. But, for our purposes, Miranda's book has more importance than de Tocqueville's because Miranda visited New Bern. During a respite from his journey over much of the East Coast by land and sea, he socialized with citizens and leaders in the city. In doing so, Miranda not only recorded his interesting observations of the day, but also saved a treasure. Yes, a genuine treasure—a remarkable and significant piece of New Bern history which has only been discovered in recent years.

Intent on seeing the liberation from Spanish colonial rule of South America in general, and his home country of Venezuela in particular, Miranda visited the newly independent United States of America to learn firsthand how the victory had been won. On his trip, he met founding fathers George Washington, Thomas Jefferson, Thomas Paine, Alexander Hamilton and others.

Arriving from Cuba, he entered the United States at Ocracoke in North Carolina. His second port of call was New Bern where he met Tryon Palace architect John Hawks and many other community leaders.

From the quality of his writing alone, it's easy to discern that Miranda was intelligent and well-educated. For a reader getting to know him through his book, he is thoroughly likable. Despite all that, it is probable that the best description of Miranda would be to quote Shakespeare's Hamlet and say he was "a piece of work."

His portraits show a handsome visage with a broad forehead and strong chin. He appears to be a well-put-together individual with thick, white hair backswept into a ponytail. Miranda is invariably well-tailored in a suit with riffled-collar shirt or in full military regalia replete with gold braid, sash and sword. Miranda was referred to by one historian as "an international Don Juan." His exploits with "the fairer sex" were many and he was not above boasting about his conquests.

And despite all his self-proclaimed altruistic motives, Miranda appears to have fled Cuba one step ahead of the law. Footnotes in the translation of his book state: "Miranda left Cuba under a cloud because of apparent complicity in

157

contraband trade." In other words, he was suspected of being a smuggler. In fact, it was an America who helped Miranda escape the Cuban authorities and suggested he go to the United States.

ON JUNE 1, 1783, Sebastián Francisco de Miranda y Rodríguez exited Cuba, "the home of vice and corruption," he said, on a voyage to the young American nation. He sailed aboard the American sloop *Prudent* arriving at Ocracoke, a small island on the North Carolina coast at the entrance to Pamlico Sound.

Miranda said residents of Ocracoke were robust and fat, attributing this to their food "which is nothing more than fish, oysters" and some garden vegetables, small gardens being "the only agriculture of these people that I know." He said the Ocracokers were particularly afraid of smallpox and at first would not allow Miranda and his fellow passengers to leave their ship.

"The smallpox would seem to be their principal enemy because before we could disembark they required us to make a thousand protests that such disease was not with us on board," he said. Smallpox was quite common, often traveled via humans and vermin aboard ships and, on a small island like Ocracoke, could wipe out everyone in a hurry. The villagers had valid reasons to be concerned.

Following the visit at Ocracoke, the *Prudent* entered "this very dangerous sound" on June 9, crossing into the Neuse River by the next morning. Miranda wrote that the Neuse River "in particular is large, its navigation pleasant, and its shores here and there covered with thick, luxuriant forests and some dwellings with little agriculture in their vicinity." The voyage took him to the state capital and small port of New Bern. He arrived at five o'clock.

The traveler took a room at the tavern of Mr. Oliver, a well-visited New Bern inn, noting that the price of one silver "peso duro" dollar per day "seemed very cheap to me considering the cleanliness and good behavior of the lodging." He immediately began to make the acquaintance of not only the local leaders, but also the international visitors in New Bern during the Revolution. He mentioned making the acquaintance of Titus or Thomas Ogden, William Blount, John Sitgreaves, Richard Ellis, Mr. Schilbeake, Mr. Goff, Samuel Johnston, and Dr. Solomon Halling and Dr. William

McClure. Also introduced were Monsieur Heró and Le Marquis de Bretigny, "a French officer in service of the state."

Miranda extolled the hospitality and good treatment he was afforded "even though their ideas are not very liberal and the social system is still in swaddling clothes."

Then Miranda, the world traveler, unleashed this amazing paragraph about the New Bern society:

"The married women maintain monastic seclusion and a submission to their husbands such as I have never seen; they dress with neatness and their entire lives are domestic. Once married, they separate themselves from all intimate friendships and devote themselves completely to the care of home and family. During the first year of marriage they play the role of lovers, the second of breeders, and thereafter of housekeepers. On the other hand, the unmarried women enjoy complete freedom and take walks alone whenever they want to, without their steps being observed."

Do you suppose the lecherous Venezuelan carefully observed some of those young women's steps? The Hispanic Lothario was less impressed by New Bern males.

"The men," he said, "dress carelessly and grossly. All smoke tobacco in pipes and also chew it, with so much excess that some assured me they could not go to bed and reconcile sleep without a cud in the mouth."

During the visit, he became acquainted with Abner Nash, who had served as governor of North Carolina during the Revolution, and Col. Richard Dobbs Spaight, then twenty-five, who would be governor ten years later. He said Spaight was clearly well-educated, had a good mind and "an excellent disposition for outstanding education." He advised Spaight to travel.

Miranda put the population of New Bern at "five hundred families." The houses are "middling and small as a rule, but comfortable and clean; almost all are made of wood." He noted that the church and assembly hall were brick.

Then he talked about Tryon Palace.

Miranda said the finest building "which really deserves the attention of an educated traveler is the so-called Palace." Miranda said that he met the "able English architect, Mr. Hawks, who came from England with Governor Tryon...and still remains in the city." He described the palace in detail saying it was entirely of brick and built in pure English styling. He called the ornamentation simple, tasteful and intelligent. He spoke of the marble fireplace in the assembly room, a gift of Sir William Draper.

"The building is situated on the banks of the river Trent in a somewhat elevated spot," Miranda said of the palace, which gives it the command of a prospectus of more than twelve miles over the river Neuse and makes its location quite pleasing."

All in all, a good and accurate description of Tryon Palace and Mr. Hawks, but something very important—as we shall see later—is missing. And what is missing turns out to be the key to the undiscovered treasure.

BEFORE LEAVING NEW BERN, Miranda was involved in a day celebrating the end of the War of Independence from Great Britain. News traveled much more slowly then, so different parts of the country heard of the end of the war days, weeks, or even months apart. The local announcement, on June 17, of the preliminary treaty with England resulted in a military parade, the sound of drums, shots from cannons, a barbecue of roast pig and the tapping of a barrel of rum. He noted that "the leading officials and citizens of the region promiscuously ate and drank with the meanest and lowest kind of people, holding hands and drinking from the same cup."

Though Wilmington had been seized and occupied by British general Lord Cornwallis, New Bern, for the most part, was spared direct military involvement. However, as the reader may remember, it was raided and briefly occupied in August, 1781 by British soldiers and Tories who shot and killed the prominent Patriot leader Dr. Alexander Gaston. For good measure, they burned some warehouses, ships and homes. The prospect of peace was warmly embraced by those here who had pulled together to make the Revolution a success.

Miranda said there "were some drunks, some friendly fisticuffs and one man was injured." There was bonfire of old barrels "at nightfall, the party ended and everyone retired to sleep."

In preparation for leaving New Bern and continuing his journey, Miranda made an inventory of all the fine women in town. He chose a dozen of the ladies by name for particular praise, saying they "retain their beautiful coloring and excellent health." He mentioned Ann Cogdell Stanly, the wife of John Wright Stanly, who he "did not have the pleasure of engaging at close range." But the one he saved for last, and commented upon with the most enthusiasm, was Ann Stanly's sister, probably Susannah Cogdell, age twenty-two. Miranda said she was "one of the best looking and most florid complexion I have seen in America."

On July 12, 1783, Miranda said farewell to his new friends, crossed the Trent River on a ferry and headed east on the road to Beaufort. At two in the afternoon, he arrived at Always Inn, twenty-three miles from New Bern near Havelock where he spent the night and appears to have seduced the innkeeper's daughter.

He lodged for a few days in Beaufort which he described as having "no commerce" and whose residents he described as "poor." He noted that Beaufort had eighty citizens and described their homes as "miserable."

Miranda soon boarded a double-masted schooner for the continuation of his East Coast tour. This time he headed for Charleston, much to the delight, no doubt, of South Carolina womanhood.

NOW BACK TO THE TREASURE. It's already been said that something was missing from Miranda's description of the palace and his meeting with architect John Hawks. Drum roll, please! Missing were a few crucial words accidentally left out of the 1963 translation of Miranda's journal.

Listen carefully because this is one of those history mysteries. There were a number of New Bern people with varying roles involved in what comes next. Instead of trying to identify everyone and explain what each one did, step-by-step, we will simply call them "the researchers." Okay?

In the 1990s, one of the historical researchers noticed something in an old New Bern history by a man named Thomas Alonzo Dill that did not match the popular 1963 University of Oklahoma edition of the Miranda journal. Dill quoted Miranda as saying the architect John Hawks had given him something. That something was a plan of the palace.

Dill was working from a rare early translation of Miranda's journal. As the researchers discovered, Dill's reference stimulated a brief search for the Miranda plan by Tryon Palace officials in the 1950s during preparation for the palace restoration. The obvious places were Spain and Venezuela.

But nothing had been found in the 1950s.

No wonder. As it turned out, the Miranda document was in England.

How did it get there?

Well, after learning all about democracy in America, Miranda returned to Venezuela and tried to start a revolution against Spain. General Miranda was captured and died in a Spanish prison in 1816 while awaiting trial for inciting a rebellion. Before he died, Miranda sent all of his papers and diaries—including the one-of-a-kind Tryon Palace plan—for safe-keeping to a nobleman he knew in England. The nobleman had Miranda's papers carefully bound in leather. Eventually, the nobleman died as well. The bound volume languished amid his family for more than two centuries. One day—a decade or so after Tryon Palace was restored—the nobleman's British heirs wondered if they might make some money off the dusty old book. They made a few calls and offered it for sale to the National Library of Venezuela. The library wasted no time. It jumped on the offer because today Francisco de Miranda is a beloved national hero in the South American country, a martyr of the revolution.

After all this occurred—and without knowing about any of it—the New Bern researchers who discovered the glitch in the 1963 translation wrote to the National Library of Venezuela in Caracas. They asked if the Miranda papers were there. But the researchers wrote their letter in English. Nothing happened. Sometime later they had a New Bern Spanish teacher translate their letter and they tried again. Or maybe they tried a couple of times. In any event, one day a letter arrived in New Bern from the National Library in Caracas, and it said, yes, we do have a plan for Tryon Palace, and here it is!

The researchers were stunned. There, in their sweaty hands, for the first time ever, was a plan of the grounds of Tryon Palace! The Hawks drawing depicted the outline of the palace buildings and the garden plan. The architectural drawings of the Palace itself had been in New Bern for a long time. No one, though, had ever seen this plan of the grounds and gardens.

This previously unknown plan was a significant historical treasure.

But wait! What's this? On the copy of the map, along its edge, were words. English words. Something had been behind the map when it was photocopied and a little bit had been reproduced accidentally along the border.

More communication flashed between New Bern and Caracas. As a favor to the researchers, an American businessman in South America went to the Biblioteca Nacional de Venezuela to have a look and, before you can say "Miranda's girlfriend," another package arrived in New Bern.

Inside was a copy of a handwritten four-page letter from John Hawks himself to Francisco de Miranda. The letter in Hawks's handwriting was a detailed description—the first one known to exist—of the interior of Tryon Palace. It talked about the use of the individual rooms. It talked about the molding trim. In it the researchers for the first time could hear the architect's own description of his finest work.

This priceless historical treasure, recovered after two hundred years by diligent local researchers, had been all around the world. And this single copy—so important to New Bern's history—was preserved because John Hawks handed it to a South American tourist in 1783.

George Washington

14

Partying with George Washington

FIFTEEN OFFICIAL TOASTS!

Each accompanied by a cannon blast!

Both were integral elements of the socializing during "the gala banquet" New Bern threw for General George Washington on April 21, 1791. No doubt it was all those toasts that made the evening at "Tryon's Palace" so remarkably gala.

Renowned and beloved as the Father of the Country, George Washington (1732-1799) was a revolutionary war hero, in fact, the architect of the rebel colonists' recent victory over their British rulers. He was elected the fledgling nation's first president, serving in office from 1789—the year North Carolina became one of the original states—until 1797, when he declared two terms was as long as anyone should serve. After all, he reasoned, we had just gotten rid of one

164

king and did not need to create another one.

It was during his first term when President Washington decided to visit a section of the country each year. Earlier in his presidency, he visited the northern and central states. The third year, he decided to go for a little ride—through Virginia, North Carolina, South Carolina and Georgia. The journey began March 21, 1791. It would last one hundred days and cover about nineteen hundred miles.

Why did he go?

In his travels, he wished to see and be seen and to hear the opinions and ideas of as many citizens as he could. He wanted to eyeball the nation he helped create, to thank those who had given service to the cause of freedom and, by his presence, reinforce the feeling of unity then current across the land.

Along the way, the President of the United States sought shelter at taverns and inns, mostly, paying his own way and thereby trying not to burden individual citizens or families with the supply of his food or lodging. He didn't make a big fuss. He traveled simply, without a guard, and assisted only by a valet and his carriage drivers. His coach was white and he called it his "chariot."

Routinely, local entourages rode out on dirt roads to greet him. Sometimes, he was accompanied for a distance by leading citizens as he left for his next destination. In one instance, a group of mounted Carolina militiamen rode out to offer an honorary escort into Charlotte. Disinterested in pageantry and showiness, the President talked to them briefly, found out they were close to their homes and sent the uniformed troops away. "I dismissed them," he wrote in his journal.

From northern Virginia, Washington entered North Carolina after visits to Fredericksburg and Richmond. In the Old North State, he made stops in Halifax, Tarboro, Greenville, New Bern, Trenton and Wilmington. His tour took him down the coast to South Carolina and Georgia and then north again with a more westerly return to his Virginia home. Much of the actual road he traveled in 1791 has faded into memory. Some of it, though, is the path of today's paved highways. In passing through this area, Washington's course approximated the route of old Highway 17.

He noted in his diary that sparsely-populated eastern North Carolina was "the most barren country I have ever beheld." That's quite a statement for such a well-traveled individual.

A small crowd of town leaders intercepted Washington at a Neuse River ferry landing before noon April 20, 1791. They rode with him into the colonial capital. Exceedingly tall, uniquely handsome with a regal bearing, the President unfolded himself from the interior of the coach. He shook hands all around and spoke quietly to the waiting throng. For the next two days, he was toured, visited and feted by New Bern's eager, adoring citizenry. He was a big hit. People haven't stopped talking about it since.

Though a detailed list of his visitors eludes us, we know John Sitgreaves, a Patriot, lawyer and jurist was on hand along with other notables like the Mayor Joseph Leech, the colonel of Revolutionary War fame, and civic leader and Masonic master Isaac Guion. Washington was paraded by two mounted forces. The local artillery company—very busy for the next two days—fired a fifteen-gun volley in welcome. Since the President was a Mason, St. John's Lodge made a big to-do sending a seven-man Masonic delegation to offer greetings. One reference indicates the general later enjoyed the shade of a mighty cypress near a Neuse River wharf at the home of Samuel Smallwood.

The townspeople sent a letter of welcome which was delivered to Washington. The national hero responded with a message of his own addressed "To the Inhabitants of the Town of New Bern."

He thanked the people for their "polite attention" and "patriotic declarations on the situation of our common country."

Referring to the aftermath of the American Revolution, he said, "Pleasing indeed is the comparison which a retrospect of past scenes afford with our present happy condition—and equally so is the anticipation of what we may still attain and long continue to enjoy. A bountiful Providence has blest us with all the means of national and domestic happiness; to our own virtue and wisdom we are referred for their improvement and realization."

It was a warm and positive message meaning circumstances were much better than before or during the Revolution, and it was up to each American to insure that the country's best days were ahead.

The general concluded, saying, his "most sincere wish"

was "that the town of New Bern may eminently participate in the general prosperity, and its inhabitants be individually happy."

Some of those happy inhabitants had prepared a fine place for the general to take his rest—the best home in town.

Wealthy Patriot-privateer-merchant John Wright Stanly— well-known to Washington—and his wife, Ann, had both died tragically in an epidemic two years earlier leaving empty their stately mansion on Middle Street one block north of Broad. Family members and neighbors made the grand residence ready for the Presidential visit with cleaning and some borrowed furniture. After pubs and roadhouses, there is little wonder Washington commented on the "exceedingly good" accommodations. Even his horses had superior quarters. Reverend L.C. Vass later reported "General Washington's war-steeds were stabled" at the Palace during his stay.

The general noted in his journal that New Bern had a population of about two thousand and that the homes were "altogether of wood" and set at widely spaced intervals. He commented that the large public and commercial buildings he saw as he toured around town looked to be in good shape.

Of Tryon's Palace, the colonial governor's extraordinary manor house on the banks of the Trent River, he described "a good brick building but now hastening to Ruins." Since the state capital had been moved to Raleigh, the Palace had been unoccupied, seldom used and had fallen into some disrepair. But it was at the Palace—still the most elegant site in town— where he was entertained with a lavish banquet and ball beginning in the late afternoon of Thursday, April 21.

The celebration that night was New Bern's social highpoint of the year, if not the decade or even the century. All the elements were there: food, drink, cheering, singing, dancing, musicians, and everyone resplendent in sartorial finery. And artillery as well because what's a good party without it?

Fueling the merriment were the after-dinner toasts; some fifteen in all. During the era, drinking without toasts was considered to be an impropriety, an indication of a lack of good taste. James Iredell, namesake of Iredell County, and one of the original justices of the Supreme Court of the United States appointed by President George Washington himself, had been highly critical of the practice.

The solution apparently was to make a lot of toasts. Therefore, toasts were an important part of celebration in the

EDWARD BARNES ELLIS, JR.

eighteenth century. Toasts might be prepared beforehand sometimes by a committee created for the purpose. They were often written, usually brief and sometimes set to verse. Frequently a toast would be followed by three cheers and sometimes nine.

Washington's brother Masons, in particular, were big toasters holding to the dictum "the bonds of friendship tighten when wet." A familiar eighteenth century Masonic toast was "Charge, Brethren! Charge your glasses to the top. My toast forbids the spilling of a drop." A typical toast to the President at the time might go something like this one: "George Washington, President of the United States of America: May the Supreme Executive of every nation be, like him, the friend, as well as the Magistrate of the People. God save Columbia's son."

The probability that the Tryon Palace toasts for George Washington's banquet were written in advance is bolstered by the fact that a list of the fifteen toasts has survived. Miss Gertrude Carraway re-discovered and published it in the 1950s. Historic documents indicate that after each toast was spoken, it was punctuated by cheers and a blast of cannon on the Palace lawn. The racket could be heard for miles.

With each toast, the goblets would be filled. Those assembled to honor General Washington stood. They raised their glasses.

And, one by one, the toasts were spoken.

First, the assembly toasted The United States.

Then they toasted the Last Session of Congress.

The President took the third turn, toasting the State of North Carolina.

They toasted Patriots of America who fell in the country's defense.

They toasted the Late American Army.

They toasted the King of France.

They toasted the National Assembly.

They toasted the Memory of Benjamin Franklin.

They toasted the Marquis de Lafayette.

They toasted the Command of the United States.

They toasted Friends of America in Every Part of the World.

They toasted the Agricultural Interest of the United States.

They toasted all "Nations in Alliance with Us."

They toasted Universal Peace and Liberty.

And finally, they toasted General George Washington, the Father of His Country, President of the United States.

Fifteen toasts!

Fifteen sips might set heads spinning. Fifteen full glasses ...well, the evening was gala, all right.

The Palace party toasted, drank and cheered. Cannons roared.

The band played. People laughed and sang. They flirted, pointed, watched and gossiped. And bowed and curtsied. And they danced. Washington counted—and noted in his diary—no less than seventy ladies of New Bern in attendance with whom to dance that night. Although the President would retire at eleven o'clock, after seven hours at his party, the festivities would go on much longer.

The next morning, Washington said his farewells and departed for Wilmington amid the firing of more honorary artillery. He was accompanied for a short distance down the forest road toward Trenton by mounted infantry and a host of the resilient "principal gentlemen" of town.

ONE HUNDRED YEARS LATER, they did it all over again... almost.

Of course, President Washington was not there having long since gone to his heavenly reward. But both he and "Lady Washington" were represented at the "Complimentary Ball" of 1891 during the "Centennial Assembly in Commemoration of General Washington's Visit to New Bern, N.C."

The fund-raiser, held in a "spacious room" at the courthouse, was filled with men and women costumed in attire of "ye olden time." There was singing. There were flags, evergreens, flowers and patriotic bunting provided by the captain of the Steamship *Winona*.

There was a court of men and a court of ladies strutting about to the "strain of sweet music from the Italian band," who presented themselves to General Washington, played by W.P.M. Bryan, and Lady Washington—who did not attend the 1791 ball—played by Miss Mary T. Oliver.

Ten couples performed a sprightly minuet. *The Star Spangled Banner* and *The Old North State* were sung by a thirty-member chorus. A flower ballet was performed by entertainers with colored lanterns. A Virginia reel was danced by most attendees. Dinner was served and money was raised for charity.

But this time there were no toasts or artillery.

Still...why stop now?

When the 2010 calendar of events was published for the three hundredth anniversary of New Bern's founding, it included an item called "The Palace by George." The calendar described the two-day commemoration as "a weekend event intended to celebrate George Washington's visit to New Bern during his Southern Tour in 1791." The calendar said there would be recreations of historical events—such as the dancing assembly held in Washington's honor—patriotic artifacts on display, and craft activities and programs for children.

No vigorous toasting or cannon-fire was slated, however.

Caleb Bradham and New Bern Pepsi plant
Joy Fisher Collection

15

The Incredible Saga of Brad's Drink

FOR NEW BERN BUSINESSMAN Caleb Davis Bradham, creating a phenomenal soft drink product proved easier than hanging on to it. Bradham had the remarkable good fortune to invent Pepsi-Cola in the 1890s. But a series of unfortunate decisions compounded by bad luck would separate the founder from his company—an enterprise today with an astounding annual net income of over six billion dollars.

Let's look at that written out: $6,000,000,000.00

Breathtaking, isn't it?

At the time of Bradham's brainstorm, soda fountains were the rage in American pharmacies and everything on the stores' shelves was being mixed into experimental "soft drinks." Soft drinks were called soft drinks as opposed to "hard drinks" like beer, wine and liquor. But some of the early concoctions included even more potent substances like cocaine.

Regardless of the formula, there were small odds of

inventing a winning product with all that competition—which makes Bradham's achievement even more remarkable.

Young Caleb Bradham wanted to be a doctor. After studies at the University of North Carolina which began in 1886, he entered the medical school at the University of Maryland. Three years later, he left school. Some biographers have said his father could no longer afford to pay tuition, but his son, George Washington Bradham, told a New Bern Historical Society interviewer that his father's part-time job at a Maryland pharmaceutical company changed his interest. In any event, he came back to his boyhood home of Chinquapin, a tiny farm community in Duplin County about twenty-five miles west of Jacksonville.

Bradham was born there May 27, 1867. His parents, George W. and Julia McCann Bradham, told him he was descended from John McCann who served as an officer with Gen. Washington during the American Revolution.

According to his son, Duplin County neighbors began calling upon the partially-trained "doctor" for treatment of their medical woes. During his few months at home, George Bradham said his father "practiced medicine in Duplin County because there was no doctors in the county."

Soon, Bradham took a job in New Bern teaching penmanship at the private Vance Avery Academy, a co-ed boarding and day school. He worked for the school's owners, Appleton and Augusta Oaksmith, for two years. With money saved, he returned to the University of Maryland and enrolled in the pharmacy program. Upon graduation, he went back to New Bern intent on going into business.

In 1893, Bradham borrowed nearly all the money necessary to buy the now-famous building at the street corner of Middle and Pollock in the center of downtown New Bern. His winning personality soon attracted a steady clientele and his soda fountain at Bradham's Pharmacy became a gathering place. The newly-minted pharmacist became well-known around the city. He joined the Naval Militia as an officer and became a Mason. He rose through the offices of the venerable St. John's Lodge No. 3 and would serve as its "Worshipful Master" in 1900, 1901 and 1927.

Pharmacy periodicals were filled, at the time, with articles about soft drink products. Formulas and ingredients were listed, and recipes discussed. The ingredients might include carbonated water, sugar syrups and flavors. One key ingredient was caffeine to give the consumer a little kick of energy. A hefty load of caffeine was available in the exotic kola nut, the seed of evergreen trees found in the tropical rainforests of Africa. From a pharmacological viewpoint, the effects of kola nut caffeine are stimulation of the central nervous system and the heart followed by increased alertness, energy and mood elevation. Kola nut is classified as a stimulant and euphoric. By adding a lot of sugar, vanilla, fruit acids, flavoring and carbonation to kola nut, Bradham soon had a crowd pleaser on his hands.

"My father was a great experimenter," said son George. "[He] liked to fool around with chemicals and flavors, so he decided to make up a drink for the boys and manufactured this cola drink. It was called "Brad's drink" because the guys liked it so much."

Pharmacists like Caleb Bradham were not engaged in creating soft drinks for entertainment. They actually believed they were formulating products with medicinal qualities. Carbonated water was believed to be healthful in and of itself, and the ingredients added to it were thought to relieve a wide range of ailments. The claims included cures for morphine addiction, indigestion, impotence, fatigue, anxiety, headache, neuralgia and depression.

Historical sources on the dates of the invention of "Brad's Drink" vary quite a bit. Many say "the mid-1890s." Others say after 1895 or "late in the 1890s." The one we like best says with maximum exactitude that Bradham invented Brad's Drink on August 28, 1898. We're surprised it fails to list the time.

In any event, his New Bern customers liked it enough that he began to keep a supply on hand. George Bradham said his father originally only had twenty-five bottles that he would fill, sell, wash and reuse in the store.

Soon he was mixing up mass quantities in the store's basement and by 1898, Brad's Drink was being sold as Pepsi-Cola. Once again, there are varying stories on the origin of the name. Some say it is unknown. Others say he bought the name "Pep Cola" from a bankrupt company for one hundred dollars. George Bradham remembers the defunct firm was in New Jersey and the name they owned was "Pepsi." Others say the name came from pepsin, an ingredient in the drink. We know the last one is plain crazy. Pepsin is an enzyme in human stomach acid, not something anyone would add to a consumable product.

Whether he bought the name or made it up, it was perfect. *Pepsis* is the Greek word for "digestion," something pharmacist Bradham would have known. And he thought the product was a cure for indigestion. The name also included the syllable "pep," perfect for an energy-stimulating beverage.

Bradham was a one-man band at first. He mixed the formula, bottled it and sold it himself at his Middle Street storefront. Things would not be so quiet for long.

Just after the turn of the century, Caleb married Charity Credle in New Bern. The marriage would produce three children: Mary in 1903, Caleb, Jr. in 1905 and George in 1907.

By the time of the first child's birth, the father had registered the Pepsi-Cola trademark, incorporated the company in North Carolina and begun to sell franchises, shipping syrup in one- and five-gallon kegs. There were dozens of bottlers in several states buying Pepsi syrup from Bradham's company. He had outgrown the Middle Street basement, turned the pharmacy over to a manager, hired employees and created a manufacturing plant in a former woodwork and coffin factory at the corner of Hancock and Johnson, diagonally across from St. John's Masonic Lodge.

Bradham's production of Pepsi-Cola syrup in 1903 was about eight thousand gallons. In 1904 sales more than doubled, reaching twenty thousand gallons. By 1907, they'd quintupled again to more than one hundred thousand gallons. In 1909, Bradham had two hundred and fifty bottlers in twenty-four states clamoring for his syrup.

George and his siblings would be raised in wealth and plenty in one of the finest homes in town. "Oh sure," George said, "everybody thought we were wealthy as the devil, and at one time we were. Wealthy men had their farms and horses and boats and dogs and everything."

Caleb Bradham bought and moved his family into the Slover House in the heart of what is now called the "historic district." The home is a magnificent three-story Greek Revival brick mansion built before 1850 by a wealthy merchant. It was so impressive that victorious Union General Ambrose Burnside chose it as his headquarters after the capture of New Bern in 1862.

By 1915, Bradham was on top of the world. The forty-eight-year-old's company was worth more than a million dollars. He was arguably New Bern's top business success.

The family enjoyed five household servants and a chauffer-driven Cadillac. He became a philanthropist and provided prizes for high-performing college pharmacy students. He was an officer of a railroad and a bank. He began investing heavily in real estate, especially farm land.

But when things went bad, they went bad quickly.

George Bradham said that at one time his father and a fellow investor, Senator Furnifold Simmons, had over two thousand acres of land under cultivation. George said his father sunk all of his liquid assets in land and set nothing aside for a rainy day. A farm recession hit the country at the same time sugar prices went through the roof. Sugar, a main ingredient in Pepsi-Cola, went from five cents a pound to twenty-two cents. A Pepsi cost a nickel so Bradham speculated and bought future contracts to protect against a further rise in sugar prices.

Then the price of sugar collapsed. It dropped all the way to three cents and then to two. With no cash, Bradham couldn't afford to cover his contracts. In one short period, he lost hundreds of thousands of dollars. He was forced to borrow money and mortgage his real estate holdings. He sold much of his Pepsi stock. By 1922, Bradham was insolvent. In 1923, his Pepsi-Cola Company declared bankruptcy. He sold what was left for a pittance. The buyers reorganized the company and prospered.

"The bottlers went broke, too," said George Bradham. "But there were two bottlers who never stopped bottling Pepsi-Cola. One was Mr. [Henry] Fowler in Charlotte and the other was the Burnette family in Durham. What they bottled we do not know, but they manufactured something. They really did. They kept selling it."

Bradham's Pepsi-Cola "had every chance to be a success," George said. "My father just did not know enough about finance and he didn't have the proper advice. Senator Simmons didn't know anything about it either, I guess."

At age fifty-six, Bradham was forced to start over. But financial fortune would not find him again. He went through several smaller commercial disappointments before the Shriners hired him as a business manager at the Sudan Temple. Bradham died in 1934.

Today, his former pharmacy is a popular tourist attraction commemorated by a state highway historic marker. And, Pepsi is the second largest selling soft drink in the world.

Possibly a portrait of Christoper DeGraffenried and a bust made from it.

16

Some Essential People of New Bern

THIS CHAPTER is intended to introduce the interested reader to some of the important cast members in the work of art that is New Bern. It also expands upon some of the main players in the book. Any listing of this type is fraught with danger because of people who may be left out. Many others could have been included, but these few are representative of those who have helped make New Bern what it is today.

John Lawson (1674?-1711)

NOT MUCH IS CERTAIN about John Lawson's early life. The name was common in England and America. It is certain, however, that the great explorer, author, surveyor and naturalist was both highly-intelligent and well-educated. He called himself "John Lawson, Gentleman" and no doubt he was. It is believed that he attended Anglican school in Yorkshire, England and Gresham College, London. What is known is that he arrived in Charleston, S.C. in 1700 and set off on one of the most remarkable adventures in American history.

Trekking with a small group through the backwoods of the Carolinas, deep into the Indian forests where no white man had gone before, Lawson amassed enough information on a wide-range of topics to produce a book that is still in print three hundred years later. Few books have the longevity of Lawson's. So, our strongest recommendation goes to *A New Voyage to America*—available at the Tryon Palace gift shop and finer book stores everywhere—a tour de force (we don't get to use that word often so we do it when we can) of science, history, ethnology, biology, linguistics, history, geography, botany (we could keep going)—and a pretty darn good read to boot.

Lawson was a sponge and almost all we know about the Carolina Indians we know from him. The book is a virtual time-machine and it gets pretty racy in parts, which is always good for keeping the reader's interest.

From 1705, Lawson lived along the Pamlico and Neuse rivers. At the future New Bern—then a Neusiok Indian Village called Chattawka or Chatooka—he lived along the creek that now bears his name. In addition to hunting, fishing, exploring, talking notes and writing, he worked as a private surveyor and soon was appointed deputy-surveyor for the Lords Proprietors of Carolina. In 1706, he helped found the first town in North Carolina—Bath—on land that he owned. Lawson laid out the street and lots, and took on administrative roles with the provincial government. In 1707, he and a woman—not his wife—named Hannah Smith had a daughter, Isabella. The following year, he became surveyor-general and soon traveled to London to publish his book, and deliver many scientific specimens to scientists. His work made a big splash. There is evidence that he had genuinely wanted to make a name for himself within the scientific community through exploration of the New World.

He would never get another chance.

While in London, he met the group of adventurer-businessmen that included DeGraffenried. He convinced them to follow his lead on the location of a colony they were planning. By the late summer of 1711, he would be dead—

the victim of the very Indians he had studied and admired so much.

In his will, Lawson left his baby daughter, Isabella, more than five hundred acres of land, free of debt and in her own name. Lawson's daughter married, had children and lived to see her own grandchildren. She was known to still be living in North Carolina in 1790.

North Carolina historian Marshal D. Haywood said of Lawson: "Amid the wilds of a new continent he lived, labored, wrote, made measurements of our seacoasts, laid out villages and promoted colonization. To wrest the soil from a fierce and warlike race of savages required men of supreme courage—men who could be killed but not cowed—and who would fearlessly face privations and death when so doing would advance the great purposes they sought to accomplish."

Christopher DeGraffenried (1661-1743)

ALSO REFERRED TO as Christoph von Graffenried, DeGraffenried is best known as the founder of New Bern, North Carolina. In 1710, two groups of settlers—mostly religious refugees from Switzerland and Germany—arrived in the Neuse River basin under his sponsorship. DeGraffenried's friendship with Queen Anne of England, and association with explorer John Lawson and the Lords Proprietors, resulted in an attempt at colonization in North Carolina.

Though challenged by a series of disasters—that may have made even the founder himself believe the little colony was a failure—the foundations of modern-day New Bern were laid by DeGraffenried. The site has been continuously occupied since those early times.

DeGraffenried was born in the village of Worb in the Canton (or State) of Bern, Switzerland about the first of November, 1661. The family had been there for generations. His father, Anton, was a government bureaucrat with the title Herr (Lord) of Worb. The father, while not wealthy, had a secure political position. Through a combination of thrift, and conservative, honest business dealings, Anton was able to accumulate a considerable estate over many years of hard work. The father has been described as unaffectionate in his family life and did not well-tolerate his son's rambunctious spirit. The father and son were never close and Christopher's independence of mind was further developed by the early loss of his mother. He was cared for by a step-mother for a short time and then sent away to boarding school. Although quite intelligent, he did not give his best effort in his studies there.

As a youth, DeGraffenried traveled and attended classes at European universities—in Heidelberg and Leyden. Popular and out-going, his family's rank gave him access to the upper echelons of society. He was introduced to kings, queens, princes, dukes and earls, as well as many of the leading business people of his day.

At fifteen, his father endeavored to arrange a marriage, but a business squabble broke off the relationship. In 1682, after a series of adventures and misadventures in England, DeGraffenried fell in love with the niece of the Duke of Buckingham. The young man had inherited twenty thousand pounds from his mother's estate, but after his travels, had spent all the money. He planned to purchase a military commission—a common practice at the time—which would provide the income necessary to support a wife. He wrote home and asked his father for a loan with which to buy the military office. The reply was for him to come home immediately. His refusal, he was told, would result in his expulsion from the family and all the future wealth and position to which he might one day be entitled.

He returned home in 1663 and the following year agreed to an arranged marriage with Regine Tscharmer. His appointment to the position of bailiff proved unprofitable, he made bad investments and fell further into debt. He soon began looking for a grand project with the potential to provide a much-needed change in fortune. Through his political connections and his charming and persuasive manner, he soon became involved in the American colonization venture.

As the reader knows, that effort ended in failure. "No good star shone for me," DeGraffenried would say in summation of his experience with the North Carolina colony. He returned to Switzerland in 1714 and died there in 1743 at age 82. He is buried in the family crypt in Worb.

One of his sons emigrated from Switzerland to South Carolina and established a line of descendents still prospering in America to this day.

William Tryon (1729-1788)

WILLIAM TRYON, best known to us today as the man who built the palace, was born into a family of British aristocrats in 1729. The son of Charles Tryon and Lady Mary Shirley, he was raised on the family's estate in Surrey, England.

The original family name is thought to have been "Trieon," a Flemish name of people from the Flanders region of southeastern Belgium. And there is a legend that an ancestor had set the family's fortunes by "escaping" from the continent of Europe with a large sum of money a century and half before young Tryon was born.

Whatever the source of his wealth, he was raised with the advantages of an upper crust family. One of the advantages was his commissioning at age twenty-two as a first lieutenant in the First Regiment of Foot, a prestigious office in the oldest infantry force in the British army.

He had a daughter out of wedlock with Mary Stanton. Nevertheless, in 1757, he married Margaret Wake, a wealthy London heiress. Her father had been governor of the East India Company in Bombay. Margaret brought a large dowry to the partnership. The marriage would produce one daughter, named Margaret after her mother.

With good and efficient conduct and with some combat experience, Tryon rose to the rank of lieutenant colonel, but in 1763, he decided to leave military service and, through the good offices of powerful friends, sought a governorship in the colonies. He was hoping for New York, but was appointed lieutenant governor of North Carolina to back up the ailing governor, Arthur Dobbs. Upon arrival in North Carolina, Dobbs made it clear that, sick or not, he was not ready to step aside. Thus informed, Tryon set out to tour the inhabited portions of the colony. It was on this trip that he first visited New Bern.

Shortly after Dobbs retired, Tryon decided to move the capital of the colony from Wilmington to a more central—and more hospitable—location along the coast. Under the guidance of a young architect named John Hawks, the extravagant government house and residence that would become known as "Tryon's Palace" was soon constructed. His intention with "the Edifice," as he called it, was two-fold: he wanted to express materially the power and majesty of the king, and prepare New Bern for commercial dominance that would bring prosperity to the new capital.

Despite his long-ranged view, Tryon's tenure in New Bern would be a short one.

The new governor was soon challenged by an uprising among a large western North Carolina contingent of disgruntled citizens who organized themselves under the moniker "the Regulators." Tryon set upon these Regulators with a well-trained force of citizen militia and defeated them in 1771 at the Battle of Alamance.

His performance with the Regulators was noted and soon he was offered the governorship of New York, which he had wanted all along. Be careful what you wish for. By the time Tryon reached New York, the American Revolution was on. He soon found himself not only back in military service with the new rank of major general, but found himself in the middle of a shooting war.

"Ocean of blood will be spilt," was Tryon's assessment of the coming firestorm.

Arguments can be found in authoritative histories saying that Tryon was ordered to declare a war of devastation against the colonists and strongly objected. Another version says that Maj. Gen. Tryon engaged in a ruthless war against women and children that shocked British sensibilities. Whichever extreme it was, Tryon's was not a winning attitude. He found himself stripped of much of his power and responsibility and soon returned to England for good.

At home, he continued to conduct the affairs of British units in America and was promoted to lieutenant general. Compared to previous adventures, the remainder of his life was uneventful. In January, 1788, Tryon died at his London home. He was fifty-six.

Today, there is little doubt that William Tryon is better remembered in New Bern, North Carolina than any other place in the world.

Richard Dobbs Spaight (1758-1802)

HE WAS BORN, lived and died in New Bern. He fought in the American Revolution. He signed the United States Constitution on behalf of North Carolina in Philadelphia in 1787. He became the first native-born governor of the state and was elected to the office three times. He lost a duel and his life in 1802.

Richard Dobbs Spaight was born on March 25, 1758, the son of Richard and Elizabeth Willson Spaight. His parents died when he was young and he was sent by the family for his education to Europe, primarily in his father's home country of Ireland. He eventually attended the University of Glasgow in Scotland.

Back in the American colonies, he served as a Revolutionary War aid to General Richard Caswell who would later become the first governor of the new State of North Carolina. Spaight saw action in the disastrous Battle of Camden, S.C. where British Lieutenant General Lord Charles Cornwallis routed colonial forces commanded by Major General Horatio Gates.

After the war, wealthy and well-educated, politics became his life. Though the list is long, his service must be remembered. His first foray into politics was as a member of the North Carolina Assembly from 1779 to 1783. Then he served two years in the Continental Congress and three terms in the North Carolina House of Commons being elected Speaker of the House during his first term. He represented the state at the Constitutional Convention thus was among the illumined group known as the "Founding Fathers" of the country.

Spaight was elected governor in 1792. During his tenure in office, Chapel Hill was chosen as the site for the state's university and a pasture with tavern at a place called Raleigh was selected as the site of the permanent state capital. He was sometimes sickly and, once retired from public life, traveled to the West Indies, and upon his return was again elected governor. In his two final offices, Spaight was tapped for the U.S. House of Representatives where he fought against the Alien and Sedition Act and voted Thomas Jefferson for President; and then served in the North Carolina senate.

In 1795. he married Mary Leech, sometimes spelled Leach, from an influential and prominent Pennsylvania family. They had three children: Richard Dobbs Spaight the second, who in adulthood would be elected governor of the state; Charles B. Spaight, a life-long bachelor who studied law, served in the legislature; and Margaret Spaight, who married Judge John Donnell, a native of Ireland.

Spaight owned more than 100,000 acres of land south of the Trent River including much of what is today the Croatan National Forest and modern Havelock. Portions of the pine forest were dedicated to naval stores production. In addition to a large slave-based farming operation, he owned several water-powered grist mills.

Following his death in the infamous duel with John Stanly, he was laid to rest in the family graveyard at Clermont Plantation across the Trent River from New Bern. Governor Spaight's grave is well-marked and clearly visible today beside Madam Moore's Lane.

John Wright Stanly (1742-1789)

SAID TO BE a descendant of Saxon nobility, John Wright Stanly arrived in New Bern in 1772. After suffering some early business failures in both Philadelphia and Honduras— one including a brief and possibly unjustified stint in debtors' prison—he grew to be the equal of New Bern's most successful men. Maybe his 1773 marriage to Ann Cogdell propelled him, but soon, in the words of family friend Judge William Gaston, he was "a merchant of great enterprise [with] the most extensive business ever known in the state." That business was ships and shipping.

His wife, Ann, was the daughter of Richard and Lydia Cogdell. Ann's family home on Middle Street was the headquarters for the local revolutionary movement headed by her great Patriot father.

Stanly, father of John, Thomas and Richard Stanly, was involved in the Revolutionary War effort sending privateers to prey upon British military and merchant vessels, laying siege to them particularly off Ocracoke and Cape Lookout. A privateer was an armed, privately-owned ship commissioned by the government to attack commercial and war ships of the enemy. In other words, it was legalized, state-sanctioned piracy. Stanly was involved with the famous *Sturdy Beggar* and owned more than a dozen other such ships. And it was all very lucrative. In fact, in 1780 his ship, *General Nash*, captured two ships containing the most precious cargoes ever sold in the Port of New Bern.

During a Tory raid here during the Revolution, several of

his valuable ships were burned at their moorings along the riverfront.

After the war, he acquired a riverside plantation worked with the labor of 60 slaves. The site included a large wharf for his shipping fleet. He also owned a molasses distillery said to have produced nearly 100,000 gallons of the dark, sugary syrup in one two-and-a-half year period of operation.

He was prominent socially and in business, but was not involved in politics. He developed a close personal friendship with Richard Dobbs Spaight who would later run afoul of Stanly's hot-tempered son.

President George Washington chose Stanly to be the first Judge of the Maritime Court following his service on an admiralty court at Beaufort. He was also a trustee of the New Bern Academy along with some of the most prominent men in town.

Both Stanly and his wife were victims of the deadly 1789 yellow fever epidemic which swept through New Bern. They left behind nine children, one of whom was but an infant. He was forty-seven at the time of his death.

His ever-humble son, John, eulogized him by saying, "My father was as much superior to me as I am to common man."

In 1791, Washington paid a celebrated visit to New Bern and found "exceeding good lodgings" at a magnificent Georgian-style home where he enjoyed several nights. That grand mansion, the John Wright Stanly House, was moved in modern times from the corner of Middle and New Street to George Street where it is now part of the Tryon Palace complex.

John Stanly (1774-1834)

LAWYER-POLITICIAN John Stanly is most famous for his 1802 duel with former North Carolina governor, Richard Dobbs Spaight, but he had a long and distinguished public career as well.

Stanly was the son of John Wright Stanly and thus was raised in New Bern with wealth and privilege in one of the finest homes in the new United States of America. His early education was through the services of private tutors. Both his parents died in an epidemic that ravaged New Bern when he was a teenager. After their deaths, he studied law at

Princeton University. He was admitted to the bar in 1799. He practiced law, served as a judge's clerk and as a master-in-equity, a sort of arbitrator making judgments in small uncomplicated legal matters.

An ardent Federalist and believer in strong government, Stanly was elected to the state House of Commons in 1798 and 1799. The next year, he was advanced by the voters for a two-year term in the U.S. Congress. He served in that body again from 1809-1811, later resuming his New Bern law practice.

He was known for his fiery and combative manner, but did not lack charm when it was called for. Everyone who knew him, friend or foe, said Stanly was brilliant.

Historian Stephen F. Miller said of Stanly: "His voice was strong, clear and musical, and his manner peculiarly graceful and dignified. In repartee and sarcasm, I never saw his equal. His efforts in that line were absolutely withering."

He served as president of the Bank of New Bern, but fell into financial straits later in life and had to be bailed out by half-brother John C. Stanly.

Local chatterers were kept busy with tales of Stanly's run-ins and his sometimes untidy personal life. One of the hot topics for scandal and gossip was a daughter who ran away with an army colonel named Armstead. Stanly vigorously objected to the pairing and the errant daughter was never forgiven by her father.

Between 1812 and 1826, he was repeatedly elected to the state House of Commons where he was chosen by the members to hold the top seat as speaker. He was in his early fifties in January, 1827 and was forcefully arguing a point in the Raleigh chamber when he suffered a severe stroke which left him paralyzed for the remainder of his life.

Though numerous sources say Stanly is buried at Christ Episcopal Church in downtown New Bern, you'll actually find his gravesite just inside the big Queen Street "weeping gate" at Cedar Gove cemetery.

John Carruthers Stanly (1774-1846)

JOHN CARRUTHERS STANLY was the son of local merchant and shipping magnate John Wright Stanly and an African slave woman of the Ebo tribe.

Men and women from the Ebo—also called Ibo or Igbo—tribe, initially captured and sold by the Aro Confederacy, were brought from southern Nigeria in the western part of Africa to American ports like Savannah, Georgia to be auctioned into the southern plantation system. Though slavery ended in the United States with conclusion of the Civil War in 1865, the Aro Confederacy operated from 1690 until 1902. It was a slave trading political union of the Igbo and the neighboring Aro tribes centered in a group of villages in present-day southeastern Nigeria. The confederacy forced travelers, pilgrims, the lower class and social outcasts of their own tribes into slavery, and sold them to European traders at African coastal port towns.

John C. Stanly was born into slavery in New Bern in 1774. At age 21, he was granted his freedom by the courts upon the petition of his owners, Alexander and Lydia Stewart. The Stewarts had tended to his education and helped to enhance his natural talents and abilities. They saw to it that he learned a trade. Stanly was nicknamed "Barber Jack" after his first occupation. Catering largely to the white customers, he made a success of his barber shop enterprise, later turning the day-to-day operation over to two of his own slaves, Brister and Boston.

Around 1800, John C. Stanly bought a female slave, Kitty Green, and two mulatto children, but freed them and married Kitty in early 1805.

Eventually, Barber Jack became one of the largest slave owners—black or white—in Craven County and the largest free black slave owner in the South. In 1830, he is thought to have owned more than one hundred and sixty slaves. One source described him as a "harsh, profit-minded task master whose treatment of his slaves was no different than the treatment slaves received from white owners."

By investing his money in local property, he eventually became one of the city's largest property owners and landlords. Using both slave and free black labor, Barber Jack created a construction and renovation company. He bought a plantation of his own and specialized in cotton, corn and turpentine. His natural thrift and entrepreneurial success made him one of the county's richest men. Well-liked and socially accepted—one witness called him "uniformly courteous and unobtrusive"—he forged political and personal alliances with many of the city's powerful and well-to-do, including his half-brother, attorney and statesman John Stanly.

Kitty Green Stanly was a social success in her own right and became a founding member of the First Presbyterian Church in New Bern.

Late in life, Barber Jack Stanly lost Kitty to illness and was hit with financial setbacks, some caused by a collapse of the nation's banking system. These woes required him to sell much of his property and his long-profitable barber shop. But at the time of his death in his early 70s, he still owned seven slaves.

William Joseph Gaston (1778-1844)

OF THE REMARKABLE New Bernian William Gaston, distinguished statesman Daniel Webster said, "The greatest of the great men of the War Congress [of 1812] was William Gaston." Gaston was arguably the greatest of the great men of New Bern as well.

The list of his honors, offices and accomplishments would fill a book. During his lifetime, he was elected to most of the major honorary, philosophical, scientific and literary societies in the country. Among the kudos were honorary degrees from the University of Pennsylvania, Harvard and Columbia, and honorary membership in Phi Beta Kappa at Yale University. Georgetown University loved him. He had been, at age thirteen, the school's first student, and, as one historian noted, probably its first drop-out when illness forced him to return to New Bern.

Above all, he was one of the nation's most gifted orators and a shining light of jurisprudence. Gaston argued some of the key legal cases in U.S. history, setting a precedent, for example, later used in rendering the famous Dred Scott decision. He was one of the most sought-after speakers for commencement addresses across the country, and many editors routinely reprinted anything he had to say, calling his speeches, time and again, oratorical "masterpieces."

Tall, blue-eyed, handsome and fun loving, Gaston was no slouch when it came to being authentic. A slave owner himself, he vigorously opposed slavery in a slave state thirty years before the Civil War. He fought for the rights of freed blacks to vote, condemned slavery as an institution and urged its abolition. He stood up for Roman Catholicism—and prevailed—in a broadly anti-Catholic region. He was described as a man with "few equals and no superiors." He was known to be a fighter for the underdog. He was nearly universally admired and loved. Gaston was a lawyer who rose to be the leader of the North Carolina Supreme Court. He was a politician, statesman, businessman and banker. Always busy, he helped to found an early library in New Bern. The judge even found time to write songs, one which became a 19th century hit.

His ditty *The Old North State*, set to the tune played in Raleigh by some visiting Swiss bell-ringers, is the official song of North Carolina. In it, Judge Gaston declared that North Carolina is "as happy a region as on this side of heaven."

Gaston owned a large plantation near New Bern worked by two hundred slaves. But it was his Georgian-style townhouse that is one of the city's architectural gems. The Coor-Gaston House at 421 Craven Street was built in 1767 and is a designated community heritage site. The double porches boasting unique Chinese Chippendale balusters helped propel the home into the National Register of Historic Places. It is one of the few homes anywhere to have its very own restoration association. On May 24, 1821, the first meeting for what would become St. Paul's Catholic Church was held in Gaston's townhouse. His miniature law office, also lovingly preserved, stands a block away just behind City Hall.

Gaston's public service creates a list as long as all the other honors. He was elected repeatedly to the state senate and the state House of Commons where he served as speaker. He served two-terms in the federal congress. He was a judge of the state's Supreme Court and was a member of the state constitutional convention of 1835. At the convention, Gaston gave a passionate two-day-long speech opposing religious tests for public office. The proposed constitution stated that office holders had to be Protestants. Through the power of Gaston's rhetoric, and in general admiration for Gaston himself, the word was changed to "Christian." His victory earned him the sobriquet "the Father of Religious Liberty in North Carolina." Gaston turned down almost as many offices as he held including several offers from presidents who sought his counsel and service.

The greatest influence on young William's life was his

mother, Margaret. After his father's death, she devoted her life to his upbringing and that of his infant sister, Jane. Mrs. Gaston, an ardent Catholic, sent her son to Georgetown to be trained by the Jesuits and later enrolled him at Princeton where he graduated with highest honors.

Gaston married three times losing two wives to illness. He was the father of one son and four daughters.

Succumbing in Raleigh to a sudden disease that would take his life in January, 1844, his last words were reported to have been, "We must believe there is a God, all wise and almighty."

In reporting Gaston's death, *The Raleigh Register* said, "For forty years he has been the ornament of his profession, the idol of his friends, the admiration of all who knew him, the able jurist, the upright Judge, the elegant and accomplished scholar, the urbane and polished gentleman, the meek and dignified Christian."

He is buried among many other lights of the city at Cedar Grove Cemetery off Queen Street.

Madam Mary Moore (1705-1761)

IT HAS BEEN SAID of Madam Mary Vail Jones Willson Moore, namesake of the winding "lane" on the east side of the Trent River, that she married once for love, once for money, and once for ambition. Whatever the case, Madam Moore was a woman of social distinction and high birth. She was the grandmother of a future North Carolina governor, Richard Dobbs Spaight, and owner of a magnificent riverfront plantation where he was buried alongside her and many other members of the illustrious family.

In her will, recorded in 1761, she left many things to her family members including the bequest of jewelry, furniture, clothing and several "servants." The paragraph for Spaight read: "I give and bequeath to my grandson, Richard Dobbs Spaight, all the [silver] plate given to me by his grandfather Wilson, that shall be found among my plates, which has his grandfather's name on it, which is as follows: two large silver tankards, two large silver kanes, one silver punch bowl, one silver teapot, two silver salts, one silver pepper box, one silver mustard pot, one silver porringer, one silver-large soup ladle, and all the silver spoons that has his grandfather's name on them as aforesaid, when he arrives at the age of 21 or marries, which shall happen first, which said plate shall be kept by my son-in-law, Joseph Leech, till then."

Leech, by the way, was a famous colonel and Revolutionary War hero, who was the pre-war commander of Gov. William Tryon's colonial militia.

Clermont Plantation was situated at the intersection of the Trent with Brice's Creek and the road through and to its 2,500 acres is still known as Madam Moore's Lane.

"Madam" was simply a title of honor and recognition of her place in society. And a high place it was. She is said to have traveled to New Bern and to visit her neighbors in a large boat rowed by a half dozen uniformed servants. She was one of New Bern's social leaders and occupied the largest pew stall at Christ Church on Pollock Street, said to be twice as big as all the rest.

Despite the long final form of her name, she began life simply as Mary Vail. The Vail family came from Long Island, New York to North Carolina where they were related to the Lillingtons who were, or were married to, governors, deputy governors, and surveyors-general of the state. Mary was kin to many of the highest ranking Tarheel families including Blounts, Dobbs, Nashes and Spaights to name but a few.

In all accounts of her life, details of her marriages seem to predominate so we shall list them here:

• The Honorable Frederick Jones of Hayes Plantation in Chowan County with whom she had a daughter, Mary, and two sons, Harding and Frederick.

• Colonel William Willson who created Clermont and left a large estate to his daughter, Elizabeth, mother of Richard Dobbs Spaight. He is the namesake of well-known Wilson Creek, a tributary of the Trent River.

• "King" Roger Moore, owner of the massive Orton Plantation near Wilmington and one of the wealthiest men in the colonies. It was this marriage that garnered for her the title "Madam." Even though Roger Moore was wealthy beyond all reason, Mary made *him* sign a prenuptial agreement in which he swore not to "intermeddle" with the inheritance of the children of her first two husbands. This marital agreement was dated January 4, 1747 and is recorded in Craven County.

George Henry White (1852-1918)

GEORGE WHITE, a New Bern Republican, delivered his final speech in the U.S. Congress on January 29, 1901.

"This is perhaps the Negroes' temporary farewell to the American Congress," said White, "but let me say, Phoenix-like he will rise up some day and come again. These parting words are in behalf of an outraged, heart-broken, bruised and bleeding, but God-fearing people; faithful, industrious, loyal, rising people – full of potential force."

It took a long time for the Phoenix to rise. White had been the last of his race in congress. No other black American would be elected to the body for twenty-seven years. And from the South? Not until the 1960s.

White served during a period of strife and turmoil in North Carolina politics. Some have called him "the last African-American Congressman of the Reconstruction era," though Reconstruction officially ended in the state in 1877. "Fusion politics," joining poor farmers, black and white, for common goals had allowed many blacks to serve in all branches of government. A powerful Democrat campaign split the Republicans around 1900 ending African-American office-holding for many years.

White was born in Rosindale, a small Bladen County farming community west of Wilmington. His father was a free farmer. His mother, Mary, was a slave at the time of his birth. As a youth, he received some education in the old one-room schoolhouse system before the Civil War. After the war, White enrolled in public school, later attending Whitin Normal School in Lumberton. But his dream was to become an attorney.

Following his 1877 graduation from Howard University in Washington, D.C., White practiced law in New Bern. He also taught school in the colonial capital and served as principal of the New Bern State Normal School, a training school for African-American teachers. During White's term in office, and with his sponsorship, four such schools had been instituted by the North Carolina General Assembly in 1881.

White, a big, hardy, mustachioed man, ran for office as a Republican in 1880. First elected to the North Carolina House of Representatives, he later served Craven County in the N.C. Senate beginning in 1884. In 1886, he was chosen to be the solicitor and prosecuting attorney for the second judicial district, serving in that post until 1894.

After selection as a delegate to both the 1896 and 1900 Republican National Conventions, he defeated incumbent Congressman Frederick A. Woodard, a white attorney from Wilson, in 1898. White, like many congressmen, used his patronage power to appoint African-Americans in his district to well-paying federal posts, as postmasters or postal workers.

Seeing the divisive future on the political horizon, White chose not to seek a third term, but instead to devote himself to the law, banking and the promotion of civil rights. He served for many years in one of the early civil rights organizations.

In 1906, White decided to leave the South. He made a new home in Philadelphia where he practiced law, ran a savings bank and prospered. As a real estate developer, he is the founder of Whitesboro, New Jersey. In 1913, he formed one of the first chapters of the National Association for the Advancement of Colored People.

He died in Philadelphia in 1918, a fighter to the end.

Graham A. Barden (1896-1967)

MANY WORTHY POLITICIANS and public servants have labored for the people of New Bern and Craven County, but few have brought home the bacon the way "Hap" Barden did. U.S. Congressman Graham A. Barden is the man who got the military bases.

Graham Arthur Barden was born September 25, 1896 in Turkey Township, Sampson County, N.C., attended public school in Pender County and was an enlisted man in the U.S. Navy during World War I. In 1920, Barden graduated with a law degree from the University of North Carolina at Chapel Hill. He opened a local practice following law school, was a New Bern High School teacher—and winning football coach—and, from 1920-24, sat on the bench as a Craven County judge. In 1933 Barden became a member of the North Carolina House of Representatives, launching a political career which would span most of the next thirty years.

But those are just the facts.

Barden had a keen ear for the needs of his constituents

and a shrewd manner when it came to navigating Washington, D.C. One colleague said Barden would reverse invitations from powerful men who asked him to fish in Minnesota and hunt in Texas by inviting them to hunt and fish in Craven County instead. "He wanted them to know that district and the people there, and to appreciate the values that made home so important to him," said D.C. attorney Edward McCabe. "It had the effect of making Graham Barden much more effective in Washington."

By a mastery of parliamentary procedure, Democrat Barden was able to block and delay enough legislation that he earned the nickname "master of confusion." He felt legislation he stopped was sometimes more important than what he saw enacted.

"He was always a tower of strength," said a southern representative who knew him well, "and has prevented more obnoxious legislation from passing than any other member of Congress..."

Elmer L. Puryear wrote Barden's biography. In *Graham A. Barden: Conservative Carolina Congressman*, Puryear said Barden "was regarded a conservative and by some a reactionary" whose views "are more acceptable today than during his time in Congress."

"The Congressman repeatedly expressed his distrust of a swollen bureaucracy, the concentration of power in Washington, corruption, inflation, giveaway programs and governmental interference in the lives of people. He was amazingly accurate in his prediction that Federal aid to education would lead to almost constant interference in state and local education. During his career, Barden warned incessantly about the dangers of delegation of legislative power to the executive branch and executive agencies, about overseas commitments, and about the certainty of inflation if excessive spending continued."

Congressman Barden became an expert in labor and education. A look at the Graham Arthur Barden Papers at Duke University shows that the congressman knew the powerful and the lowly, and had his hand in a myriad of issues of his day—from the U.S. census to commercial fishing, to the minimum wage on the island of Guam. But it was his seizure of the opportunity for the placement and construction of military bases that has been his most lasting legacy, and the one with the most impact on eastern North

Carolina. Specifically, his role in the acquisition of the Cherry Point Marine Corps Air Station at Havelock, the Camp Lejeune Marine base at Jacksonville and the Seymour Johnson Air Force base at Goldsboro have offset devastating losses in the tobacco, textile and manufacturing sectors by supplying steady, recession-proof employment for thousands of East Carolinians, and billions of dollars for the local economies over nearly seventy years. In one seven-month period in the early 1940s, Barden procured three major military bases.

Hap Barden most often ran for office unopposed. It was his choice not to seek re-election in 1960. He was succeeded by Congressman David N. Henderson.

Barden spent his final years in New Bern among his large well-known and well-respected family. He died in 1967 and was buried at Cedar Grove Cemetery.

There is an inlet named for Barden near Harker's Island, a school named for him in Havelock, and he has his own highway historic marker on Broad Street in New Bern.

Maude Moore Latham (1871-1951)

THE GOLD COINS came as a surprise to James Latham. He had been giving them to his wife, Maude Moore Latham, on birthdays and anniversaries for many years. But here she was, with more than one hundred of the shiny ounces, asking for his advice on investing. James E. Latham was a very successful businessman, but his wife had created a little horde and was now planning to make some money of her very own. Through the rest her life she would exhibit both skill and willpower in handling her money...and in getting husband James to help.

One of those uses would be to breathe life into the restoration of Tryon Palace. In January, 1944, with her husband's assistance and support, she established the Maude Moore Latham Trust Fund making an initial deposit of $100,000. She stipulated that if the State of North Carolina acquired the land necessary for the re-construction of the colonial capitol, she would give even more.

In 1949, as the project progressed, she increased the endowment by $150,000. She also donated $125,000 worth of antiques to furnish the palace.

Maude Moore was born in New Bern on December 16, 1871. Her parents were James Washington and Sarah Jane Gordon Moore. She was a recognized honor student in New Bern public school. Later, she lived with her grandmother in New York City where she attended public schools and Hunter College. Mrs. Latham enjoyed many types of sports and is even said to have participated in a few Virginia fox hunts.

She and James were married in the summer of 1892 at the First Presbyterian Church in New Bern. They had two children, Edward and May Gordon. In 1904, the family moved to Greensboro where the Mr. Latham had important business interests.

In 1939, when she was president of the prestigious Garden Club of North Carolina, Mrs. Latham helped fund the publication of a ground-breaking book, *Old Homes and Gardens of North Carolina*. In the book, the eminent Dr. Archibald Henderson called for the restoration of Tryon Palace, reminding the readers that it had been the most beautiful building in colonial America.

A generous benefactor for many worthy causes, she and her husband supported hospitals and homes for the aged. She helped restore Governor Charles B. Aycock's birthplace near Goldsboro and supported many other historic preservation organizations and projects. Mrs. Latham made the largest donation toward the acquisition of the original Carolina Charter of the Lords Proprietors issued by British King Charles II.

The Latham's son, Edward, died at Fort Thomas, Kentucky in military service during World War I. Upon Mrs. Latham's death in 1951, her daughter took on the mantle of leadership for the Tryon Palace Commission. Mrs. Latham's son-in-law, John A. Kellenberger, became commission treasurer.

In her will, Maude Moore Latham bequeathed $1.15 million more for the New Bern landmark. The Latham Fund continues to generate revenue for operation of the palace to this day.

Mrs. Latham, prime benefactor of Tryon Palace, is buried in Greensboro.

May Gordon Kellenberger (1893-1978)

MAUDE MOORE LATHAM'S DAUGHTER, May Gordon Latham Kellenberger and her husband, John A. Kellenberger, were hands-on workers in the restoration, furnishing, opening and administration of Tryon Palace. She served as "chairman" of the Tryon Palace Commission for twenty-seven years.

Among other things, May Gordon, as she was always called by family and friends, oversaw the purchase, in Europe and America, of exquisite antique furniture, artwork, china, carpets, and silverware—all the things that made the palace beautiful. Her choices were not always historically accurate, but her taste was impeccable.

Asked once if she wanted the palace furnishings to be authentic—in keeping with what might have been there during Governor Tryon's reign—or if she wanted it to be beautiful, she responded, "By all means, make it pretty."

She and her husband were also instrumental in the purchase of the first four historic homes still included in the palace complex. They were involved in the restoration and furnishing of these homes as well. Mr. Kellenberger has also been given credit for working with local real estate professionals to ensure that owners displaced by the palace were fairly compensated for their homes, businesses and land. As many as seventy pieces of property were acquired by the state. These were assembled to create the twenty-two acre Tryon Palace site.

May Gordon Latham was born in New Bern June 3, 1893. Her father, James Edwin Latham, was a cotton merchant. Her one brother, Edward, died in an influenza epidemic during World War I.

In early childhood, she attended a New Bern kindergarten and a private school, as well as classes in the old Academy building. The Lathams moved to Greensboro in 1904. Her parents set an example for their daughter with service in cultural, civic and patriotic organizations.

Mrs. Kellenberger later attended Greensboro public schools, and New York and Salem Academies. She studied at Greensboro, Converse, and Barnard colleges. She also had exposure to music, art history, and language education in Europe.

During World War, she served as executive secretary of the Red Cross Home Service in Greensboro where she completed every course offered by the American Red Cross. Her duties included handling the myriad messages that flowed through the field office during a raging war-time flu epidemic. One of those messages brought word of her brother's critical illness in Kentucky. Sadly, he died before family members could reach his base. Throughout the epidemic, she worked tirelessly with the volunteer nurses in a Greensboro emergency hospital dedicated to the care of the victims. Her husband, John, a Pennsylvania native she met in Greensboro, often helped in her Red Cross duties. They married September 11, 1920.

Later in life, through association with her mother's charitable work and their shared love of historic preservation, she became involved with the Tryon Palace project. May Gordon assumed the leadership role when her mother died in 1951. She missed only four meetings of the Tryon Palace Commission in three decades. All four were related to her or her husband's illnesses. Upon her death, she left sixty percent of her estate, about three million dollars, to the Tryon Palace Restoration. She left substantial bequests to ten other historical, education and religious groups.

The research facility within the main branch of the New Bern-Craven County Public Library on Johnson Street is named in her honor. The Kellenberger Room houses a local history and genealogy collection and features a beautiful oil portrait of May Gordon Latham Kellenberger.

Miss Gertrude S. Carraway (1896-1993)

Be thou faithful unto death, and I will give thee the Crown of life.
—Revelations 2:10

SHE'S BEEN CALLED the "first citizen" of New Bern, the premier historian of the city, and, in her time, one of its most well-known and beloved people in town. Gertrude Carraway—"Miss Carraway" to many—was all that and more.

And without her motivation and organizational savvy, there may not be a Tryon Palace Restoration today.

A New Bern native, she was a newspaper woman, a publisher, and a historical researcher of such note that the *Sun Journal* once said she "made history while studying history."

She discovered John Hawks's original early-1700s architectural drawing for Tryon Palace gathering dust in a New York archive. She created the North Carolina Highway Historical Marker Program. She was a tireless speaker, writer and promoter of all things New Bernian.

She was the daughter of John R. and Louise E. Carraway. The family lived at 207 Broad Street in the home where Miss Carraway was born and would occupy her entire life. After graduating from the University of North Carolina at Greensboro, she studied at Columbia University in New York City. She taught history, English and French, became a feature writer, and authored hundreds of articles, news stories, dozens of booklets and six books. For her achievements over the years, she was awarded three honorary doctorates.

Therefore, we can say Dr. Carraway received the keys to eight cities, was named a Kentucky Colonel, an Arkansas Traveler, a North Carolina Admiral, an Honorary Citizen of New Orleans, New Bern's Woman of the Year, North Carolina Citizen of the Year, Tar Heel of the Week by *The News & Observer*, and received awards for historical preservation, enhancement, promotion, knowledge and research too numerous to mention. She was listed in *Who's Who* in the United States and in about two dozen other national and international volumes of biography.

She was editor of the city's newspaper, the *Sun Journal*, from 1924-37. Miss Carraway is said to have used personal money to keep the paper from failing during the Great Depression.

During World War II, she conducted bond drives, served in the Red Cross, christened a Liberty ship and received twelve awards for patriotic service.

She was a diligent proponent of the National Society of the Daughters of the American Revolution. She served as state regent, and on the national level as President General. During her three-year terms in Washington, D.C., she "invented" Constitution Week.

According to the DAR's website, "In 1955, the President General of the Daughters of the American Revolution,

Gertrude S. Carraway, adopted a project to promote the observance of the U.S. Constitution with a memorial week beginning on the anniversary of the signing of this document, September 17. She asked DAR chapters, committees, and members to study, teach, and discuss the U.S. Constitution. Carraway also encouraged members to invite their governors and mayors to issue proclamations celebrating the Constitution. Constitution Week was officially declared by President Eisenhower on August 2, 1956."

And, after all that, her friends would say that "Gertrude didn't think she was doing anything out of the ordinary."

Miss Carraway published "The Flying Marines at Cherry Point" and the "Historic New Bern Guide Book." She said the profits allowed her to travel to many countries of the world.

But there was one cause for which she put forth the most effort. She is repeatedly pointed to as one of the key people in the success of the Tryon Palace restoration. She was among a small group promoting the idea for three decades. From its inception in 1945 until the palace restoration was complete, she was diligent in her duties as secretary of the state-appointed Tryon Palace Commission. In 1956, she became the first director of the Tryon Palace Restoration, crafting the image and working the day-to-day machinery via a disciplined system that came naturally to her. She continued to put both the palace and New Bern on the map in big bold letter by industriously promoting tourism and history until her retirement in 1971. Even after retirement, the governor of North Carolina re-appointed her to the commission and she served as vice chair of the Kellenberger Historical Foundation. Tryon Palace's four thousand volume research library is named in her honor.

Among the books she authored are histories of St. John's Lodge, No. 3, entitled *Years of Light*, and Christ Episcopal Church called *Crown of Life*.

Miss Carraway passed away May 7, 1993 in the New Bern home at 207 Broad Street where she had been born ninety-six years before.

The kidnapping of John Lawson and Christopher DeGraffenried
North Carolina Collection, University of North Carolina at Chapel Hill

17

Kidnapped: The Baron in His Own Words

STUDENTS, you will get extra credit for staying the course here as we move into serious, genuine, original historical material. But you've gotten this far and doubtless you can handle it.

What follows was written by the man himself, New Bern's revered founder, Christopher DeGraffenried. Published in 1920, the book *Christoph von Graffenried's Account of the Founding of New Bern* was edited by two professors, Vincent H. Todd and Julius Goebels. The text below is but a portion of DeGraffenried's whole book.

The account has been further edited by this author to make it more readable for the intended audience and more relevant to our subject matter. When any of DeGraffenried's words have been deleted, three dots like this "..." have been inserted. [This author's few comments are in brackets like this.] Readers who wish to see more, may find the entire book in the Kellenberger Room of the New Bern-Craven County Public Library or on its website.

In this excerpt, DeGraffenried describes his kidnapping and escape from the Indians in which John Lawson lost his life. It is important to remember that his is the only testimony and the one source from which much of New Bern's early history has been drawn. A careful reader may agree that the writer at times goes to great lengths to appear both blameless and noble. DeGraffenried paints Lawson as reckless, condescending and fool-hardy, and William Brice as a dishonest conniver "that gave me great trouble." Even his own colonists are a "seditious gang" of ungrateful cowards who have unfairly turned against him. Some scholars wonder whether Lawson, Brice and the colonists might have a different story to tell if they were still around. Regardless, DeGraffenried's account makes fascinating reading and is a valuable addition to the historic record.

So, acknowledging the predisposition of most human beings to cast themselves in the best possible light in any given situation, but otherwise having no reason to doubt his account, here's the Baron in his own words:

Account Written to Mr. Edward Hyde, Governor in North Carolina, The 23d of October, 1711, With Reference to My Miraculous Deliverance from the Savages

Honored Sir:

Through the wonderful and gracious providence of the Most High, I have at last escaped out of the barbarous hands of the wild Tuscarora Nation, and have arrived at my little dwelling at New Bern; but yet half dead, because for two whole days I had to travel afoot, as fast as ever I could, out alone through the forests which lie towards Catechna, [near present-day Grifton, N.C. between New Bern and Greenville on what is now called Contentnea Creek, a Neuse tributary] compelled to take up my quarters by a frightful wild ditch in which there was deep water, because the night overtook me and I could not go farther from weariness.

How I passed this night can well be imagined, in no small fear of being caught by the savage or strange Indians, and of being torn to pieces by a number of bears which growled the whole night close about me. In addition I was very lame from walking, without a gun, yes, I did not have a knife with me with which to strike a fire, and because the north wind blew very hard it was a cold night. In the morning when I tried to arise my limbs were so stiff and swollen by the cold and hard lying that I could not go a step. But because it had to be I looked me up two sticks upon which I could walk, but with great difficulty and pain. I had enough to do to get myself over this water, which was full of snakes. I did it by climbing over on a long limb.

At last I reached home. When I, at a little distance from home, came within sight of a dwelling, fortified and full of people, I was somewhat comforted, because I thought that everything there had been burned out and destroyed by the Indians, as well as the houses of the other colonists; yes, also that I should find few of my people, because the terrible expedition of the savages was only too well known to me, when they burned, murdered, and plundered whatever they found along the rivers Pamtego [Pamlico], Neuse and Trent. When my good people got sight of me, black and looking like an Indian, and yet looking like myself as far as my size and blue coat were concerned, they did not know what to think. But thinking, all of them, that I was dead, they were firm in the opinion that it was, rather, an Indian spy who had put on my coat and wanted to spy out something there; and so the men folks put themselves into an attitude of defense. But when I came toward the house walking very lame on two sticks, they saw by my countenance and posture that I was no Indian or savage. Yet they did not recognize me till several came out to look at me better. When I saw that they were in anxiety I began to speak from a distance, with a very broken voice, to be sure. This shocked them so that they retreated several paces, crying to the rest to come forward, that it was their master, whom they supposed murdered. So they all came running pell-mell, men, women, and children, with loud exclamations, some weeping, some completely dumb with amazement, saluting me as a marvelous spectacle. There was mourning, joy, and bewilderment mixed, and this went to my heart, so that it forced out abundant tears...

The next day I asked what had happened in my absence, but so many vexatious things came out that it makes my heart heavy. The worst was that, besides sixty or seventy Palatines who were murdered, the rest who could save themselves were plundered, and the survivors of these Palatines had left my house, in which were their own goods, and the little city.

A certain William Brice, an unthankful man to whom I had shown much kindness, yes, whom the money and goods belonging to myself and the poor colonists had brought out of poverty, had drawn them away from me with all sorts of promises and cunning and had brought them to himself upon the Trent River, by means of whom, with some English Planters or inhabitants in addition, he had succeeded in getting together a garrison to defend his house. So I had to be satisfied with a number of women and children. In armed soldiery there were no more than forty. These all I had to support for twenty-two weeks. So all my grain, which luckily I had in store, my cattle great and small, were all gone. If we do not soon receive the necessaries, we shall have to starve to death or give up the post. Therefore, Honored sir, we urgently beg you to send as soon as possible and in all haste the needed provisions, military stores, and armed troops, in order that we may drive back these barbarian murderers, otherwise the evil will become greater, and it is to be feared that the whole land will be destroyed...

Honored Sir, the above is only as a report how I came home. But to free and justify myself it will be necessary for me to tell how I came into this barbarous nation.

Because of the fine and apparently settled weather, the Surveyor-General [John] Lawson came to invite me to travel up the Neuse River, saying that there was a quantity of good wild grapes, that we could enjoy ourselves a little with them. But that was not enough to persuade me to go there. So the above mentioned Monsieur Lawson came again soon, pled better reasons, namely that we could at the same time see how far up the river was navigable; whether a shorter way might be made to Virginia, in place of the ordinary way which is long and difficult, and in like manner see what kind of land is up there. This, and how far it is to the mountains, I had been for a long time desirous to know and to have seen for myself. So at this I resolved upon a small journey and took everything that was necessary, including provisions for fourteen days. I asked Mr. Lawson in particular whether there was danger from the Indians, especially with those with whom we were not acquainted. He gave me for an answer that this was of no consequence, that he had already made the trip and it was entirely safe, that he knew of no wild Indians on this arm of the river, but that they were tolerably distant. But that we might go the more securely, I took besides two negroes to row, two neighboring Indians whom we knew, to whom I had shown much kindness. And since one understood the English language, I thought if we had these two Indians with us we should have nothing to fear from the others, and so we traveled right on up. It had not rained for a long time; the water was not deep; the stream or current of the water was not strong. The whole day we were upon the river; at night we spread our tent upon the land by the water and rested; in the morning we proceeded again...

It was already late... We were landing at the first spring to take up our quarters for the night. We met already two armed Indians there, who looked as though they were coming from hunting. Upon this I said it did not please me that we would not remain there, but would go back. He, the Surveyor-General, laughed at me, but before we turned around it became serious so that his laughter disappeared. In a moment there came out of all the bushes and swimming through the river such a number of Indians and overpowered us that it was impossible to defend ourselves, unless we wanted to have ourselves wantonly shot dead or frightfully tortured. We were forthwith taken prisoners, plundered, and led away.

By this time we had gone three good days journey up the river, not far from another Indian village, called Zurutha. The river is there still rather broad, but the water not more than two or three feet deep, and it is still far from the mountains. We asked that they should leave us there this night, with a guard if they doubted us, giving as reason that I could not go so far afoot, that early in the morning we would go by water to the king at Catechna [Indian Chief Hancock's main village], promising that we would be there. But it was not to be done since I was such a rare and important capture; for they took me for the Governor of the whole province. Their barbarous pride swelled them up so that we were compelled to run with them the whole night, through forests, bushes, and swamps, until the next morning about three o'clock when we came to Catechna where the king, Hancock by name [Some of the Indians adopted or were given English nicknames], was sitting in all his glory upon a raised platform; although the Indians are accustomed at other times to sit upon the ground. After a consultation and a sharp speech by the leader or captain of our escort the king with his council left and came to us very politely with his chief warrior. But he could not speak with us. After a short time the king went into his cabin or hut; we remained by a fire guarded by seven or eight savages. Toward ten o'clock there came a savage here, another there out of his hut; council was held, and it was disputed vigorously whether we should be bound as criminals or not. It was decided no, because we had not been heard yet. Toward noon the king himself brought us some food in a lousy fur cap. This was a kind of bread made of Indian corn, called dumplins and cold boiled venison. I ate of this, with repugnance indeed, as I was very hungry.

In the evening there came hither from all the villages a great number of Indians with the neighboring kings, upon a fine, broad, open space, especially prepared for the festivities or executions. And there was appointed an assembly of the chiefs as they call them, consisting of the most prudent, sitting after their fashion in a ring around a great fire. King Hancock presided. There was a place left in the ring for us, where were two mats, that is to say pieces of wickerwork woven of small canes or reeds, laid down to sit on, which is a sign of great deference and honor. So we sat down, and our spokesman, the Indian that had come with us, who could speak English well, sat at our left. The king gave a sign to the orator of the assembly, who made a long speech with much gravity. And it was ordered that one of the youngest of the assembly should represent and defend the interests of the council or of the Indian nation. He, so far as I could discern, did it in due form. He sat right next to our interpreter and spokesman. The king always formed the question, and then it was debated pro et contra. Immediately after that came a consultation and decision.

The first question was, what was the cause of our journey? Our answer was, that we had come up there for our pleasure, to get grapes and at the same time to see if the river were convenient so that we could bring goods to them by water; to have good business and correspondence with them. So the king asked us why we had not paid our respects to him and communicated our project to him. After this there came into question a general complaint, that they, the Indians, had been very badly treated and detained by the inhabitants of the Pamtego, Neuse, and Trent Rivers, a thing which was not to be longer endured. And they named the authors of it in particular, and among others, the Surveyor-General was accused. He being present excused himself the best he could. After considerable disputing and deliberation which followed, it was decided that we should be set free, and the next day was appointed for our journey home.

The next day there was a considerable delay... Meantime there came some of their chiefs and two kings who were curious to know what grounds of justification we had. And so we were examined again in King Hancock's hut two miles from the village, and gave the same answer. Unfortunately the king of Cartuca was there, who reproached Lawson with something, so that they got into a quarrel on both sides and became rather angry. This spoiled everything for us.

However much I tried to keep Lawson from disputing, I could not succeed at all. The examination finally ended, we all rose up, we two walked together and I reproached him very strongly for his unguardedness in such a critical condition. Immediately thereafter there came suddenly three or four of the chiefs very angrily, seized us roughly by the arms, led us back and forcibly set us down in the old place. There were no mats laid for us, they took our hats and wigs away from us and threw them into the fire. After that some malicious young fellows came and plundered us the second time, searching our pockets, which they had not done before when they confined themselves to the larger things.

Hereupon a council of war was held and we were both condemned to death, without knowing the cause of it. And so we remained the whole night, sitting in the same position upon the ground till morning. At the break of day we were taken away from there and again led to the great judgment and assembling place, a bad omen for us, and I turned toward Mr. Lawson bitterly upbraiding him, saying that his lack of foresight was the cause of our ruin; that it was all over with us; that there was nothing better to do than to make peace with God and prepare ourselves betimes for death; which I did with the greatest devotion.

When we arrived at the place mentioned, the great council was already together. By chance I saw an Indian dressed like a Christian before we were called into the ring. He could speak English. I asked him if he could not tell us what was the cause of our condemnation. He answered me with a very disagreeable face, why had Lawson quarreled with Core Tom and why had we threatened that we would get revenge on the Indians? At that I took the Indian aside, promising everything I could if he would listen to me and afterward tell of my innocence to some of the chiefs... And so I told him I was sorry that Monsieur Lawson was so imprudent as to quarrel with Core Tom; that the councilors could themselves see very well that I was not to blame for that; and about the threatening, there was not the least thought of that, it was a misunderstanding or else Monsieur Lawson complaining at my negroes for disturbing his rest the first night. At this I threatened the negroes sharply because of their impudence, and this was all. After the Indian had heard me he left me, I repeating my promises to him.

Whether he spoke very much in my favor I do not know, but a quarter of an hour after the old chief came, led us out upon the place of judgment and bound us there hand and foot, and the larger of my two negroes as well. And there began our sad tragedy which I would like to relate with your leave, if it would not be too long and sad. Yet since I have begun I will continue.

In the middle of this great space we sat bound side by side, sitting upon the ground, the Surveyor-General and I, coats off and bare headed; behind me the larger of my negroes; before us was a great fire and around about the fire the conjurer, that is, an old gray Indian, a priest among them, who is commonly a magician, yes, even conjures up the devil himself. He made two rings either of meal or very white sand, I do not know which. Right before our feet lay a wolf skin. A little farther in front stood an Indian in the most dignified and terrible posture that can be imagined. He did not leave the place. Ax in hand, he looked to be the executioner.

Farther away, before us and beyond the fire, was a numerous Indian rabble, young fellows, women, and children. These all danced in the most abominable postures. In the middle was the priest or conjurer, who, whenever there was a pause in the dance, made his conjurations and threats. About the dance or ring at each of the four corners stood a sort of officer with a gun. They beat time with their feet and urged on the other dancers and when a dance was over shot off their guns. Besides this, in a corner of the ring, were two Indians sitting on the ground, who beat upon a little drum and sang, and sang so strangely to it, in such a melody, that it would provoke anger and sadness rather than joy. Yes, the Indians themselves, when tired of dancing, would all run suddenly away into a forest with frightful cries and howling, but would soon come back out of the forest with faces striped black, white, and red. Part of them, besides this, would have their hair hanging loose, full of feathers, down, and some in the skins of all sorts of animals: In short in such monstrous shapes that they looked more like a troop of devils than like other creatures; if one represents the devil in the most terrible shape that can be thought of, running and dancing out of the forest. They arranged themselves in the old places and danced about the fire. Meanwhile there were two rows of armed Indians behind us as a guard, who never left their post until all was over: Back of this watch was the council of war sitting in a ring on the ground very busy in consultation...

Let the Governor consider what a mournful and terrifying sight that was for me to die, yet I had my mind made up for it. I was, thus, the whole day and night in ardent devotion. Oh what thoughts I had! Everything that happened to me so far back as I could remember occurred to me. I applied and made use of everything that I had read from the scriptures and the Psalms and other good books. In short, I prepared myself as well as I could for a good and blessed end; yes, the merciful

God gave me so much grace that fearlessly, calmly, I waited what my end might be. After the anguish of soul I had endured, worse than the fear of death, nevertheless there remained in me I hardly know what kind of hope, despite the fact that I saw no sign of any rescue. Although, as I said before, my sins hovered before me, still I afterwards found great consolation in considering the miracles which the Lord Jesus did in His times on the earth. This awakened such a confidence in me, that upon this I made my ardent prayer to my Saviour, in the strong confidence that my prayer was heard, and that these savage minds and stony barbarian hearts would perhaps turn, so that at my pleading and explanation they would change their minds and be led and moved to mercy; which also happened through God's wonderful providence.

For as the sun was going down the council assembled once more, without doubt, to make an end of this fatal, terrible, and sad ceremony. I turned myself somewhat around, although bound, knowing that one of them understood the English language rather well, and made a short speech, telling my innocence, and how if they did not spare me the great and mighty Queen of England would avenge my blood, because I had brought the colony to this land at her command, not to do them any harm but to live on good terms with them; and what else seemed to me good to say to engage them to kindness; with the offer of my services and all sorts of favors if I were liberated.

Now after I had finished talking, I noticed that one of the leading Indians, who before this seemed entirely inclined to me, the one, indeed, who had once brought me food, and who belonged to King Taylor, from whom I had purchased the land where New Bern now stands, was amazed and spoke very earnestly; I had no doubt in my favor; which turned out to be the case, for it was hereupon decided to send some of their members immediately to the neighboring Tuscarora villages; and with them the result was that I should have my life, but the poor Surveyor General would be executed.

I passed the night between life and death, bound all the time in the same place, in continual prayer and sighs...

In the morning about three or four o'clock the deputies came back from their mission bringing the decision regarding their errand, but very secretly. One of them came after a while to loose me from my bonds. Not knowing what that might mean, I submitted patiently to the will of the Lord, the Most High, arose and followed. Oh how dumb-founded I was, when, some paces from the old place, the Indian said to me in my ear, in broken English, that I should not fear, they would not kill me, but they would kill General Lawson. This went to my heart.

About twenty paces from the place where I was bound the Indian brought me to the cabin or hut and gave me food to eat, but I had no appetite. Soon there came a great number of the Indian rabble about me, who all evidenced great joy at my deliverance. The very same man brought me again to the clear space, but a little further in advance, where the whole council sat, and they congratulated me in their way and smiled. Meantime I was forbidden to say the least thing to Monsieur Lawson, not even to speak a single word to him.

They let my negro loose also, but I never saw him again. Poor Lawson remaining in the same place could easily guess that it was all over and no mercy for him. He took his leave of me striving to see me in his danger; and I, not daring to speak with him or give him the least consolation, indicated my sympathy by some signs which I gave him.

A little while after this, the man who had spoken for me in the council led me to his hut, where I was to remain quietly until further orders and in this interval the unfortunate Lawson was executed; with what sort of death I really do not know. To be sure I had heard before from several savages that the threat had been made that he was to have his throat cut with a razor which was found in his sack. The smaller negro, who was left alive, also testified to this; but some say he was hanged; others that he was burned. The savages keep it very secret how he was killed. May God have pity on his soul.

The day after the execution of Surveyor General Lawson the chief men of the village came to me with the report that they had it in mind to make war on North Carolina. Especially did they wish to surprise the people of Pamtego, Neuse, and Trent Rivers, and Core Sound. So that for good reasons they could not let me go until they were through with this expedition. What was I to do? I had to have patience, for none of my reasons helped. A hard thing about it was that I had to hear such sad news and yet could not help nor let these poor people know the least thing of it. It is true, they promised that Caduca, which is the old name of the little city of New Bern, should receive no harm; but the people of the colony should come down into the little city, otherwise they could not promise much for the damage. These were good words, but how was I to let the poor people know? Since no savage would take the warning to them, I had to leave this also to the Most High.

There were about five hundred fighting men collected together, partly Tuscarora, although the principal villages of this nation were not involved with them. The other Indians, the Marmuskits, those of Bay River, Weetock, Pamtego, Neuse, and Core began this massacring and plundering at the same time. Divided into small platoons these barbarians plundered and massacred the poor people at Pamtego, Neuse, and Trent.

A few days after, these murderers came back loaded with their booty. Oh what a sad sight to see this and the poor women and children captives. My heart almost broke. To be sure I could speak with them, but very guardedly. The first came from Pamtego, the others from Neuse and Trent. The very same Indian with whom I lodged brought a young boy with him, one of my tenants, and many garments and house utensils that I recognized. Oh how it went through my heart like a knife thrust, in the fear that my colony was all gone, and especially when I asked the little fellow what had happened and taken place. Weeping bitterly he told me that his father, mother, brother, yes, the whole family had been massacred by the very same Indian above mentioned. With all this I dared not act in any way as though I felt it.

For about six weeks I had to remain a prisoner in this disagreeable place, Catechna, before I could go home. In what danger, terror, disgrace, and vexation is easily to be thought...

After these heathens had made their barbarous expedition they came home and rested for a time. Then I watched the opportunity and when I found the chiefs of the village in good humor I asked whether I might not soon go home. To bring them to a favorable disposition I proposed to make a separate peace with them, promised at the same time each chief of the ten villages a cloth coat, something in addition for my ransom; to the king, two flasks of powder, five hundred bullets, two bottles of rum, a brandy made of sugar...

They wanted that I should send my smaller negro to New Bern, so that everything that I had promised should be brought up to Catechna; but yet not a savage would go with him although I wanted to give him a passport or safe conduct. I told him that none of my people who survived would come back with him, because they were so frightened at the robberies and murders, and my negro could not come alone against the current with a loaded boat. Since we could not come to an agreement, I referred it to the Indian with whom I lodged, who gave a sensible decision about our strife so that we were satisfied on both sides...

[During this time more Indian attacks on the settlers occurred.]

So the savages came back two days afterwards to Catechna with horses, food, hats, boots, also some coats. When I saw all this, especially a neat pair of boots with silver trimmings belonging to me, I was much dismayed and greatly feared that they had plundered my house and store, but there was no damage done. Why my things were among them is this. My people used the things of which they had need for this expedition.

So these wild warriors or murderers who were in great glory came in triumph home; and we also went out of our place of concealment in the evening, and traveled the whole night through, back again to our old quarters in Catechna. They made great fires of rejoicing, especially in the place of execution, on which occasion they hung up three wolf hides, representing as many protectors or gods...

After the Indian celebration was over I began to become impatient, asked certain of the chiefs whether now they would not let me go home, because they were victorious and possibly all of my people had been slain. One of the troop answered laughing, that they would see what to do, and he called the king and his council.

Two days after, early in the morning, they brought me a horse. Two of the chiefs accompanied me, armed, but afoot, until about two hours distant from Catechna. There they gave me a piece of Indian bread and left me. Because I saw a long way before me I begged them to leave me the horse, saying that I would send it back without fail, or they should go somewhat nearer to my quarters with me. But I could not prevail upon them. They remained at the place where I left them and made a big fire, to signify to me that there were strange Indians in the woods, and I should hasten and walk swiftly; yes, for two hours run as fast as ever I could, which I also did, until night overtook me and I came to my frightful, desolate ravine, over which I could not go in the dark on account of deep water; but on the contrary I had to stay over night there until morning. The rest of the journey I have already told to the Governor.

Snow on Pollock Street, Christ Church at right
Norm Kellum Collection

18

Tidbits, Morsels and Leftovers

IN A CITY full of remarkable things, one of the most remarkable things in New Bern is a cannon buried point down in the sidewalk at the corner of Pollock Street and Middle Street. If you've never seen it, go there today. It serves as the corner post for the fence around Christ Episcopal Church. The big black iron gun is a souvenir from the British ship-of-war *Lady Blessington* seized "in a sharp engagement during the [American] Revolution" by a bunch of New Bern bad boys under the leadership of John Wright Stanly. That's right! These Patriot privateers sailed out the Neuse and grabbed themselves a warship! The cannon was later handy as a starting point for surveying the city.

HISTORY IS CURIOUS. Attentive students will remember Duke Berthold V of Zähringen from the beginning of the book as the man who shot the bear from which Berne, Switzerland took its name. Well, some sources say he was a count, not a duke. The major citations place the date of the duke's or count's historic bear kill as 1191. Others say he arrived and dispatched the beast in 1160. We just thought we would point this out to add to the confusion.

ALBERT EINSTEIN was living in Berne, Switzerland in 1905 and working in the Swiss Patent Office when he published the paper *On the Electrodynamics of Moving Bodies* which expounded his famous Theory of Relativity.

A BERNESE BEAR is hidden in the logo of Toblerone chocolate. The legendary triangular-shaped Swiss treats originated in Berne. It is named for the inventor, Theodore Tobler, and the combination honey and almond nougat called "torone." Each chuck of Toblerone is called an "Alp" because of its Matterhorn shape. In one of those curious twists of history, the candy was patented in 1909 at the Federal Institute for Intellectual Property, the very patent office where Albert Einstein was then employed. The next time you see the triangular Toblerone box, look at the "mountain" logo on the left and there you will find the hidden bear shape, representing the family's home town of Berne, Switzerland, namesake of you-know-where.

NEW BERN CITY HALL and old Firehouse Number One are not the only buildings to ever have an animal sticking out of them. The Elks Temple Building, our "skyscraper" at the corner of Middle and Pollock Street, had a huge elk head gracing its top floor for many decades. The elk featured light bulbs at each of its antlers tips. When the Benevolent and Protective Order of the Elk's New Bern Lodge #764 moved to a new location across town, the elk went with it to be mounted on the brick wall near the entrance where today it keeps watch, no doubt, for bears.

FOR THE RECORD, there is no known portrait of colonial Gov. William Tryon. You'll see one labeled with his name in authoritative books. You can see the image on the Internet. But, it's not him. History detectives are still looking though.

THE RAINS BROTHERS loved to blow things up. Gabriel James Rains and George Washington Rains became the leading experts on explosives for the Confederacy during the Civil War. They were raised on Craven Street and attended New Bern Academy. George made the explosives and Gabriel turned them into bombs, including the first land mines and underwater anti-ship mines called, at the time, "torpedoes." Gabriel became a brigadier general.

DO YOU KNOW about Berne, Indiana? Wikipedia tells us: "Berne is a city in Monroe and Wabash townships, Adams County, Indiana, thirty-five miles south of Fort Wayne. Berne was settled in 1852 by seventy devout Mennonite immigrants who came directly from Switzerland, and named for the capital of Switzerland. The population was 4,150 at the 2000 census. Berne and the surrounding area have become known for their large Amish population." The City of Berne bills itself as the "Furniture Capital of Indiana." The city logo, by the way, is a cross between and New Bern bear and a Berne, Switzerland bear. It is depicted in a walking stance as opposed to the climbing angle of this city's coat-of-arms. Curious readers can see it on the Internet.

TINY NEWBERN, VA., "founded in 1810, was the Pulaski County seat through much of the 1800s. The historic district—a national historic landmark—encircles the entire community and contains twenty-six of the original log or wooden buildings, including a jail, hanging house, store, churches, private residences and inn, which served as a stagecoach stop," according to its website. It's just off I-81 in western Virginia. Don't miss that Hanging House!

SIXTEEN PEOPLE were killed in Newbern, Tennessee when it took a direct hit from an F3 tornado April 2, 2006. Newbern is a town in Dyer County in the far western part of the state near the Mississippi River. As of the 2000 census, the town population was 2,988. Newbern is a stop for Amtrak's famous train Number 59, the *City of New Orleans.*

NEW BERN, Kansas was a fictional city in the short-lived CBS television drama, *Jericho*. The choice of the name may be related to the fact that Jericho's head writer and executive producer, Carol Barbee, is a native of North Carolina who grew up in Concord. In the series, the also-fictional town of Jericho, Kansas was attacked by hungry residents of New

Bern after a nuclear war. There is a real Newbern in Kansas, however. It's a township in Dickinson County with a recent population of 349.

NO BOOK about New Bern would be complete without something about Blackbeard. Many scholars of the matter say Blackbeard once lived in New Bern and even had a riverside house downtown. Other equally meritorious scholars say he never set foot here. Having diligently considered all the evidence, we take a firm stand and boldly proclaim our agreement with the scholars.

AS WE HAVE SAID EARLIER, two of the many World War II Liberty ships were named for New Bern's famous Spaight and Stanly. Most of the nearly three thousand vessels built nationwide were named after prominent Americans starting with Patrick Henry and the signers of the Declaration of Independence. Eighteen were named for outstanding African-Americans. Of local interest, listed by Wilmington keel number along with their fates, are the USS Zebulon B. Vance (1) which survived the war; USS William Gaston (15) torpedoed and lost in the South Atlantic, 1944; USS Abner Nash (41) survived; USS Furnifold M. Simmons (66) survived; USS Sturdy Beggar (111), christened by Gertrude Sprague Carraway, survived; USS Arthur Dobbs (168) survived; USS John Lawson (169) survived and converted to liquefied natural gas carrier; and USS Thomas Pollock (185) survived the war but sunk in 1956.

AN ADVERTISEMENT for "a few good" Marines and sailors to serve aboard the original Sturdy Beggar was published in the North Carolina Gazette at New Bern, August 8, 1777. It read: "Wanted immediately for the celebrated and well known Brig of War, Sturdy Beggar, under Command of James Campbell, Esq; now fitting out at this place for a short Criuze against the Enemies of the Thirteen United States, a few good seamen and Marines. The Sturdy Beggar is allowed to be the handsomest Vessel ever built in America, is completely furnished with all kinds of warlike Stores, Ammunition &c. is remarkable for fast sailing, having never chased a Vessel but she came up with."

AT THE TIME of the Civil War, Queen Street was the edge of

New Bern.

COASTAL CAROLINA REGIONAL AIRPORT, formerly Craven Regional Airport, formerly New Bern Regional Airport, was originally to be called Simmons Airport in honor of New Bern's ultra-powerful politico and U.S. Senator Furnifold M. Simmons. With Simmons and a crowd of hundreds on hand for the air field's dedication, November 21, 1931, U.S. Marine Lt. Joel Benedict Nott lost his life when his plane crashed. Nott and four fellow Marines from Quantico, Va. were flying the type of performance that would one day be the art of the Navy's Blue Angels. Inexplicably, during a five plane loop, Nott's Curtiss Hawk aircraft went out of control suddenly and augered into the field. The crowd reacted with horror at the loss of the twenty-six year old, recently–engaged former football team captain and honor student. The son of a New York City judge, Nott seemed destined for a stellar career at the time of his untimely death. The cause of the crash was never determined. Following the tragedy, Senator Simmons agreed that the young Marine flyer's sacrifice be recognized by including his name at the airport. Thus, the field was Simmons-Nott Airport for the next fifty-seven years. Even after the many name changes, a bronze plaque on the terminal grounds commemorates both men.

FOR A BRIEF SPAN during World War II, Simmons-Nott Airport did duty as an out-lying field for the nearby Cherry Point Marine Corps Air Station with several squadrons stationed there. Called Camp Mitchell, the field was also used as a base by the Army Air Corp to hunt Nazi subs off the Outer Banks.

DEMOCRATIC U.S. Senator Furnifold M. Simmons of New Bern was the main proponent of the federal income tax in 1913. The one percent tax on income over four hundred thousand 2009 dollars was buried deep in a tariff bill called the Underwood-Simmons Act. Simmons, who lived on East Front Street, is also the "father of the intracoastal waterway."

ONE OF THE PEOPLE who spelled New Bern with a "u" was prolific French novelist Jules Verne, author of *20,000 Leagues Under the Sea* and *A Journey to the Center of the*

Earth. In his 1896 science fiction thriller *Facing the Flag (Face au drapeau)*, Verne main character, Thomas Roch, a crazed genius invents the "Fulgerator," an enormously powerful bomb mounted on a missile similar to a modern atomic ICBM. Roch is kidnapped from a "Newburn," North Carolina insane asylum where he has been sequestered and is then secreted away aboard a submarine on the Neuse River. Verne is not known to have visited either Newburn...or the center of the Earth.

TRYON PALACE wasn't called Tryon Palace until modern times. It was nicknamed "the palace," but not Tryon Palace. In Governor Tryon's time, it was called "the Government House." Tryon is known to have referred to it as "the Edifice." When Tryon's name was first associated with it, around the turn of the last century, it was called "Tryon's Palace."

VANCE COUNTY, in the central part of the state on the Virginia border, was named for Governor Zebulon B. Vance, one of the Confederate commanders at the Battle of New Bern.

TRYON COUNTY, near Charlotte and originally named for colonial Governor William Tryon, ceased to exist in 1779 shortly after the American Revolution when it was divided into Lincoln County and Rutherford County.

GOV. TRYON
'S remarkable and vivacious wife, Margaret Wake, is the namesake of Wake County, location of the state's capital, Raleigh. Governor and Lady Tryon lived in the brand-new "palace" at New Bern 1770-71.

SPAIGHT STREET in the middle of Madison, Wisconsin is named in honor of New Bern's Richard Dobbs Spaight. Many of the streets there are named for signers of the United States Constitution.

STANLY COUNTY, North Carolina, also near Charlotte, was formed in 1841, and named in honor of New Bern's John Stanly, the infamous duelist.

GASTON COUNTY, just west of Charlotte, is named for

Stanly's friend and fellow New Bernian, William Gaston, as is its county seat, Gastonia. Apparently a county and city were not enough, so a thirty-five-mile-long lake near the Virginia border was also named in Judge Gaston's honor.

IN ANOTHER of those weird curiosities of history, New Bern's most famous "firefighter," Fred the Fire Horse, was born in Gastonia which is named for New Bern's most famous judge.

NEW BERN almost became an automotive capital. Buggy maker Gilbert S. Waters built one here in 1899. It was a great car and Gilbert drove it around town for the next thirty-six years. It would go thirty-five miles an hour and got forty MPG. He originally wanted to set up a factory and build what he called Buggymobiles, but two—count 'em!—two New Bern bankers told him a horseless carriage was the dumbest thing they had ever heard. Henry Ford's bankers had a little more imagination.

THE VENERABLE Miss Gertrude S. Carraway was quite fond of making lists of New Bern "Firsts." First school, first printing press and so forth. We add to the list the pardon of John Stanly for the killing of Richard Dobbs Spaight, the first pardon of its kind ever issued in North Carolina.

NOW, from local court records, here's your Separation of Church and State moment: *The jurors of the State of North Carolina, upon their oaths present that Richard Fen and John Den of the Town of New Bern, in the county and state aforesaid, did within the limits of the Town of New Bern aforesaid on the 23rd day of April, being the Lord's Day, commonly called Sunday, then and there were guilty of the vile practice of Cock Fighting to the manifest and evil example of morality and against the peace and dignity of the state. New Bern, N.C., 26 April, 1815, Signed: H. Carraway foreman, Meshack Always, John Jones, James Dickson, Gideon Sparrow, Abijah Davis, Clement L. Davis, Jos. Physioc, Elijah Scott, Cla. Ivey, Richardson, D. Shackelford, Enoch Simons, Will P. Moore, Thomas Wadsworth, Frederick Foy, Sen. Wm. H. Herritage, David A Murdock and John C. Mansfield, witnesses.*

IN COLONIAL DAYS, North Carolina justices of the peace were charged with investigating crimes including "all manners of felonies, witchcraft, enchantments, sorceries, magic arts..."

EDWARD HYDE was sent from England to North Carolina in 1711 to become its colonial governor. Hyde contracted yellow fever the next year in an epidemic that killed many and caused the illness of Christopher DeGraffenried as well, according the North Carolina historian William Powell. Hyde died of the disease in 1712, but DeGraffenried recovered.

THE BOOK about Venezuelan visitor Francisco de Miranda, *The New Democracy in America*, translated by Judson P. Wood, and published by the University of Oklahoma Press, is still in print and can be easily ordered on the Internet.

MRS. MARGUERITE ARMSTRONG, mentioned at the beginning of the book, was said to have been the best first grade teacher of her time in New Bern. Upon her retirement, she made a deal with the local school board to open a private first grade class for children who failed to make the age cut-off for public school. In the 1950s, children had to be six years old by October 15 to enter first grade. Her class included youngsters who missed the date by one day to three months. To enter public second grade from her class, the students were required to take a special test agreed upon by Mrs. Armstrong and the school board. Her class, held in the now-demolished white masonry education building at First Presbyterian Church, was sponsored by the ministerial association. Records vary on the dates, but one said she taught her class from 1955 to 1961 after which she permanently retired from teaching. We also found her name spelled Margeurite.

BORN IN NEW BERN in 1875, Mary Bayard Morgan Wootten became not only a remarkable photographer, but was a ground-breaker for women's rights. Faced with the daunting task of making her way in a profession dominated by men, she founded an association of female photographers and sealed the deal by producing some of the most striking images of North Carolina and the South from that era. Bayard Wootten began her career in 1904 with a studio at her parent's New Bern home where she was born. Since her death in 1959, she has been recognized as "perhaps North

Carolina's most significant photographer during the first half of the twentieth century," according to the University of North Carolina.

OH, YEAH. Almost forgot the football game...that eastern state championship between New Bern and Sanford that had so many people out of town on December 1, 1922 when the whole dang town almost burned down—well, New Bern won! Team Captain Redmond Gill hurled this long bomb that was pulled in by the fine hands of Nicky Simpson. Nicky made it into the end zone. Final score: New Bern, 6; Sanford, zip. Coaching credit went to a future congressman, Graham A. "Hap" Barden.

FOR THOSE READERS longing for a moment of irony, you're in luck. The largest contribution to the Raleigh Relief Fund set up to aid the victims of the Great New Bern Fire of 1922— ninety-some percent of whom were black—was the $800 sent by the Robeson County Ku Klux Klan. The Wilmington Klan also made a donation.

THE FIRST BLACK BABY born in the wake of the big fire was delivered by Dr. Joseph Latham who worked tirelessly for thirty-six hours straight during and after the fire. Dr. Latham had helped set up a makeshift emergency hospital in St. Cyprian's Church on Johnson Street. The baby boy was named St. Cyprian's Emergency Dillahunt. He went through life with the nickname "Cyp."

ONE OF THE HOMES dynamited during the Great Fire of '22 was on George Street. According to a newspaper report, the blast rocketed a white goat twenty-five feet into the air. Believe it or not, witnesses said the goat landed on all-fours and skedaddled.

ANOTHER CURIOSITY of history: Two opposing generals at the Battle of New Bern died six months afterwards in the same manner within a few days and a few miles of one another. Brigadier General Jesse L. Reno, a Union commander, was killed by a Confederate sharpshooter in Maryland on September 14, 1862. A Union sharpshooter killed Brigadier General Lawrence O'Bryan Branch, the Confederate commander, in Maryland three days later.

JAMES CITY, across the river from New Bern, was established and named for the third "superintendent of the poor" appointed by the local Union commander during the Civil War. When Union troops occupied New Bern in 1862, it became quickly apparent to slaves in the surrounding region that freedom awaited them within the federal lines. Soon they were coming in droves. They traveled on foot through woods and swamps, arrived by boat and even swam the rivers. Sometimes slaves fell into step behind Union patrols and followed them to town. Eventually, ten thousand would make it through the lines. In 1863, Gen. Ambrose Burnside selected Rev. Horace James, a Massachusetts minister, for the superintendent's post. James succeeded in settling the majority of the freedmen on land across the Trent River from New Bern. The property was owned by James A. Bryan, an heir of Richard Dobbs Spaight, but the northerners considered the Bryan land abandoned because of his service as a Confederate officer. Rev. James saw to the provision of basic shelter, food, medical care, education and the establishment of churches for the freedmen. In recognition of his service, the settlement was named for James.

INITIALLY OVERWHELMED by the needs of the freedom-seeking slaves, Union Gen. Burnside appointed two men in succession to superintend the needs of "the poor," as he called them. Neither predecessor of Horace James would last long. The first, Vincent Colyer, soon ran afoul of President Abraham Lincoln's appointed North Carolina governor, Edward Stanly. Stanly said feeding, clothing and sheltering the escaped slaves was justified, but educating them was just too much. Colyer quit over the schools dispute. The next superintendent of the poor, Army chaplain James Means, died of yellow fever in early 1863.

MANY OF THE FREEDMEN who entered the federal lines at New Bern were put to work as laborers. The pay rate was eight dollars a month and one meal per day. These workers rebuilt the railroad bridge over the Trent River which burned during the Battle of New Bern. They also built the massive earthen Fort Totten west of the city and constructed or improved other fortifications.

JAMES WALKER HOOD (1831-1918) arrived in Union-occupied New Bern in 1864. The traveling missionary of the African Methodist Episcopal Zion Church would stay three years and serve as the pastor of St. Peters A.M.E. Zion Church. Bishop Hood traveled as much as twenty thousand miles per year and is said to have once preached forty-five sermons in thirty-one days.

FOR MANY YEARS there was a fishing pier called the Iron Steamer on Bogue Island a few miles to the west of Atlantic Beach. The pier was built over the wreck of an old Confederate blockade-runner—the 224-foot-long side-wheel steamer, *Pevensey*. The *Pevensey* was making a run from the island of Bermuda to Wilmington, N.C. with a load of arms, blankets, shoes, silk, cloth, lead and bacon when it got lost and approached the U.S. coast near Beaufort. An armed federal supply ship spotted the mysterious vessel, gave chase and fired on it seventeen times. At least one shell blew up on the deck of the *Pevensey*, before the captain decided to run her aground in hopes that he and his thirty-six man crew might avoid prison. Before abandoning ship, they blew up the huge steam engine. One of the smugglers drowned in the surf. The other thirty-five, including three Confederate officers, were captured on the beach by cavalry from nearby Fort Macon. And the ship that ran the *Pevensey* aground? Why, it was the *USS New Berne*, acquired by the U.S. Navy in 1862 and named in honor of the recent capture of this fair city.

BARON DEGRAFFENRIED'S business partner in the settling of New Bern, Franz Ludwig Michel, aka Francis Louis Mitchell, though the specifics are unknown, is said to have "died among the Indians."

IT HAS BEEN NOTED repeatedly that early surveyor, settler, explorer, author and murder victim John Lawson lived for about three years on the local creek which bears his name with a young Indian fellow and a bulldog. History writer Fred Sloatman suggested in a 1992 edition of the Journal of the New Bern Historical Society that—if this city ever wants a companion mascot for the beloved bear—a bulldog would be just the thing. He suggested the dog's statue might look nice right next to the bust of Baron DeGraffenried near City Hall.

We would lend our support to the initiative...but only if the canine's tongue is sticking out.

AND, though it's not historic—yet—it is history-making. Beverly Eaves Perdue, the seventy-third governor of North Carolina, is our state's first woman governor. Dr. Bev—she earned a doctorate in education administration—calls New Bern her hometown.

THE HISTORIC DISTRICT is full of white wooden historic plaques. The scrolled shadowboxes identify important homes and events in carefully hand-lettered black script. Our absolute long-time favorite is one at 226 New Street bragging:

On this site on
September 9th
in the year of
our Lord
1782 absolutely
nothing occurred.

AFTERWORD

THERE IS REASON to consider New Bern a miracle. So many things had to fall in place to make it what it is today, and if any one of them hadn't, New Bern would not be New Bern.

If John Lawson had not known about this place on two mighty rivers called Chattawka, or never met DeGraffenried in London, or if he had not convinced DeGraffenried that it was *the* place, or if Christopher DeGraffenried had died or stayed in Switzerland or thought the whole thing was too risky, he would have never gotten here with his colonists. Well, you say, someone else would have come and built a city. Yes, probably, but it would not have been New Bern. It would have been settled differently. It would not have had their plan of organization or the skilled craftsmen who set the standards for architecture from the earliest days. They didn't build crude one-room log cabins here like those at Jamestown. They started building plank-sided frame houses, some of them two-stories tall, from the earliest days. And it certainly would not have been called New Bern. Lawson and DeGraffenried. What a pair. But, together...miraculous.

It was indeed a miracle that the Tuscarora failed to annihilate everyone here. If the Indians had not been divided, they would have. If William Brice hadn't stepped up and saved most of the settlers...if Col. John Barnwell had not come....if not, no New Bern.

Then it took someone with the personality and the very unusual drive of William Tryon to even conceive of building an extravagant structure like Tryon's Palace in a backwater coastal town of a sparsely-inhabited colony. Then again, to conceive is one thing, but to execute is something quite different. To actually build a structure at a great enough cost in taxation that it could be the spark of a rebellion, and to face the rebels and put down that rebellion with a firm hand...well, that takes some miraculous mixture of genius and mania. And William Tryon had whatever it was in full. Without William Tryon's Palace, New Bern would not be New Bern.

The Tories could have burned New Bern. So could the Yankees. Fortunately, the Tories just came for a pound of flesh and then went away. The federal forces occupied the city during the War Between the States. It was thus protected from destruction in a war that saw many cities of the South, large and small, go up in smoke. Now, Yankee soldiers *did* try to steal everything here, but some things *were* nailed down.

What if Chief Bryan had not resorted to dynamite in the great fire of 1922? All of the homes in the historic district were threatened, but he and his firemen blew up part of the city to save the rest. Twenty-five percent of New Bern was lost that day. It's a miracle the whole city didn't burn down.

And, maybe the biggest miracle of all...what if all those ladies in the 1930s, 1940s and 1950s had simply admitted, had faced the fact that the restoration of the palace was impossible—because it was impossible. At least it seemed impossible.

But, they did it anyway

They rerouted the highway and moved the bridge and moved a hundred things and got the money and built it back as good as new. Don't tell those tough women anything is impossible.

Without Tryon Palace and the historic district, and the rivers, and the legacy of heritage, and without the energy generated by it, and the energy created around it, and the synergies cooked up and brought to full boil by all of it, well, New Bern would not be New Bern.

All those things and more had to happen.

It's a miracle.

—Edward Ellis

ADDENDA

A Chronology of New Bern History

c. 1690	European settlement begins on Neuse River
1700	Explorer Lawson treks across the Carolinas
1710	DeGraffenried's settlers arrive at New Bern
1711	Tuscarora War begins
1713	DeGraffenried returns to Switzerland
1715-18	Tuscarora War ends
1767	Construction begins on original "palace"
1770	Governor Tryon moves into palace
1771	Battle of Alamance – "the Regulators"
	Tryon transferred to New York
1775	American Revolution begins
1776	Halifax Resolves in North Carolina
	Declaration of Independence
1781	British troops raid New Bern
1783	Francisco de Miranda visits
	American Revolution ends
1791	President George Washington visits New Bern
1798	Tryon's Palace burns
1802	Spaight-Stanly duel
1861	Civil War begins
1862	Battle of New Bern – March 14
1865	Civil War end
1898	"Brad's Drink" becomes Pepsi-Cola
1920s	Palace restoration movement begins
1922	Great Fire of New Bern
1929	New Bern Historical Pageant
	Stock market crash begins Great Depression
1941	World War II begins
1945	World War II end
	Establishment of Tryon Palace Commission
1959	Tryon Palace Restoration opens to public
1960	"The Third Frontier" presented at 250th
	Anniversary of the founding of New Bern
2010	300th Birthday Celebration

The Old North State

THE OLD NORTH STATE is the official song of the State of North Carolina. Written by New Bern's own Judge William Gaston (1778-1844), it became a favorite statewide and was particularly popular during and immediately following the Civil War. Gaston's tribute was adopted as the state song by the North Carolina General Assembly in 1927. Here are the lyrics:

Carolina! Carolina! Heaven's blessings attend her!
While we live we will cherish, protect and defend her;
Tho' the scorner may sneer at and witlings defame her,
Still our hearts swell with gladness whenever we name her.

Hurrah! Hurrah! The Old North State forever!
Hurrah! Hurrah! The good Old North State!

Tho' she envies not others, their merited glory,
Say whose name stands the foremost, in Liberty's story,
Tho' too true to herself e'er to crouch to oppression,
Who can yield to just rule a more loyal submission?

Hurrah! Hurrah! The Old North State forever!
Hurrah! Hurrah! The good Old North State!

Plain and artless her sons, but whose doors open faster
At the knock of a stranger, or the tale of disaster.
How like the rudeness of the dear native mountains,
With rich ore in their bosoms and life in their fountains.

Hurrah! Hurrah! The Old North State forever!
Hurrah! Hurrah! The good Old North State!

And her daughters, the Queen or the forest resembling
So graceful, so constant, yet the gentlest breath trembling.
And true lightwood at heart, let the match be applied them,
How they kindle and flame! Oh! none know but who've tried
them.

Hurrah! Hurrah! The Old North State forever!
Hurrah! Hurrah! The good Old North State!

Then let all those who love us, love the land that we live in,
As happy a region as on this side of heaven,
Where plenty and peace, love and joy smile before us,
Raise aloud, raise together the heart thrilling chorus.

Hurrah! Hurrah! The Old North State forever!
Hurrah! Hurrah! The good Old North State!

Miss Gertrude Carraway's List of New Bern "Firsts"

AS WE HAVE MENTIONED, New Bern's devoted chronicler and booster of all things historic, Gertrude Carraway, kept a list of firsts for the city and published it in various forms over the years. Below is a compilation of superlatives from the 1957 edition of her *Historic New Bern Guide Book.*

FIRST In America to record officially the legal principle that a legislature in limited in power by the Constitution.

FIRST in America for a provincial convention called and held in defiance of British orders.

FIRST in America to celebrate George Washington's birthday.

FIRST in North Carolina and *THIRD* in America, next to Boston and Philadelphia, in celebrating Independence Day.

FIRST incorporated school in North Carolina and *SECOND* private secondary school in English America to receive a charter.

FIRST town to get a bequest and start free trade school for orphan girls.

FIRST free school for white children in North Carolina.

FIRST public school for Negroes in North Carolina.

FIRST printing press, *FIRST* pamphlet, *FIRST* newspaper and *FIRST* book published in North Carolina.

FIRST revolving gun made here.

FIRST death sentence by a Federal Court in the United

States.

FIRST federal hanging.

FIRST capital of Independent State of North Carolina, following 34 years at different times as provincial capital; and capital of the Federal Department of North Carolina during the War Between the States.

FIRST state capital inaugurated here. Tryon Palace, the *FIRST* state capital building.

FIRST State Legislature met here.

FIRST four-faced clock on a building in the State, if not the world.

FIRST ship in state, or one of the first, constructed and launched here.

FIRST steamboat owned in North Carolina.

FIRST railroad to be 100 per cent Diesel operated.

FIRST torpedo put to practical use invented here.

FIRST modern minesweeper made in State, launched here in 1942.

FIRST internal improvement in North Carolina, Indians cutting an early canal from near the mouth of the Neuse River to Core Sound.

FIRST road and *FIRST* ferry in North Carolina led from New Bern to Bath.

FIRST postal service in North Carolina.

FIRST post office in State under the Republic.

FIRST in North Carolina to decorate streets in vari-colored electric lights during the Christmas season.

FIRST motion picture theatre built from the ground up in the State.

FIRST in State to organize County Drama Association, with branches in all high schools.

FIRST in State to sponsor programs and offer essay prizes on highway safety in all County schools.

FIRST public banking institution for State of North Carolina, 1778. One of the *FIRST* two banks chartered in the State, 1804.

FIRST steam sawmill in area.

FIRST macadamized [paved] road in the region.

FIRST in the State and *SECOND* in the country to organize Girls' Hi-Y Club.

FIRST in North Carolina to observe Local History Month, mark historic spots, issue free guide books, and offer guide service.

OLDEST theatre in America still in regular operation here.

OLDEST benevolent society still in existence in State and perhaps *SECOND* in the United States.

OLDEST school building still in use in North Carolina and one of the oldest in America.

OLDEST Roman Catholic parish in North Carolina

OLDEST Christian Science Church in East Carolina.

OLDEST Presbyterian Church organization and building in Presbytery.

OLDEST fire company in State with the earliest charter still in existence. Several World records have been broken by local firemen.

OLDEST instances of paternity on official medical records.

ORIGINAL Self-Kicking Machine.

SMALLEST city in the United States to confer all Masonic degrees except the 33rd, and have a Shrine Temple.

LARGEST lumber barge ever made in North Carolina was built on Trent River in 1900.

MOST magnificent Post Office and City Hall for town of its size.

MOST historic communion equipment in the country—silver communion service, Bible and prayer book presented to Episcopal Church in 1752 by King George II of England; and one of three communion cloths in America made of memorial laces from over the world.

MORE fine original examples of early American architecture than any other town of size.

MORE genuine antiques and local relics than any other town of region.

ONE OF FIRST towns of its size in the nation to own its electric light plant and start rural electrification.

ONE OF FIRST cities anywhere to organize a modern Community Council to aid unemployed and needy.

ONE OF FIRST places in North Carolina to start a public library.

ONE OF FIRST ten Coast Guard Cutters of the United States was built here.

ONE OF FIRST mutual fire insurance companies.

ONE OF FIRST pulp mills in the State.

ONE OF OLDEST gasoline buggy-automobiles that still runs was made here.

ONE OF OLDEST Episcopal parishes in the South.

ONE OF OLDEST hotels, the Governor Tryon, in the South.

ONE OF LARGEST collections of ancient weapons, at Anderson's Drug Store.

ONE OF LARGEST collections of dolls, owned by Mrs. Ralph B. Warrington.

ONE OF TWENTY most historic trees of America.

BEST AIR SERVICE for any town of its size.

ONLY town in state with three railroads, water and air transportation.

ONLY town to have founder with title of nobility bestowed for America.

ONLY town in State and perhaps America to adopt and own a City flag presented by the European capital for which it was named.

ONLY town to have distinguished namesake, settled and named by its aborigines—Tuscarora Indians from here giving the Indian name of their local village, "Chattawka," to the now-famous Chautauqua, N.Y.

Miss Carraway's "Personages of Note"

IN ADDITION to "firsts," Miss Gertrude Carraway kept and published a list of important people with New Bern connections. Below, slightly edited, is her list from the 1957 edition of her *Historic New Bern Guide Book.*

MARTIN HOWARD, Chief Justice of the Royal Colony of North Carolina from 1767 to 1773, resided on his plantation, "Richmond," near New Bern. He was founder and first Master of St. John's Masonic Lodge.

SAMUEL CORNELL, a prosperous merchant who lent money for the construction of Tryon Palace, had strong Tory leanings which led to the famed Bayard-Singleton court case. His grandmother was Daniel Webster's second wife. A family descendant started Cornell University.

MARQUIS De BRETIGNY, who commanded the N.C. Cavalry at Guilford Court House, lived here and was on the Governor's Council in 1783.

WILLIAM BLOUNT, who became Governor of the Territory South of the River Ohio and Senator from Tennessee, owned property in New Bern. He and Richard Dobbs Spaight were two of North Carolina's five delegates at the Constitutional Convention of 1787 in Philadelphia and were two of the three signing the Constitution. The third signer, Dr. Hugh Williamson, came to New Bern during the Revolution.

BISHOP GEORGE W. FREEMAN of Arkansas, Episcopal clergyman, served previously here as assistant to his brother, Rev. Jonathan Otis Freeman, principal of New Bern Academy, early in the nineteenth century.

THE REV. FRANCIS LISTER HAWKS, Episcopal minister, became Supreme Court Reporter and President of the University of Louisiana. He was a noted orator and historian, three times elected to be Bishop.

THE REV. CICERO S. HAWKS was named Bishop of Missouri.

DR. FREDERICK DEVEREAUX LENTE, born in New Bern, December 28, 1823, invented an early instrument for blood transfusion.

THE REV. DRURY LACY, Presbyterian pastor here 1834-36, served as President of Davidson College and he and his wife opened Raleigh school that became Peace College. His son, Dr. Ben Lacy, Sr., was long State Treasurer, and a grandson, Dr. Ben Lacy, Jr., President of Union Theological Seminary at Richmond.

RUSSELL H. CONWELL, Baptist minister, who built the largest Protestant church in America, founded Temple University and two hospital in Philadelphia.

GEORGE BROOKS, Massachusetts soldier and brother of the noted Phillip Brooks, died of typhoid fever in Stanly hospital here February 10, 1863.

GEN. JAMES JOHNSTON PETTIGREW, Confederate leader killed in 1863, lived here during his youth. His mother, nee Shepard, was born here.

HANNIS TAYLOR, Minister to Spain and authority on International Law, was born September 12, 1851, in the Blackwell-Bray House, 218 Broad St., built 1774 by Josiah Blackwell. It was war headquarters of the Cadet Band, 45th Massachusetts Regiment. Taylor's brother, Richard V. Taylor, was long a member of the Interstate Commerce Commission.

DR. DAVID BANCROFT JOHNSON, local school superintendent, was founder and first President of Winthrop College, 1886.

MRS. BROWNIE HANKS EBY, of Raleigh, formerly of New

Bern, became here the first woman bank teller in North Carolina.

MRS C.D. BRADHAM was the first registered nurse in North Carolina.

MS. CHARLOTTE RHONE was the first African-American nurse in the state.

DR. CHARLES G. VARDELL, Presbyterian pastor here 1891-96 was first President and is now President Emeritus of Flora McDonald College. His son, Dr. Charles Vardell, Jr., directs the Salem College Music Department.

The Halifax Resolves

THE HALIFAX RESOLUTION, later called the Halifax Resolves, was the first official step by any of the thirteen colonies "in declaring Independency" from Great Britain. On April 12, 1776—a date that appears to this day on the North Carolina state flag—the fledgling state authorized her delegates to the Continental Congress to vote for independence. The vote was unanimous. All eighty-three delegates present in Halifax at the Fourth Provincial Congress agreed to adopt the Halifax Resolves. The original is today preserved in the National Archives in Washington, D.C. It read as follows:

> The Select Committee taking into Consideration the usurpations and violences attempted and committed by the King and Parliament of Britain against America, and the further Measures to be taken for frustrating the same, and for the better defence of this province reported as follows, to wit,
>
> It appears to your Committee that pursuant to the Plan concerted by the British Ministry for subjugating America, the King and Parliament of Great Britain have usurped a Power over the Persons and Properties of the People unlimited and uncontrouled; and disregarding their humble Petitions for Peace, Liberty and safety, have made divers Legislative Acts, denouncing War Famine and every

Species of Calamity against the Continent in General. That British Fleets and Armies have been and still are daily employed in destroying the People and committing the most horrid devastations on the Country. That Governors in different Colonies have declared Protection to Slaves who should imbrue their Hands in the Blood of their Masters. That the Ships belonging to America are declared prizes of War and many of them have been violently seized and confiscated in consequence of which multitudes of the people have been destroyed or from easy Circumstances reduced to the most Lamentable distress.

And whereas the moderation hitherto manifested by the United Colonies and their sincere desire to be reconciled to the mother Country on Constitutional Principles, have procured no mitigation of the aforesaid Wrongs and usurpations, and no hopes remain of obtaining redress by those Means alone which have been hitherto tried, Your Committee are of Opinion that the house should enter into the following Resolve to wit,

Resolved that the delegates for this Colony in the Continental Congress be impowered to concur with the delegates of the other Colonies in declaring Independency, and forming foreign Alliances, reserving to this Colony the Sole, and Exclusive right of forming a Constitution and Laws for this Colony, and of appointing delegates from time to time (under the direction of a general Representation thereof) to meet the delegates of the other Colonies for such purposes as shall be hereafter pointed out.

Recommended Reading

READERS wishing to learn more about New Bern and North Carolina history may wish to consider some of the following books available at libraries and from booksellers in stores and on-line:

The Civil War in North Carolina by John G. Barrett; University of North Carolina Press (Paperback - 1995) (Hardcover - Jan 1, 1963). Comprehensive, excellent.

The Burnside Expedition in North Carolina by Richard A. Sauer; Morningside House, Inc. (Hardback – 1996). A valuable resource for the Civil War buff.

James City, A Black Community in North Carolina, 1863-1900 (Research reports from the Division of Archives and History) by Joe A Mobley (Paperback - 1981). The only thing wrong with this little gem is its title. It is so much more than just the story of the James City settlement; it's a history of African-Americans in eastern North Carolina. Fascinating.

The New Democracy in America: Travels of Francisco de Miranda in the United States, 1783-84 by Francisco de Miranda and John S. Ezell (Paperback - 1963). Great insights into the colonial period from a truly remarkable man.

A New Voyage to Carolina by John Lawson and Hugh Talmage Lefler (Hardcover 1967; Paperback - 1984). The one best way to truly understand what Lawson was about.

A History of New Bern and Craven County by Alan D. Watson Tryon Palace Commission (Hardcover - 1987). An amazing accomplishment and *the* comprehensive history.

A New Bern Album by John B. Green III (Hardcover – 1985). This visual trip down New Bern's rich memory lane is a classic, a keeper.

The Historic Architecture of New Bern and Craven County, North Carolina by Peter B. Sandbeck (Hardcover - 1988). Nothing about the city's rich architecture appears in *New Bern History 101*, because Sandbeck already said it all.

The Crown of Life: History of Christ Church New Bern, 1715-1940 by Miss Gertrude Carraway (1940). Beautifully and lovingly written with great local insight.

A Walking Guide to North Carolina's Historic New Bern by Bill Hand (Paperback – 2007). In fact, read anything by Bill Hand.

In This Small Place: Amazing Tales of the First 300 Years of Havelock and Craven County North Carolina by Edward Barnes Ellis, Jr. (Paperback - 2005). Previously unreported history of eastern Craven County, plus insights about New Bern and the Civil War.

INDEX

Clarendon, 39
Clark, John, 51
Clark, Mayor Edward, 98
Clermont Plantation, 90, 183, 190
Code Duello, 78
Cogdell, Lydia, 183
Cogdell, Richard, 66, 68
Cogdell, Susannah, 161
Coleman, Robert, 51
Colyer, Vincent, 223
Contentnea, 58, 201
Cornwallis, Lord Charles, 62, 182
Cox, Capt. John, 72
Craig, Major James, 70, 73
Craton, Capt. M.D., 117
Craven Street, 20, 32, 91, 92, 188, 216

D

Daughters of the American Revolution, 111, 198
Davis, James, 64, 102
Deal, A.L., 92
DeGraffenried, Christopher, 9, 10, 15, 17, 19, 32, 34, 36, 39, 40, 41, 42, 43, 44, 45, 46, 47, 48, 51, 52, 54, 56, 57, 59, 150, 151, 152, 153, 154, 177, 178, 179, 200, 201, 221, 225, 226, 228
Dill, Alonzo, 161
Dill, Emily, 7, 85
du Pont, Mr. & Mrs. Henry Francis, 113
Duffy, Minnette Chapman, 107, 108

E

East Front Street, 19, 128, 218
Ebenezer Presbyterian Church, 19, 95
Elks Temple, 215
Ellis, Gov. John W., 117
Ellis, James, 64, 66
Ellis, Richard, 64, 69, 158

Ellis, William, 32

F

Faulkenberry, Chuck, 17
First Missionary Baptist Church, 95
First Presbyterian Church, 18, 187, 195, 221
Forrest, Craig, 18
Fort Thompson, 125, 128
Foster, Gen. John, 122, 132, 145
Fred the Fire Horse, 19, 89, 99, 220

G

Gale, Christopher, 54
Gaston House, 138, 188
Gaston, Alexander, 61, 62, 65, 72, 73, 160
Gaston, Margaret, 73
Gaston, William, 9, 80, 87, 183, 187, 217, 220, 229
George II, 233
George III, 65
George Street, 18, 95, 99, 107, 184, 222
Germany, 35, 36, 37, 38, 39, 178
Ghosts, 9, 148, 149
Goldsboro, 16, 56, 115, 116, 117, 118, 130, 146, 194, 195
Goldsboro Rifles, 117
Goodgroom, Alexander, 51
Graham, Edward, 78
Great Fire of 1922, 90
Green Springs, 16
Green, John B. III, 7, 238
Greene, Lt. Charles, 124
Guion, Isaac, 166

H

Halifax Resolves, 67, 68, 228, 236
Hancock Creek, 51
Hancock Street, 16, 89, 100, 118
Hancock, King, 42, 55, 205, 206

About the Author

EDWARD ELLIS is a journalist and author who spends much of his free time in libraries dusting off history books. Although a specialist in Craven County history, he has haunted archives from New England to New Orleans and created a special historical collection at East Carolina University. Eddie is an avid accumulator of documents, maps, books and artifacts related to local heritage. He is involved in several historical societies and has been Havelock's historian for twenty-five years.

In the newspaper profession, he was a staff member of a number of North and South Carolina newspapers, where he labored as an award-winning photographer, graphic artist, reporter, columnist, managing editor and publisher. In 1986, Eddie founded the *Havelock (NC) News* and was publisher of Cherry Point's *Windsock* for eight years. Over the past few decades, he has written thousands of newspaper and magazine articles, dozens of short stories and several book length projects. But he still types with two fingers.

A native of Craven County—raised in New Bern and Havelock—he has also worked as a lobbyist in the North Carolina General Assembly representing state employees, and owned and operated a variety of business enterprises. And, if worse comes to worse, he has skills as a master carpet layer.

He and his wife, Veronica, are commercial and residential real estate developers who split their time between homes in New Bern and Raleigh while keeping track of five children and—at last count—five grandchildren.

Eddie's first book *In This Small Place: Amazing Tales of the First 300 Years of Havelock and Craven County, North Carolina* was a runaway hit, once reaching 66,485th place on the Amazon.com sales rank list, just a little behind a Harry Potter book which was Number 1 that day.

For more information visit
www.edwardellis.com

$17.95

ISBN 978-0-975-87009-9

51795

9 780975 870099

McBryde Publishing
NEW BERN, NORTH CAROLINA USA